A MODEL OF POLITICS

A MODEL OF POLITICS

WILLIAM P. KREML

University of South Carolina

MACMILLAN PUBLISHING COMPANY
New York

Collier Macmillan Publishers
London

ACKNOWLEDGMENTS

I wish to thank Peter Sederberg, Thomas Waldrep, and Tracy Sonafelt for their assistance with the editing of this work. I also wish to thank Elizabeth Thomas for her careful typing of the manuscript and Bill Clark for his assistance with the glossaries and graphics.

Macmillan Publishing Company
866 Third Avenue, New York, New York 10022

Collier Macmillan Canada, Inc.

Library of Congress Cataloging in Publication Data

Kreml, William P.
  A model of politics.

  Includes index.
  1. Political science.   I. Title.
JA66.K68 1985   320   84-3867
ISBN 0-02-366470-3

Printing: 1 2 3 4 5 6 7 8   Year: 5 6 7 8 9 0 1 2 3

ISBN 0-02-366470-3

To

James MacGregor Burns
with deep appreciation

PREFACE

The world of politics is vast and sometimes confusing. Yet so much of what goes on in the modern world is subject to the public decision making that we call politics that whether or not you as a student choose political science to be your major field, you should at least know how politics affects your daily life. There are many ways to introduce the subject of political science to students, but I have found that two methods are extremely important to a student's ability to both understand and retain what a course in political science offers.

The first has to do with how the student is addressed. After many years of teaching, I am convinced that a simple description of political principles and concepts is not sufficient. You, the student, will understand me and what I have to say far better if I engage you directly in a full discussion of politics. In the classroom, I have found that the asking of questions that challenge a student and help him or her move from one level of understanding to the next is vastly superior to a recitation of what we mean by such concepts as democracy, freedom, conservatism, and the like. This text will, therefore, ask you questions as you go along. In response, you should attempt to answer these questions in your mind.

The second method of this book is also one that I have found to be helpful to students. It would be an exaggeration to say that the real world of politics is one well-organized whole. There are many things within politics that have only the most remote linkage with other things in politics. Yet there are still certain unifying themes within the real world of politics. The best way to teach political science is to attempt, as nearly as possible, to unite at least the fundamental principles of politics into a relatively unified model.

What is a model? Those who write about political science explain it as a kind of representation of what the reality of the world is. One definition describes a model as "a simplified picture of a part of the real world."[1] Certainly there is a good deal of truth to this definition, but I prefer a more dynamic definition, one that includes the observer of the model more actively within the modeling process. Alan Isaak, in his discussion of models, differentiates models from theories. Theories, according to Isaak, are used primarily to "explain" political facts. Models, on the other hand, are used primarily to "discover" political reality.[2] The difference is a large one, for what this book is designed to do is to have *you* build a conceptual network or a pattern of understanding about politics. To see a model as a discovery fits well with what education is all about. As Mortimer Adler and so many others have pointed out, education is more than simply the learning of facts. Education includes the two additional stages of (1) refining the student's analytical skills and (2) building patterns of understanding or discovering models that place knowledge within useful and expandable frameworks.

The pattern of this book should be clear to you from the beginning. It is an attempt to build a model of politics that weaves each strand of material into every other strand. In this sense, this book is very different from what you are used to. It is, I assure you, designed to be a different kind of book, for it will stress the interrelationship of concepts, that is, the conceptual network that we will try to build within your mind. If you read this book carefully, and if you weave the material that it presents into a model, you should come away with one relatively unified understanding of the principles of politics. This model should both explain a good deal of what is going on in the public discussion of politics, and permit additions to your own model that more advanced political science courses will bring.

W. P. K.

1. Charles A. Lave, and James G. March, *An Introduction to Models in the Social Sciences* (New York: Harper and Row, 1975), p. 3

2. Alan C. Isaak, *Scope and Methods of Political Science* (Homewood, Ill.: Dorsey Press, 1975), p. 136.

CONTENTS

Preface   *vii*

1   *The Problem of Valuation*   *1*

2   *The Element of Reason*   *16*

3   *Capitalism and Its Modifications*   *32*

4   *The Socialisms*   *51*

5   *The Modern Valuational Debate*   *66*

6   *The Building Blocks of Structure*   *92*

7   *The Modern Political Structure*   *123*

8   *The Principal Institutions*   *145*

9 *Pluralism and Elitism Evaluated*   *168*

10 *The Grand Equilibrium*   *180*

11 *Political Psychology: The New Perspective*   *208*

Epilogue   *219*

Index   *221*

A
MODEL
OF
POLITICS

CHAPTER 1
THE PROBLEM OF
VALUATION

Remember Robinson Crusoe and the difficult time he had on his island—his loneliness, the limits to his activity, his fear that he might not return to civilization? Yet Crusoe was free of one of the great problems that faces humankind. He was free of politics. This is because politics requires people, at least two people, and it involves the intertwining fates of persons living within what the ancient Greeks called a *polis*.

What is a *polis*? It is the arena in which public decisions are made, that level of a cohesive community where government actively makes the choices that affect the members of that community. A *polis* may cover a large area and a large number of people or only a small area and a few people. No matter how many people it includes, however, a *polis* is the arena in which they deal with their public concerns.

THE MATTER OF DISTRIBUTION ▬▬▬▬▬

The question of how much each of our fortune is part of everyone else's fortunes and, therefore, how much we want the *polis* to make decisions for us is one of the central questions of politics. As long as more than one of us is living within any political jurisdiction, there will have to be some distribution of the common wealth of that society. Distribution means who gets how much of whatever the total productivity of society is.

There are two ways that most writers have looked at politics; that is, there are two general models of understanding that most commentators have used to understand what goes on within the

1

public arena. One of those models is a *power* model; the other is a *value* model. Without question, power is important. But consider the concept of value. Value asks us to search for the kind of political society of which we would like to be a part. It tells us what we want out of that society, and if we know what our separatre values are, it tells us that we can each go into the public arena and attempt to acquire those things that we want for ourselves. If we know what it is that we value, then we, as a part of a political system, will respond to the question of who will receive what out of that system. Harold Lasswell, a prominent political scientist, defined politics as "who gets what, when, and how."[1] Lasswell pointed out that values in the minds of the citizens of a *polis* and the ways by which these values compete within the political society form the essence of real-world politics.

Let us look first, then, at value as the dominant political characteristic because value attempts to define what it is that we are arguing over. Indeed, in this book, unlike most texts that introduce political science, we will postpone detailed discussions of particular political institutions, such as legislatures, political parties, chief executives, and so forth, until we have a very clear understanding of what it is that the citizens of a polity are arguing over.

Thus, as we proceed with our model, we should start with a thorough discussion of distribution or the patterns of who gets what out of the system. Should a few people receive a lot and the rest only a little? Should the distribution be more evenly divided? We need not answer these questions here but we should remember that these are the principle distribution questions.

Some Preliminary Definitions

Before we initiate our more complete look at the political model, let us pause to make sure that we know what we mean by the terms *politics* and *political science*. Simply put, politics concerns the battle over such things as distribution, and political science generally concerns the study of such controversies. Politics involves the clash of values, whereas political science, at the very least, attempts to take students of politics outside of the biases that all of us have and helps them see that people have different views about how a political society should distribute its well-being. Throughout the building of our model, therefore, we are talking of different views. Political science, that is, the more or less formal study of politics, requires that we understand the ranges of views that people have about politics.

RESOURCES AND WORK ▬▬▬▬▬

Let us look at the distribution question more closely now. If you are alone on a desert island, what will determine how well you live? The answer is fairly simple, really, because there is only one major factor that will determine your well-being—the availability of resources that are present on the island. What food is available? What material is there for shelter? What will protect you from the danger of hostile animals, and what opportunities will there be for you to invent enjoyable pastimes or games that will entertain you?

Suppose, however, that you are not alone. Suppose that the available resources will be shared by you and another person. The scarcity of resources makes politics more difficult, yet the heart of politics asks how a governmental system allocates its resources among the members of the *polis*. It is the political interaction within the *polis*, the scramble over resources and the arrangement for the production and the distribution of wealth, that determines how well each citizen will live. Thus, it is an interactive factor, and at different times it sets citizens against one another in a *competitive* way or it asks citizens to be *cooperative* for the good of all.

The Two-Person Community

What, then, if you are not alone on the desert island? Suppose that there is one other person on the island with you and that there are ample supplies of nuts, berries, fruits, and fresh water. Suppose also that both you and the other resident are reasonably healthy and that you are both reasonably capable of performing certain life-sustaining tasks. Suppose too that the two of you are getting along with each other reasonably well and that you are therefore willing to engage in the joint decision making that we are calling politics.

What, you might ask, will be your standard of living on the island? How well shall each of you do in the quest for whatever foodstuffs, comforts, and so forth that are available? Most important, how will you decide who does how well in the distribution of what is on the island for your sustenance? It may be, for example, that you agree to share equally whatever is gathered on the island. That is one possible result of the allocation question, but we need not necessarily come to that conclusion or any conclusion about how things will be divided right away. Let us examine, rather, an entire range of possibilities for how the island's wealth could be apportioned, and let us consider how you would feel about a variety of different allocations.

Perhaps, as a hint of where we are going, think about how much work each of the island residents or each of the citizens of a larger society has performed or is willing to perform. Would the capacity for work have something to do with what you feel constitutes a just return of wealth?

The Realities of Distribution

The problem has deliberately been kept simple. We have talked of one island and of two residents. We have placed ample food on the island and have given reasonable health and capability to both residents. The real world, as you know, is never quite that simple. Before we proceed, we need to recognize that even in the simplest of political societies, some rules of distribution are needed.

Consider the "authoritative allocation of values," which involves two, not one, components: (1) *contribution*, and (2) *reward*. As we look at these two elements more closely, let us clearly remove one consideration that would take politics out of the entire island situation. Let us assume that the two island residents decide not to split the island down the middle and go their separate ways without any further interaction. Even that alternative, the decision process that would surround even that judgment of separation, would itself involve a small amount of what constitutes politics. Yet the resulting total separation of the two would then remove the political question from further consideration.

Thus, we are going to say that the island is not divided and that each resident will contribute some of the work, which will foster the well-being of both on the island. Again, the key word is "contribute," because, as we said, the relationship between contribution and reward is the heart of the political question.

How much should you, as one individual, receive from a political system? How much are you entitled to ask for from what has been produced by the entire system? In the simplest of terms, what is your fair return for the contribution that you have made?

As is true for most great political questions, this issue has been around for a long time, and its answer has been wrestled with by some of the best political thinkers of the ages. Aristotle, one of the first Western thinkers to ponder the questions of politics systematically, thought a good deal about the issues of contribution and reward. Dismissing the idea of everybody's receiving equal return from the bounty of the community, Aristotle decided that the relationship between contribution and reward was such that everyone should receive the same proportion of return from the society as what that person contributed.

Think about this as a theoretical principle, but also think about it in a very concrete sense too. Should anyone get more out of something than they put into it? Should anyone get less? Neither of these alternatives makes any sense, and, in fact, the notion that everyone should get just about what they put into something has a kind of universal appeal. Many different thinkers and many different political societies have adopted the idea.

Of course, there have been those who have argued for privilege, although most of those who have argued that way were the ones who were already a part of a privileged group. But among thinkers who were not part of privilege, there is a recurrent thought, a feeling that has lasted down through the centuries that contribution and reward should be about the same. Justinian, the great Byzantine thinker and one of the first Western philosophers to talk about a naturally based, self-evident set of principles, said that contribution and reward should be equal, that everyone was entitled to his or her due. What Aristotle and Justinian said was mirrored years later by the English philosopher John Locke, who said that everyone was entitled to the fruits of his or her labor. The similarity of these thoughts is abundantly evident, yet the trick is to comprehend their meaning in a society whose contributions are mixed together or at least not identified as belonging to a single person.

Consider as a typical day on the island that the food gathering, the water gathering, the building of a stronghold, or the construction of any recreational facility are all being done simultaneously by both residents. Each gathers berries; each climbs back up to the fresh water source; and, in great part because all these things are joint projects, each works at more or less the same pace with almost identical records of productivity. Under these circumstances, the problem of allocation or reward is not difficult. The work performed by both parties is about the same, and the reward for both parties should also be about the same. The problem is that working alongside someone else is more than likely not the way that an individual would choose to work on the island. Even more clearly, it is not the way that we work in the larger, modern world.

What, then, are the characteristics that distinguish modern work, that is, work performed in an industrial or what some now call a postindustrial setting? There are many characteristics, but there are two that are very clear. One is that modern work is rarely simultaneous; that is, it is rarely done with people doing identical things side by side. Neither is the work that some people do in the modern world similar in intensity to what other people do. We know that some people work harder than others. Some people work at more skilled tasks than others, and some work longer hours than others. Therefore, rarely are two jobs anywhere as close in valuation as, say, the job of a berry picker and a coconut tree climber would be on the desert island.

HOW WORK IS REALLY PERFORMED ━━━━━━

Even on the island, it is probably not realistic to think that both residents are going to work together on every project, standing side by side and doing similar work simultaneously. As a practical matter, work will be allocated, and both parties will split up during the workday, returning periodically to a home base with whatever each has gathered.

Why do we distribute work, even on a desert island? There are a variety of reasons, but the most important is that the work itself is done more efficiently that way. Even on the island, it is probably a better usage of both inhabitants' time not to have both pick berries and then both go up to the source of fresh water. It is probably better to have one go to the spring and bring down the water and the other gather the solid food so that the total time spent on those tasks will be less all around. Such a principle is certainly true for the postindustrial work world, for there is an incredible variety of jobs that need to be done today. Without question, society has found that the sorting out of these jobs—specializing—has contributed to the overall production of wealth.

The Idea of Specialization

On the island, the decision to specialize is made for the same reason. "You go up and get the water today and I'll get the berries," you might say, and both may agree tomorrow to switch jobs and let the other get the water. It is specialization in work that we are talking about. It is on a small scale to be sure, but you may notice that another complicating factor should be added to our analysis. Consider why it is that the jobs might better be switched every so often. Maybe a reason for switching has to do with the boredom of the jobs, for you may wish to create as much variety in your life as you possibly can.

Variety is a consideration, and though it has something to do with contribution and reward, the fact is that there is a much more important reason for the rotating of jobs that relates to the contribution-reward equation. The fact is that both fellow island residents probably decide to engage in job switching because they suspect that certain jobs are more difficult than others. Perhaps, on a particular day, both inhabitants believe that the person who had to get the water contributed a little more to the entire productivity of the island than did the person who picked the berries by the ocean front because more time and physical exertion were required to complete the task. Perhaps, because the water source was located beyond jungle growth, the task was also more dangerous. In any case, the agreement between the two parties reflects the notion that the jobs to be done are at least a bit different. Since one job was tougher than the other, then the real reason for the work switch was to not deal with the difficult task of allocating contributions and rewards based upon the assumption that one inhabitant was contributing more than the other.

Let us pause because we have reached a key plateau of understanding that needs to be solidified before we can continue. The simple fact is that although little tricks like job switching can be used in a two-person, desert island situation, these tricks are largely impossible in the modern world. Let me ask you to remember one simple principle here. It is that some jobs are more difficult than others. Also, if you adopt the classical notions of Aristotle, Justinian, Locke, and others that each citizen should receive from the system about the same reward as what he or she contributed, then you should come to the conclusion (which we did not need to reach on the desert island) that some people are going to get more of a reward than are others.

The Concept of Proportionate Reward

The importance of this idea of proportionate reward cannot be overstated. It is one of the most fundamental in all of politics, for some citizens will do better than other citizens, at least in their returns from the society, and all systems in varying degrees accept the inequality of reward among their citizens. They accept, in short, some notion of proportionate return to those who contribute either more or less to the overall well-being of the system.

Let us build from there. Let us find out how much more we want certain occupations to receive, and let us, at the same time, begin to try to understand what the standards will be for who gets what out of each political system. Within these two questions—How much differentiation should there be? and What are the standards of differentiation?—are the core of what we generally call *ideology*. Ideologies are nothing more than systems of belief about politics. Although we want to talk much more about them later, we already need to have a sense of how each of us feels about the degree of differentiation of work value and about what standards should be used in what valuation. These are the value questions that we spoke of earlier. Both of these questions, I would suggest, have something to do with how we feel about work. They also have something to do with how people allocate the rewards of a political system.

THE CORE OF IDEOLOGY

Beliefs about value, that is, those sets of feelings that each of us has about the valuation of work and other concerns, are what make up what is generally called *ideology*. For now, let us stay with the value question: How is it that some people are judged to be contributing more to a society and are thus held to be worth the higher amount of return that they receive?

Take two professions in the modern world as examples—a physician and a street sweeper—both everyday occupations. Each is important in its own way, and a goodly number of people perform each task. Yet there is a clear distinction between the two tasks in most people's minds, and it is a distinction that certainly is evidenced by the differentiated pay of the two jobs. One of these careers traditionally receives a considerably higher salary than does the other. Most citizens accept the differentiation, and they do so partly because they have a sense that one of the tasks contributes more than the other to the well-being of the entire system. Some citizens might feel that the street sweeper's task is less pleasant and, therefore, that it should receive a higher payment than a physician's. In reality, however, most people would probably not reason that way. An argument for an equal return for the two employments would probably not appeal to many observers.

Before we proceed much farther, there is an important reservation that must be made, namely, that agreement does not mean unanimity. More simply, even though there is a general agreement on the ranking of some occupations with respect to others, the question of *how much* the difference in reward should be is still very significant. As you have probably already figured out, there is substantial disagreement over how much more the physician should get than the street sweeper. Again, the argument over the degree of differentiation and the argument over the standards used for such differentiations are part of an understanding of ideology. To begin our analysis of that differentiation, think of a number that you believe is the fair representation of how much more the physician should get than the street sweeper. Should the physician get twice as much as the street sweeper, three times as much, or maybe even ten times as much?

There is no right answer, of course. Just think about the problem for a minute. Do you remember when you were asked to think of ranges of values? Here is one of those times when we will do that because what we are asking is how much more valuable to a society is the physician than the street sweeper. To put it in a somewhat more systematic way, we might ask, how high do you believe the pyramid of distribution in a society should be between those who earn a great reward and those who do not earn very much? We are now at another plateau of understanding, for nearly everyone agrees that there will be a pyramid of distribution of some kind. Yet the question that begins to touch on ideology is the question of how high each of us believes that the general differentiations of the society, or how high the distribution pyramids that reflect those beliefs should be. Clearly, there is no agreement on that, and you know that understanding the range of different views will go a long way toward understanding the differences in political views.

By now, you should have thought of your number. You should have arrived at some figure that, in a rough sense, says "I think that physicians are worth two, three, ten, or whatever times more than street sweepers." Now, in a rough sense, by extending the physician–street sweeper comparison over the society as a whole, we all have an idea of how high we want the distribution pyramid to be. How great, in other words, do we want the differentiations between the valuation of work of some people and other people to be? If on the desert island one person climbed a coconut tree and brought down protein-rich coconuts while another either could not or would not climb a tree, would we not agree that the first person should receive a higher return? Again, the ratio of what the differentiation would be could run from 2 to 1, up to, say, 10 to 1 or beyond (see Figure 1–1). Yet we can be assured that, in the modern world, there will be different justifications for different ratios of unequal returns. What we need to do now is discuss what these justifications are.

FIGURE 1–1.
Evaluations of contribution and reward for different occupations.

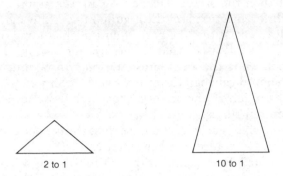

2 to 1   10 to 1

Have you ever played poker? If you have, think about when you played and, more particularly, about who it was that you played with and what your relationship to that person or persons was. Some people play poker for money, and for them it's a serious business. The competitiveness of the game is important, and these players hold their cards close to their chest and try to win as much money as they can. Other people play for only a little money, maybe pennies, or maybe even for no money at all, as when people used to play for wooden match sticks. Maybe you have played in both kinds of games. All you need to do is think about how you related to the other players in each of the two kinds of games.

Probably in the penny ante game, the people that you played with were just good friends. You were no doubt enjoying an evening and mostly enjoying the company of those friends. The evening had some worth to you all by itself, and the social commonality of the evening was far more important than having the chance of coming home with several large betting pots. In the competitive game, your fellow players may not have been such good friends, and whether or not you enjoyed the evening probably depended upon whether or not you won or lost money.

THE HUMAN NATURE QUESTION

Let me suggest that these two poker playing orientations, by analogy, are at the core of how we relate to our fellow citizens and how we feel about distributions of reward generally. In doing so, let me reintroduce two fundamental terms. Let me also ask that you think of these terms as representing a continuum or spectrum of beliefs and not just two separate categories of views that have no relation to each other. The terms to concentrate on are *cooperative* and *competitive*, for all of us, in our unique ways, fall somewhere along a cooperative versus competitive continuum in how we relate to our fellow citizens.

Is the world a dog-eat-dog place? Do I, in order to succeed, have to watch out for you and make sure that you do not take advantage of me as I believe you want to do? On the other hand, do I feel that the world is a reasonably generous and friendly place? Do I look to my fellow citizens as partners in the general society? If I see confidants and partners in my work and in my social life, I am generally of a cooperative view about human nature, and I prefer to trust my fellow citizens at least most of the time. Again, if we can think of this vital sense of how we all fit in with the rest of our fellow human beings as a continuum, or as a conceptual line that stretches all the way from those whose views of human nature are very cooperative to those whose views are that humans are essentially competitive, then we have reached another plateau of understanding.

There is a linkage here, of course, and it is the tie-in between (1) how you feel about human nature (that is where you fit yourself on the competitive versus cooperative continuum of relationships to your fellow citizens), and (2) how you feel about the degree of differentiation that should be made among various contributions. Think about what your relationships to others are and ask yourself whether it is the competitive or the cooperative personality that wants the high differentiation of reward, the 10-to-1 rather than the 2- or 3-to-1 ratio between the physician and the street sweeper (see Figure 1-2).

FIGURE 1–2.
Human nature assumptions underlying different contribution and reward ratios.

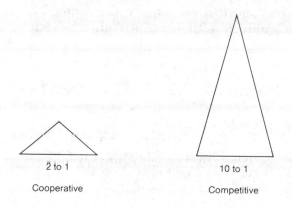

You will probably reach only one conclusion, that the competitive view prefers high differentiation of income between the two occupations and the cooperative view wants minimal differentiation. Again, the competitive personality wants the physician to be making ten times more than the street sweeper, whereas the cooperative personality will want a considerably smaller separation in income, perhaps two or three times what the street sweeper makes. What causes the difference in these views again? It is that each view of human nature reflects how high the differentiation of reward among people ought to be within the larger society. The competitive view argues largely that, because we are separated and distinct from each other in the society and concerned only with our own well-being, the rewards of the economic poker game should be well stacked in favor of the winner of the contest. The cooperative view believes that since we are all basically in the society together and have a great deal in common as part of the larger humanity, the division between the extrinsic contributions or the rewards of each of us should never be terribly great.

You will notice the use of the word *extrinsic* here; it is used because to some degree, what is going on in this competitive versus cooperative or high pyramid versus low pyramid of distribution analysis is that different ideologies are really valuing different things. This differentiation of our personality should also be a part of our understanding for, without question, the purely competitive view values only the productivity of the work itself. It does not value the worker so greatly as a member of the community, as a social being, or as a valued *intrinsic* member of the society in any non-economic sense. The holder of the cooperative view clearly includes these intrinsic considerations in his or her evaluation of someone's worth. The subscriber to the cooperative view says, in effect, that the world should not be a dog-eat-dog place or, in a somewhat more sophisticated way, that people are valuable in and of themselves and that economic contributions should never be the sole determiner of valuing contribution to society.

DIFFERENT KINDS OF CONTRIBUTIONS ———

By now, you should see clearly how the competitive view would lead to something like a preference for a 10 to 1 differentiation between a physician and a street sweeper and how the cooperative view would argue for a lesser ratio. You should also be able to tell that we expect to build a better understanding of what we mean by political ideology. Human nature and the range of views about human nature are clearly at the core of the issue. In other words, relatively competitive and cooperative views value economic contributions in relation to other noneconomic kinds of contribution in a very different way.

Of course, pure economic contribution makes up a great deal of any contribution to a society. Yet, if at one end of the continuum the competitive view of human nature tends to value extrinsic, economic valuations as being about all that the system should consider, we can see that at the other end of that continuum, at the cooperative or harmonious side, a number of noneconomic kinds of contributions will also be valued. What will these valuations be? They will be very close to the cooperation and friendship that is valued at the poker game played among friends who play for pennies or for match sticks. They are the values other than economic productivity that you would want to find on an island with another resident. Generally, we call these the *values of association* or the *intrinsic values* of human worth, and they are the glue or cohesion that holds any society together, be it two people on a desert island or an entire modern political system.

All societies have many tasks, and we have now talked about productivity in a way that attempts to emphasize economic values and noneconomic values. Surely, the economic contributions are as important as they are responsible for the material well-being that everyone in the society needs to sustain themselves. But the other end of the human nature continuum argues that a society also needs to be bound together, to work effectively as a whole, and to foster a spirit of joint purpose and a social togetherness for its own sake (see Figure 1–3). We do that when we think of our families, our friends, our neighborhood, or even our love of our fellow human beings. The motivation for this kind of association or identity comes from the cooperative side of the human nature continuum.

You should be able to see that a citizen's human nature orientation, or the balance of individualistic versus associative values within the interaction of citizens in the *polis*, along with the relative importance that is placed upon economic as opposed to noneconomic needs within society, will dictate how high the pyramid of reward will be. The more competitive, more individualistic, and more economic side of the continuum will generally argue that the pyramid should be tall. The more cooperative, associative, and noneconomic side will argue for a pyramid that is rather flat.

FIGURE 1–3.
Political policy preferences and contribution evaluation differences.

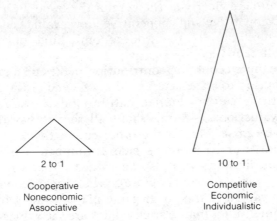

2 to 1	10 to 1
Cooperative Noneconomic Associative	Competitive Economic Individualistic

CONCLUSION

Again, we are at one of the plateaus of understanding. What you have been introduced to is not simply that the height of the pyramid depends upon different orientations toward economic activities but that political ideology is also a part of different people's valuations of economic contributions versus noneconomic contributions. This question is directly related to ideological conflict because it is the question that asks you to look at (1) the differences in what is being evaluated (that is, the economic versus noneconomic values) along with (2) the differences in the evaluator's views of human nature (competitive versus cooperative attitudes). If we understand that there are differences in the competitive versus the cooperative view and if we understand further that we are not only arguing over the degree of different economic contributions but about the differences between material, concrete, and extrinsic contributions and those contributions that are more bonding and associative for the society, then our understanding is a good one. It is hoped that you see this process of valuation as really nothing more than a preference for different views of human nature, and that this process works itself out in politics in a relatively predictable way.

In closing this chapter, let us acknowledge that some political issues fit into the model of lower and higher pyramids and economic and noneconomic values much more closely than do other issues. The debate over valuation that we are introducing represents the core of most political debate as well as what the major political ideologies have argued over throughout recent history. In one form or another, almost all political issues can be understood with this model, but some issues certainly are more directly applicable than others.

Reference Note

1. Harold Lasswell, *Who Gets What, When and How?* (New York: P. Smith, 1936).

Glossary

TERMS

polis

power

value

distribution

politics

political science

competitive

cooperative

contribution

reward

ideology

extrinsic value

intrinsic value

NAMES

David Easton

Harold Lasswell

Aristotle

Justinian

John Locke

CHAPTER 2
THE ELEMENT OF
REASON

As we look into this process of political evaluation more deeply, let us determine what it is that specifically makes up the estimate of how particular economic work should be valued. The essence of what we are talking about, again, is human reason. It is the idea that human beings are capable of arriving at sensible conclusions about things and, further, that there is at least some commonality to the elements of reason within all of humankind. We will discuss the specific elements of reason shortly, but first let us briefly review the history of reason since the feudal period of the middle ages.

EARLY ATTITUDES TOWARD VALUE

What we should concentrate on is closely linked to our idea from Chapter 1 that different citizens have at least some commonality in their views. This commonality, as a practical matter, was very much in evidence in the feudal period of history because, at that time, the very question of the value of work was not much debated. How was work evaluated in the feudal period? The answer is quite simple, for how well you profited from your labor was very much determined by the accepted orders of the feudal estate that typified the Middle Ages. What did your parents do? What was their station in the feudal order? These were the questions that determined your standing. The feudal order was so stable that where you fell within it was the result of generations of understandings among the lord, his serfs, the church, the orders of knighthood, and the deep social and economic interrelationships that bound that static system together. Further, what you received was rarely paid in some form of money or currency but, instead, was a payment of protection by the lord along with some percentage of the produce of his estate. Yet, even within that period to some degree and more particularly near the close of the feudal age, the question of the valuation of the independent craftsman or merchant was becoming more significant.

As the feudal period came to a close, more and more workers labored outside the feudal order. These workers were paid for the goods that they sold on the basis of something other than a percentage of their production or the physical protection within the walls of the feudal city. With the increase of tradespeople of this kind, serious new questions as to how work should be rewarded had to be faced.

What should be done with the reward for work that was done outside of feudalism's orders? Clearly, the dominant religious teachings of the time were important for the answer to this question. Regarding how specific work should be valued, religious figures such as Martin Luther said that the aggregate citizenry should dictate a work's particular value. The carpenter, the blacksmith, the tanner, or the cooper or barrel maker, according to Luther, should in a general sense receive what the *polis* as a whole thought their work was worth. Importantly, these craftsmen were not, according to strict religious tenets, supposed to charge whatever they could for their goods or their services. They were to charge a reasonable rate for their products or services, one that the society as a whole would commonly agree truly represented the contribution to the society.

Let us make sure that we understand what we mean about the inclusion of the entire society in the question of economic valuation. Understand that the essence of the linkage of any political society to the valuation of particular work requires that humankind, all of humankind, has at least some notion of reason within it. Since reason does not mean that all will think alike, that is, that we are still dealing with only an approximation of a just order, it certainly cannot always generate a single, exacting notion of what the just or fair order of the world should be. The perceptions of all citizens will always vary somewhat, but, again, there will be at least some degree of agreement among everyone's view. With the aggregate of all citizens' viewpoints, some reasonable estimate should be able to tell us what various endeavors are worth compared with other endeavors.

REASON IN VALUATION

Let us try now to be specific about the elements of reason. The fact is that a number of criteria or standards of judgment emerge that tend to structure the idea of reason and structure how it is

that we think about the contribution and reward of different occupations. Going back to the physician and the street sweeper, it
will help if you are specific about why it is that the physician is
seen as being more valuable to the society. There are some very
clear reasons why you probably do, and, if you haven't thought of
them in detail, we should begin to do so now.

What is it about the physician that is more valuable than the
street sweeper to the modern society? Some of you may say *skill*,
and certainly most would agree that the physician's task is more
difficult than the street sweeper's. We might all reason that the
person in the society who performs the task with greater skill
should be rewarded over the person who has a less skillful job.

Closely related to skill is the question of *training*. It is reasonable,
is it not, that a person who spends many years within an educational process that makes that person skillful should be rewarded
more than one who can learn a job in a few days or weeks? The
period of training is usually a period of sacrifice, and any political
society, as a part of its general reasonableness, will tend to say that
the contribution of being willing to suspend more gainful employment for a period of training should be rewarded for that suspended
time.

A third component of reasonableness, and remember that we are
talking about specific component parts of the general valuational
view of the society, might have to do with *risk*. We would expect
to find general agreement in a population that if one job involves
a greater danger of injury or loss of life than does some other occupation, then the worker in that job should be rewarded more
substantially than should the worker in a less dangerous occupation. Again, such a conclusion is something that almost everyone
would consider reasonable.

A fourth component of reasonableness might be *scarcity*, that
is, the absence of other citizens in the society who can do a similar
task. It is thought to be appropriate to reward a physician more
than a street sweeper because almost anyone could perform the
task of the street sweeper, whereas we clearly would want only a
select, highly qualified portion of our citizenry involved in the
business of caring for our physical health. The very scarceness of
that talent and intellect throughout the population makes us more
ready to reward those that we do have more generously.

There are certainly qualities other than skill, training, risk, and
scarcity that we might wish to include as standards for the differentiation of contribution and reward. Rather than go on with the
list, however, let us reassert that what we are saying is probably

generally understood within the reason of all humankind. It is certainly not accurate to say that each and every citizen, in each and every case, will look upon the reward for tasks that their fellow citizens perform in the exact same way. No society will ever agree, with perfect uniformity, upon the numbered ratios or will accept the height of the pyramids of return that the various occupations receive. Again, some will say that physicians are two times more valuable than street sweepers while some will say ten times. But, at the same time, we do know that there will be substantial agreement within the citizenry that some occupations are at least more important than others.

Two processes, in a sense, are going on at the same time here. There is agreement in general that physicians are more valuable than street sweepers and disagreement on the specifics as to how much more valuable. The degree of agreement permits a political society to be one society, bound together by some commonality of human reason. The disagreement, as we have said, means that there will be ideology in society, as there is ideology in every society, because there is never perfect agreement among the values of all citizens (see Figure 2–1). The ideological question, in the case of the physician and the street sweeper, is the heart of the question of how tall the pyramid should be.

But the ideological question becomes more complicated when other, less clearly differentiated occupations become involved in the analysis. We should now concentrate on this more subtle portion of the ideological question, and, to do so, we shall contrast two other occupations and consider them in ways that use your own emerging understanding of reward and contribution.

FIGURE 2–1.
Agreement and disagreement in political argument.

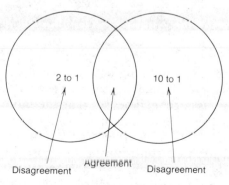

THE QUALITATIVE VARIABLE ———————

What do you think of the relative contribution and reward of two occupations such as engineer and psychiatric social worker? This is a more difficult question than the physician–street sweeper question, isn't it? Why is it more difficult? It is more difficult, we suggest, because the capabilities or the skill, training, scarcity, and risk components that we just introduced as the elements of reason are certainly much more clearly differentiated in the physician–street sweeper case than in the engineer–psychiatric social worker case. The skill, training, and scarcity of both jobs may be fairly high, whereas the element of risk, apart from the risks of taking one job over another, is really quite low for both. The aggregate valuation for both, therefore, might be about even.

Yet when we think of it, we can guess that there will be disagreement, perhaps considerable disagreement, over the valuation of these two new occupations. How do you feel about the relative value of the two occupations? Perhaps your answer lies in great part in the essence of your own ideology, perhaps even in the belief that you hold about the competitive or the cooperative view of human nature. What is the nature of what the engineer contributes? It is a structure, is it not, a physical contribution? It is very important in any modern society, and it directly relates to the external and tangible needs of society.

What is the nature of the contribution of the psychiatric social worker? It is more intangible, is it not? It is more abstract, not related directly to the external needs of society, and it is generally more intrinsic or internal in the sense that it is important to the linkages or bonds of a society. Such linkages are a part of the common values of a society. They promote a sense of association or a sense of belonging. They are, most certainly, not economic kinds of contribution, at least in a direct sense. By contrasting these two occupations, you should begin to see what we mean when we contrast the economic with the noneconomic contributions to society.

Let us pause for a moment. Once again, I need to ask you to keep the distinctions we are making between occupational valuations on a continuum, rather than within two separate categories. The fact that we say, in a general sense, that the more individualistic and competitive view of humankind values the engineer more highly than the psychiatric social worker does not mean that there is no worth placed upon that contribution by those who favor the engineer. Similarly, even the most noncompetitive view of human nature should and usually does acknowledge the value of an oc-

FIGURE 2–2.
Political valuation and contribution preference.

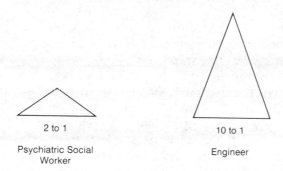

2 to 1	10 to 1
Psychiatric Social Worker	Engineer

cupation such as that of an engineer (see Figure 2–2). The more cooperative personality can enjoy a bridge or a building or any physical object that is well constructed. Yet there is still a difference in the two kinds of recognition. It is a difference that has a good deal to do with the human nature view of the citizen and a difference that ultimately has a good deal to do with political ideology.

An Example

Let me present you with a simple example. Have you ever been to a diving meet? Or, better yet, have you ever participated in a diving meet? You know that all the divers are scored for their efforts and, of course, that the best total score wins the event. But, if you recall, the score for each individual dive is derived from a combination of two subscores. The first score is usually called something like "the degree of difficulty," and it is the result of a long history of supposedly expert valuation that says that some dives are more difficult than others. Clearly, a dive involving three revolutions of the body should be weighed more than a dive involving only one.

But what about the difference between a tuck and a layout, a rollover, or a body spin? The valuation of these is more qualitative, is it not? Such valuations are more subject to a preference for one kind of performance over another. What if, in a diving meet that you entered, the valuation of the dives and the first scores were all changed around from what they usually were? What if the dives that you felt most accomplished in were downgraded and the dives that you performed the least well were now considered more important? Worse yet, what if you came to the diving meet and were told that there were no set scores for any of the dives and that you, the diver, had to set the "difficulty" scores on the night before the meet began?

Now you are dealing with everyday politics, and you can understand the actual mechanics of evaluation that go on with real contributions in a modern society. The question is not simply a matter of how much more physicians will be valued over street sweepers, two occupations that are far apart in the elements of skill, scarcity, and the like. It is now a question of which kind of arguably closely equal contributions you prefer to value more highly, the engineer and the psychiatric social worker being reasonably equal in risk, and so on. The differential is that because of their own values, some people value one occupation more highly than the other.

THE HISTORY OF VALUATION

Now, let us pause for a moment. What we have done so far is develop a framework, a more or less ideological framework, for the valuation of different kinds of contributions to a society. We now know that all societies have people living within them who have different valuation preferences. Your understanding of this problem has progressed from the desert island up through more complicated work situations and into qualitatively different kinds of work. We have thus fairly well covered the fundamental elements of what various perceptions or various views of the human reason would argue are a fair distribution of reward. The ideological identification should now be fairly clear to you, and thus what we need to look at next is a brief political history of how those orientations toward contribution and reward have developed themselves in modern times.

Remember that ideology is not going to leave our analysis. In fact, at the end of the next phase of the analysis, the major modern ideologies will spread themselves out before us in terms that we should be able to understand quite readily. What we are going to do now is go back into history and examine both how work has been valued and, to a lesser degree, what choices have existed over what kinds of work people chose to do.

If we begin with the feudal period, that is, the period that roughly extends from the fall of the Roman Empire to the beginning of the Renaissance or the modern age, we know that there was not a great deal of choice about the kind of work that individuals engaged in.

The static and closed nature of the feudal system left lord and serf locked into the occupations of their fathers, and with the minor exceptions of the clergy and a comparative handful of skilled trades-people, feudal citizens tilled the fields, raised a few animals, and shared the bounty of their work with the manor lord.

Valuation in the Feudal Period

What was the value of the work of the feudal serf? As we have said, the analysis of work that we have developed would not have made much difference. The lesson of the first chapter would not have applied because the distributions of the fiefdom were well fixed, with little that the serf could do about it. Also, the serf did not receive any compensation in the form of currency or money. The serf received only a prescribed share of what was produced. Yet feudalism presented a tiny glimpse of modernity, because for the practitioner of the skilled trade, or for the seller of wares who moved from one feudal estate to another or who appeared at the annual fairs, there was a monetary price charged for goods. The price could be determined in two ways, both of which are very important for us to understand because they still make up the principal ways in which a political society values economic contributions today.

Later Methods of Valuation

The first method of valuation, and the one that was particularly important for the skilled artisan of the day, had to do with an evaluation of what the quantity and quality of work was that the worker put into a product. Let us call that method of valuation a *rationalistic* interpretation because it has to do with how human reason, or the combination of different human reasons, adjudges a product of work to be valued. Let us go back to Aristotle, Justinian, and Locke and their notions of natural value, for the views of all three are relevant in the sense that the notions of "contribution," "giving everyone their due," and earning the "fruits of one's labor" are representative of the natural sense of the worth of certain goods.

In those days, the artisan worked on a product, maybe as a carpenter or in some other trade, but there was always a determination of the risk, skill, training, scarcity, and the like of such work. However, such rationalistic notions were not exclusive to the idea of the determining value. They were not exclusive because the producer and the seller of wares was sometimes able to charge a little bit more or a little bit less than what might have been the rationalistic price. What caused this variation from the rationalistic notion of work? The answer is very simple, and it had to do with what we would today call the sales *market*. It had to do with the relative price of one product with another similar product that was being sold within the same area.

Thus, the market, our second valuation technique, is an altogether different standard for determining valuation than is the rationalistic method of determining worth that we saw in the last chapter. It is a complex, competitive mechanism; rather than relying upon a notion of the risk, training, skill, and scarcity of a particular product, the market relies upon the bidding up or down of the value of different goods as they move through a marketplace. It centers the attention of the marketplace upon the movement of such goods through a vehicle by which people try to buy and sell various commodities.

In a word, the key to the concept of a market price is the relationship of that price to other prices to which it is being compared. In that sense, the market price is worked through by an analysis of the demand for the product and the supply of the product. To review, there are, again, two methods of evaluating the worth of anything. There is the rationalistic view, incorporating in some systematic way what the valuable qualities of something are, and there is the market view, which incorporates the direct result of the immediate competitive bidding for that object. A key thing to remember is that, in the real world, there is probably no price of any single commodity that is ever purely the result of either the rationalistic or the market method of valuation. There is always a little of both in the sales price of anything, but one of the political arguments that has continued to dominate political debate is whether one method or the other should be the principle method of valuation.

Mercantilism

As we have said, during the feudal period the market method played only a very small role in the valuation process. Most value was determined by the very nature of the work relationships that existed in the feudal system. But this began to change as history moved out of the feudal period. The next period of history was what is called the *mercantile* period, and during that time the modern nation-state was born, and the French, the English, the

Dutch, the Spanish, and others began to engage in manufacturing and trade in a way that benefited these new nations.

What exactly was mercantilism? Mercantilism was an economic and political set of policies that, in those countries that practiced it, actively encouraged private business in both manufacturing and overseas trade. In those places where mercantilism was practiced, feudalism was already giving way to a new prominence for artisans, and particularly for the new manufacturers who were becoming a more prominent part of the economy. The advanced nations, in short, were encouraging people to produce products that would go beyond the immediate area where they were made for sale in world markets. The noted historian Sir Henry Maine was later to call this shift out of feudalism a part of the long-term movement from *status* to *contract*. What he meant was that the role of work and the status of particular kinds of work was increasingly not a matter of one's station or one's forebearers' station in life as it had been in feudal times. What replaced that traditional notion of station was a matter of looking at what one as a worker was presently producing and what one as a seller of a product could get for that product in a pure economic setting.

When you think about it, the valuations that are possible with a more "open" economic system, that is, the possibilities for ways of valuing things that are for sale outside of a feudal arrangement, are more numerous when the number of different occupations becomes greater. As the status-arranged distributions of productivity were being replaced, the battle between market methods of valuation as opposed to the traditional rationalistic methods of valuation began in earnest. Because of the temptation to sometimes charge "what the market would bear," it was here that several clerics of the time, including Martin Luther, lashed out strongly against the evils of the economic market. For Luther, and for the orthodoxy of the mercantile period that he saw coming, the natural valuations of the aggregated populace were a far more appropriate method of valuation than was the market. The general sense, that is, the sense within the population as a whole of what the valuation of skill, risk, scarcity, and training were thought to be, was of a far better moral quality than was a finding of whatever price a product might bring on a market because of supply or demand.

The Emergence of the Market

Nonetheless, whether it was considered ethical or not, the market was becoming ever more dominant. Indeed, as the emerging nation-states competed more vigorously with each other during the mercantile period, it was the rising importance of the new national trading companies themselves and not the preachings of figures like Luther that kept the market system of work valuation from becoming altogether dominant.

Why were the trading companies not willing to go over to the market completely? On the one hand, the rush of business was picking up in the seventeenth century as mercantilism was reaching its greatest fruition. The trading companies of the English, the Dutch, and the others were extending themselves around the globe. Surely, the early merchants were adventurers and entrepreneurs, and their efforts continued to win greater political favor as they both contributed to the wealth of their countries and challenged the decaying status of the often idle aristocracy and the hated monarchy. Change was in the wind, and the protections that were written into the cause of private property were welcomed by the new entrepreneurs. Soon, the commercially oriented writings of such people as John Locke would be applauded as merchants sought to protect the new commercial and market-oriented forms of private property.

On the other hand, however, the changes that the period of mercantilism brought about were still quite minor compared with the changes that were right around the corner of history. The business interests of mercantilism still preferred controlled markets, not totally open to the competition of supply and demand. They were happy to have their exclusive franchises and subsidies that kept competitors away from established businesses.

Yet in the latter part of the eighteenth century, two circumstances occurred that, without exaggeration, affected everything that we have talked about so far more dramatically than any other set of events either before or since. It is not an exaggeration to say that when these new changes took hold, nothing that had to do with how economic productivity was arranged or evaluated would ever by the same.

The two events, quite simply, were the Industrial Revolution and the corresponding eventual acceptance of the market that denied rationalism as the primary evaluation device. We are now at another plateau of our understanding (and you should have all that we have talked about so far well understood). What we are now adding builds directly upon that earlier knowledge, for the Industrial Revolution was nothing less than a true historic milestone, an event that altered so much of the entire rest of history.

The Industrial Revolution

It happened only a little over 200 years ago, and its impact is still being felt today. When exactly did the Industrial Revolution begin? It is hard, of course, to give it a specific date, but it was during the 1760s and the 1770s that the water frame, the spinning jenny, Mr. Watt's reciprocating steam engine, and a number of other key industrial inventions were introduced. These devices made it possible for what were previously only "cottage," or small, often home-based manufacturing facilities to begin to take on the form of the modern industrial factory.

Do you remember reading the story of a miserly old weaver and his daughter? Do you recall that he was put out of his home-based business when a modern textile factory moved into his town? His name was Silas Marner, and the importance of his story is that he had done his work in a way that was radically changed by the modern factory. Silas Marner had performed all the processes of manufacturing himself—spinning the yarn, weaving the yarn on a loom, and even selling the finished product. But when the factory came, Silas Marner could not sell his material at a price that could compete in the market. He wasn't able to compete because the way that work was organized in the new factory meant that work was finished more quickly and more cheaply than Marner alone could do it.

What was this new and different way of organizing work? It was probably the most important of all the changes brought about by the Industrial Revolution, or at least every bit as important as the industrial inventions that the new factories utilized. To understand what happened, consider who, within the modern factory, controlled the way in which the work was organized? The answer is that the owner controlled the organization of work. The very way that this work was controlled by the entrepreneur and was then parceled out among the workers was radically different from any way in which work had ever before been organized.

How was it different? It was different in that the work was broken up into little segments, with one person spinning yarn all day, another operating a loom, another replacing yarn onto the loom, and so forth. Most of the political argument that has taken place over the valuation of work in the last 200 years has concerned the fairness of the valuation of work when each worker only performed little segments of entire tasks and performed these tasks for someone else. From the time of the Industrial Revolution, the machinery, the tools, the material that was being worked on, along with the work place itself were owned by someone other than the worker. What this now meant for the valuation of the worker's work is what we will concentrate on in the next few pages.

The Modern Valuation of Work

From where, specifically, was the new efficiency of work supposed to come within the new factory system? It came, more than from any other place, from the idea that an individual who learned a specific task such as wool cleaning, spinning, or weaving could do that work more efficiently and quickly if the worker only had that segment of work to do. Under the new industrial work process, again, each worker did only that single segment of the work and did it over and over again before passing it along to the next worker who would, in turn, do another section of work on the product.

This entire process, again, was an attempt at a greater efficiency of work, and without question, the new method did seem to demonstrate that more work could be done by fewer people in a shorter period of time. This new concept was called the *division of labor*, and what it meant was that, from this industrial period of industry on, the wage-earning worker would never again be responsible for the manufacturing of an entire product.

The effect on the evaluation of such work, of course, is what we are principally concerned with, since it is the valuation of work in a manufacturing setting that has led to the ideological controversies of the modern period. To be sure, the factory system surely existed and still does exist within other kinds of valuational systems. Yet it was the factory system's role in the formative period of capitalism that raised the issues that made the factory system so controversial.

Let us recall that the element of factory ownership was what changed the worker's condition and made the entire valuation issue so different after the Industrial Revolution. What, again, was the difference? Before the Industrial Revolution, the person who worked on a product usually owned the materials that went into the product and almost always owned the tools that were used in the production of the good. The importance of these simple facts is that the valuation process could thus be seen as one process, the essence of which could be contained within the scope of the quality and quantity of each person's work. The preindustrial artisan could take unfinished material, such as wood, leather, wool, or whatever, and, because that artisan went through all the stages of improvement, there was never any doubt about to whom the finished product belonged.

This method of work, and this way of looking at work, of course, changed in the modern factory. The entrepreneur's ownership of the materials, along with the breaking up of the work of the factory worker, was truly a dramatic change in work routine. Our main interest is to understand what effect all this had on the valuation of the now divided labor. By now, you should see that the work of that individual laborer was so totally separated from not only the traditional ownership of the worker but also from the traditional value standards that rationalistic evaluation had always encouraged. It would not be as easy now for labor to be evaluated on the basis of the skill, training, scarcity, and risk of what the creation of that product required. Now, labor itself was being bought and sold. Labor was a part of the market, or as some have said, labor was a commodity.

THE MARKET AND LABOR COMBINED: ADAM SMITH ━━━━━━━━━━━━━━━━

We said earlier that two major events occurred at approximately the same time. The first was the coming of the Industrial Revolution with its change in the nature of work and the valuation of work. The second was an intellectual acceptance of market valuation, beyond the practical use of the market. How did the idea of market valuation become so accepted? It became accepted, in great part, because of the writings of a man named Adam Smith, a writer who supported the newly emerging system of production and labor. Smith, with some real concern for the welfare of all citizens of his native Britain, still believed that large amounts of private capital provided a genuine opportunity for nations to increase their material well-being. A fair reading of Smith would reveal that at some time he wanted that wealth to be spread throughout all the community, even down to the workers.

Yet Smith was a realist, and he knew that, for a while at least, wages would not be bountiful for the new industrial worker. Smith therefore filled most of his now famous *The Wealth of Nations* with talk of the promised increases in productivity and the pricing mechanisms for products, but not with what workers should be

paid. Yet let us look at one portion of Smith's thought rather carefully, for it is one that is largely misunderstood today as the labor
valuation question continues to be argued over by the great political
ideologies.

Some will say that Smith was a pure market theorist and that
he believed in permitting the competition of products and the amount
of supply and demand in the market to exercise full power in
determining the price of each product. Some might say that a rational method of valuation should not be considered and that the
contribution question should be decided solely by what the price
of labor is in a labor market. Yet Smith's ideas were often misin-
terpreted. Philosophically, Smith's entire notion was derived from
the rationalist rather than from any independent market value
notion of valuation. His arguments in favor of finding fair prices
for products as well as for labor, call for a recognition of what he
referred to as "natural" prices and "natural" values for things.
Smith, in other words, was not in favor of having the market run
away with prices, in either a higher or lower direction according
to the supply and the demand of whatever was being bought and
sold. He never argued that the price of something should be based
upon "what the traffic would bear," and in fact, he contended that
prices for goods would rise and fall according to economic laws
that would keep those prices within reason.

Smith's model, again, is truly rationalistic, with supply and demand vacillating only slightly, and doing so around a point that,
without question, was still dictated by the larger laws of natural
or rationalistic valuation. The skill, risk, training, and scarcity of
an occupation were still to be taken very seriously, as Smith fully
intended to keep the rationalistic valuation notion at the core of
the contribution question.

Of course, and as you might have guessed, much has happened
to Smith's theory since he wrote his work, and what has happened
to the labor market has left the idea of capitalism open to substantial criticism. Let us remember that Smith spent most of his
time talking about the pricing mechanism of commodities, goods,
and services, and that the adaptation of his argument to the industrial wage of the worker was not paramount in his thinking.
The use of something like a market involving laborers who worked
for an entrepreneur was a substantial step from rationalistic valuation, and the debate over the industrial wage, which again was
the core of the argument in political ideology for nearly 200 years,
began with the attempt to apply Smith's thinking to the matter of
the industrial wage.

CONCLUSION ━━━━━━━━━━━━━━━━━━━━━━━━

In sum, it is hard to overstate the importance of the dual happenings of the Industrial Revolution and the justification that came along for a market valuation of labor after the writings of Adam Smith. The debate over the industrial wage, or the height of the modern distributional pyramid, began in the late 1700s and has continued until the present time. This was so even though, until quite recently, a majority of citizens in Western industrial nations still made their livings in agricultural or farm-related enterprises. Yet, as we will see, those agricultural occupations made increasingly little difference within the ideological battle of politics. The dispute over the contribution and the wage of the factory worker was the single most important issue that divided people ideologically and defined their politics. Although the last few years have seen additional modifications of the debate, it is from these early arguments over the fairness of the industrial wage that we still understand much of today's political ideology.

Glossary

TERMS

skill

training

risk

scarcity

ideology

rationalistic valuation

market valuation

mercantilism

status

contract

division of labor

Industrial Revolution

Silas Marner

The Wealth of Nations

NAMES

Adam Smith

James Watt

Martin Luther

St. Thomas Aquinas

CHAPTER 3
CAPITALISM AND ITS MODIFICATIONS

The new industrial order created many new kinds of employment. Yet just as there were new employments, so too there were varied notions of what was fair payment for the industrial worker. The economic world was becoming more complex, and it was changing so rapidly that the role of the old social structures such as the church and the small farm village changed. These stable institutions, which had in great part insulated political systems from widely varying political ideologies, were now less important than they had been.

From one perspective, the very fact that the matter of the industrial wage could become a public issue was a sign of great change in politics, a change that in good measure was the result of a growing political spirit of democracy. We will talk a good deal about the evolution of democracy before long, but we are now at a point in our model where we should continue with the valuation question as it grew within the Industrial Revolution.

BEYOND THE INDUSTRIAL REVOLUTION ⸺

Generally speaking, the ideologies that came out of the debate over industrial valuation can be grouped into four overarching categories. Of course, there are more than four ideologies in the modern world, but as the argument over fairness of the industrial wage evolved, four major ways of valuing industrial labor emerged prominently. The four ideologies are (1) *pure* or eighteenth-century *capitalism*, (2) *liberal* or twentieth-century *capitalism*, (3) *democratic socialism*, and (4) *Marxist socialism* or *communism*. The first ideology, capitalism, is what originally grew from the early industrial period, particularly as that industrialism developed in both England

and the United States. Apart from Smith's admonitions, capitalism as a political ideology held that the market, not rational valuation, took precedence in the battle over the industrial wage. Capitalism as practiced, in short, meant that the labor valuation question was left alone by society and the distributions of the society or the pyramid of reward moved to whatever height it found on its own.

A key phrase that explains early pure capitalism is the French term *laissez-faire*. It is an expression that, we think, grew out of the mythical response of a French industrialist to a French government official who asked him how the government could help his industry. The official's question was not an unusual one, because before capitalism, as we have noted, government worked hand in hand with businesses of the time, assisting them generously in their mercantilist battles with other nations' subsidized enterprises. The economic theory of that earlier period was not one that would leave business alone. It was one that encouraged government and business to work together.

The French industrialist's request for freedom from government involvement in business was a radical one. The idea that franchises, subsidies, restrictive tariffs, and all the other arrangements that previously assisted business would now be abandoned was revolutionary indeed. As a matter of historical notation, it should be mentioned that the English, and later the Americans, took this issue of removing the government from business more seriously than did the French or other countries of the European continent. Yet even on the European continent, there was a change in business-government relationships in the late eighteenth and early nineteenth centuries, and it meant that the relationship between the public and economic sectors was substantially more distant.

The result of this new separation of government and business was that the very capital of the new entrepreneurs (the money that was invested in new enterprises) often came from sources other than government. These new industrialists in large part felt that they owed little to the existing governments. (Remember that governments at that time, particularly by today's standards, were still only marginally democratic. Also, a significant tension existed between this newly burgeoning industrial class and the old monarchies and landed aristocracies that were still influential in their representation of the hereditary social and political orders of earlier times.)

In England, as early as the close of the seventeenth century, the philosopher John Locke was already attacking the lack of productivity that came from the traditional titled landed aristocracy. Locke also attacked the Anglican church and its vast untaxed land holdings on the basis of their economically unproductive nature. Nonetheless, the manufacturing breakthroughs of the Industrial Revolution meant that the factory-style companies could be independent of the government and could thus control all of their internal business operations such as the hiring and firing of workers.

It seemed that the promise of Adam Smith was being realized. The new economic separation from government, along with the increasing economic influence of market valuation, was leading to a substantial increase in total wealth. Factories boomed out new levels of productivity, and the old methods of manufacturing were soon forgotten. What the new arrangement also did, however, was to restructure the entire argument over contribution and value. It began, in short, the modern ideological debate over the distribution of wealth within the new industrial states.

MODERN VALUATION OF WORK

England, in particular, evidenced this new debate, and the arguments surrounding the industrial wage questioned whether modern factory workers were receiving fair payment for their work. We should now consider an important question as part of this analysis. If the government and society at large were separated from the economic productivity of that society, and if work itself was broken up so that wages were largely dependent upon a commodity-like notion of the market, what then dictated the condition of that market? The answer, though unfortunate for the worker, was rather simple. With the increasing movement of former agricultural workers into the city and with the usage of child and female labor, the condition of the market was such that the *supply* of labor was nearly always in excess of the *demand* for that labor. In other words, although the equilibrium between supply and demand for commodities was usually stable and prices remained close to "natural" prices, the supply and demand imbalances for labor nearly always reflected an oversupply in the market.

What was the impact of this oversupply on the "price" of labor? What did this mean for the industrial wage of the worker? It meant that the price of labor was nearly always very low, even well below what Smith would have predicted. When there were more people ready to work than there were jobs available, the worker was forced to take the wage that was offered or be replaced by someone waiting outside the factory's door. This kind of labor market became the standard in early or "pure" capitalism, particularly since both the product and labor markets were very open. The labor markets were not influenced by government or even by ethical norms, and, when it came to the industrial wage, Smith's hope that all prices would approach a "natural" or rationalistic level was never realized.

Yet, if an unbalanced supply and demand for labor during the Industrial Revolution made things difficult for the worker, another event soon worsened the market condition for that worker still further. The English government, close on the heels of industrialization, engaged in a policy that drove even more workers into the overcrowded industrial labor market.

Consider the series of legislative acts known as *the enclosures*. The Enclosures were, simply, the sale of a good deal of what had long been public English lands or what were called *commons* to private investors. It was the closing of what had long been public lands.

This was an important event in the matter of the industrial wage because the land in question had been worked on by farmers and shepherds, sometimes for generations and, with the Enclosures, these people could no longer work them. Again, as lands were sold, a large number of rural workers, mostly farmers and shepherds, were thrown from the land and into a now even larger pool of potential industrial workers. The expulsion had caused a great movement into the manufacturing cities, and, of course, the result of such an urban migration only furthered the disequilibrium of supply and demand. As you can guess, the pyramid of distribution for the entire industrial society, and the differentiation between the reward of the entrepreneur and the worker, went even higher still (see Figure 3–1).

In summary, the period of early or pure capitalism brought forth

FIGURE 3–1.
Early industrial distribution and criticism of those distributions.

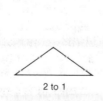

2 to 1

Critics of Early Industrial
Revolution Distribution

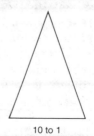

10 to 1

Early Industrial
Revolution Distribution

the first blush of political ideology that grew out of the Industrial
Revolution, and that promised to bring wealth to the inhabitants
of industrializing nations. As for the industrial wage, it would not
be fair to say that capitalism, by an original design, kept the wages
of the new, fragmented, and largely unskilled industrial worker as
low as it did. It would be fair, however, to say that things turned
out that way. If we consider that the excessive height of the pyramid may have been unintentional, we should also acknowledge
that the peak of the pyramid was very high indeed. The notion that
any citizen was at least theoretically able to become an entrepreneur was not much comfort to the everyday worker who entered
industrial work with no capital and little skill. The former farmer
or shepherd who was newly arrived in town, had to take what he
could from wherever he could get it. He had to work in the new
factory or not work at all.

THE HUMAN NATURE CHALLENGE

Having reviewed the essential elements of the Industrial Revolution and the changes that it brought to the valuation of work, we
should now return to our opening assumptions about human nature. Remember that you were asked to consider the competitive
versus cooperative view of human nature and to view such things
as being a part of a single continuum? Would you agree that the
underlying human nature assumptions of early capitalism were
decidedly competitive and that they rested toward one end of the
human nature continuum? Adam Smith certainly thought so. Smith
spoke glowingly of economic self-interest, and our model of politics
would acknowledge that, in fact as well as in theory, the more
competitive, individualistic notions of human nature were the very
notions that led to the highest pyramid of distribution and reward.

Remember, too, the two kinds of poker games we discussed and
the "high-stakes" poker players who believe in high pyramids of
distribution and large differentiations between winners and losers.
These kinds of citizens, as you may guess, want the larger game
of politics to be similar to that high-stakes game. Their viewpoint
reflects the image of a competitive world that contrasts with the
world view that embraces a more cooperative view of humankind.
The cooperative view, again, prefers a reduced pyramid of distribution and holds that the pursuits of humankind are not entirely
economic. This last point deserves special emphasis, for what we

should be thinking of here is not simply the contrast between the good and thus the successful economic players of the game and the not so successful players. You should also consider the contrast between people who value the entire economic pursuit greatly and those who value such things less highly.

Consider the difference between the valuation of the engineer and the psychiatric social worker again. It is a different kind of valuation that we are talking about than with the physician and the street sweeper. Early capitalism not only extended the pyramid of distribution skyward, it also welded the affection for economic gain itself into something that, with the help of Adam Smith, approached a full-blown political theory. Self-interest became more than an isolated political or economic concept. It became the core of an ideology.

LIBERAL CAPITALISM ━━━━━━━━━━━━━

What happened to pure capitalism? We know that it ran into almost immediate opposition as many considered it to rest upon a severely competitive notion of human nature. Many considered it to violate the classical notions of a worker being entitled to a reward "in proportion to contribution" or according to "the fruits of one's labor," or in receipt of one's "just due." Many also considered it to violate ethical principles of what was fair and just in a largely Christian society. Let us now examine these criticisms of early capitalism.

One of the earliest thinkers to believe that pure capitalism violated traditional valuation standards was the economist David Ricardo. Ricardo, writing in the early nineteenth century, argued that the oversupply of working people, along with the fragmentation of work within the new industrial order of factory labor, meant that workers' wages were excessively low. Importantly, he also argued that these wages would continue to be at or near the subsistence level that existed following the Industrial Revolution. Ricardo called his theory the *iron law of wages* by which he meant that the oversupply of workers that existed in the early days of industrialism would continue to exist into the future.

Ricardo reasoned that in any period, a certain number of people were needed to work in factories and that as the next generation grew to working age, the supply of labor would be kept high enough that wages would remain low. Perhaps, during hard times, there would be an increase in infant mortality, and infant mortality might even be severe enough that perhaps, for a short period, there might be too few workers. Under those conditions, wages (under the influence of supply and demand) might rise a small amount. Yet, Ricardo argued, as soon as the wages rose a bit, the children of the industrial worker would be better fed and infant mortality would consequently drop. Ironically, the very prosperity that would feed, clothe, and house these children would put more of them on the labor market, with the consequent growth in the labor supply inevitably bringing labor's wages crashing back down to subsistence levels.

Ricardo, as you might have guessed, was sympathetic to the new industrial worker. He argued, for example, that the worker's labor should continue to be valued on rationalistic (risk, skill, etc.) grounds or on the notion of what he called *labor embodied*. There was, he argued, a kind of inherent value to labor, one that existed apart from the market for work. Ricardo, even today, is known among economists as a "value theorist"; that is, he is recognized as one who endorsed the notion of a stable, rationalistic standard of value contributed within the labor market. His views, incidentally, are often contrasted to those of his contemporary, Thomas Malthus, who believed in the idea that labor has no inherent or rationalistic value and that it is only worth what it can command in the labor market.

Certainly, with early or pure capitalism, the views of Malthus were winning out over those of Ricardo. But the writings of Ricardo had a significant effect on people's thinking about the industrial wage, and the beginning of the reform of pure capitalism was very much in tune with, if not also inspired by, Ricardo's early nineteenth-century work.

Let us now examine the first of the three alternatives to early capitalism. Again, it is sometimes called liberal or state capitalism, and it represents the least radical set of changes in early or pure capitalistic practice. It is also the model of capitalism that is prominent today in many of the modern nation-states, most significantly the United States.

We shall discuss three aspects of liberal or state capitalism. All these aspects will be representative of the kinds of changes that altered early capitalism in order to redress some of the imbalances of the early model. They respond, in other words, to the major criticism that was made of pure capitalism. The first, one that we have already talked about, is what many considered to be the *unfairness of the industrial worker's wage*. The second has to do with the *safety of the industrial worker*, and the third has to do with the *stability* or the *survivability of capitalism through its cycles of prosperity and depression.* Let us begin with the question of industrial safety, realizing that the safety of the modern workplace was not simply an issue that concerned early capitalism alone. It was, however, one of the problems of early capitalism that many critics cited as an early weakness of the capitalist arrangement of productivity.

Industrial Safety

Industrial safety became an issue in the early days of capitalism. The long hours and the poor training of workers who wrestled with crude and often unreliable machinery endangered both the life and limb of the worker. To understand the evolution of industrial safety standards better, we should first know something about the law of the late eighteenth and nineteenth century.

Essentially, the kinds of worker protections that we now take for granted did not exist in this early time because the traditional law of the period was thought to protect the rights of an injured worker. That law, the common law, although embracing a generous body of personal protections often expressed in "writs," was based solely upon an individual's rights and obligations. At first blush, such a foundation for law looked fair indeed, for if you as a worker were injured you could sue your employer in a common law court, and at least theoretically, you were on an equal footing in claiming your rights.

Yet, unfortunately for the worker, every claim of negligence against a company that a worker might make was faced by rigid common law *defenses* that were available to the employer. The bulk of those defenses came from an earlier time in the common law when there were no factories and when injuries caused by one party to another were easily adjudged as being a result of someone's negligence. In a factory system, the injury to a worker was nearly always more indirect, the harm coming from a machine that was owned by, but not directly under the control of, the owner. In effect, the work situation itself had changed, but the law that surrounded the worker had not.

The common law provided for a number of defenses to a legal claim, and these defenses became rather notorious in the industrial era, known as *the unholy trio.* The elements of the unholy trio were (1) contributory negligence, (2) assumption of risk, and (3) the fellow servant doctrine and, as we review each of them briefly, let us concentrate on how they effectively deflected the injury claim of the worker.

The first, contributory negligence, is a very simple concept. It is a defense that is still used prominently today, particularly in such personal injury cases as automobile accident claims and other claims for negligence. What it means is that if any portion, that is, *any* portion of the cause of the accident was the result of the actions of the injured and suing party, the defense against that claim would be absolute and no compensation would be rewarded. Think about this for a moment. Contributory negligence is a very difficult rule to overcome because in the days of crude machinery, when a worker, for example, would work a loom or a press for many hours, the chance of making a mistake at some time was very great indeed. Yet, under the defense of contributory negligence, there would be no compensation for an injury from an operating error. As you can see, contributory negligence in an industrial setting was highly beneficial to the employer and very inhibiting to the injured industrial worker's attempt to receive compensation for an injury.

The second defense of the unholy trio was known as the assumption of risk, that is, if the worker knew, or should have known that the work undertaken was inherently dangerous, then this knowledge could be used by the employer as a defense against the worker's injury claim. We have already stressed that virtually all the occupations of the early industrial period were dangerous. If you were injured while operating a steam engine or an automated loom, it was assumed that you knew the task was dangerous. According to the law, if you were hurt in such a job, you had consented to that risk of injury.

The third component of the unholy trio was known as the fellow servant doctrine. What it did was permit an employer to say that if the injury sustained by an employee was in any way the fault of another worker and not the entrepreneur, then the employer, again, would not be liable. Consider the situation in an early factory setting. At a time when hours were long, training was short, and the young and the very old, along with those who were sometimes ill or too infirm to work, worked alongside you, the chances that an injury could occur because of the fault of a fellow worker were very great indeed. If such fault was the cause of injury, then the injured worker, again, could not successfully sue his employer.

These three concepts, again, were known as the unholy trio. They constituted a devastating use of traditional, preindustrial law within an industrial setting. When added together, few workers were ever able to sue their employers successfully. Further, consider the difficulty of receiving compensation for an industrial injury in view of the legal expenses that had to be incurred as well as how much time the worker had to be away from work.

There is one more point to consider with regard to industrial safety. Think of the extent to which a worker's suit would encourage an employer to build and maintain a safe factory. In other words, why would an employer, protected as he was by the unholy trio, pay the additional expenses to have a factory that would not injure people. The incentives would seem to run in the other direction; in fact, it would be cheaper to have the least protection for the worker since it was unlikely that the employer would ever be successfully sued.

Remember, again, that we are looking for the differences among early and pure capitalism and the liberal or latter-day capitalism that we see today in a country like the United States. What is different about factories today? What has changed since the time of the unholy trio? Factories, as you know, are safer now, and if you look to the current laws of modern nations, you will find that in virtually every one of them there are what are known as *workmen's compensation laws*. That is, an injured worker can apply to a government labor office to receive compensation for an injury without legal contest. The money that pays the worker under workmen's compensation comes from a pool or general fund of money that is provided by the employer.

Clearly, the incentives of the employer to have a safe workplace have thus turned around completely. Unlike the case under the pure common law, the current arrangement now puts the employer and the employee on the same side of the issue, each trying to prevent the injury from happening in the first place. The increased safety of the workplace, enhanced even further in recent years by legislation on specific industrial safety standards, is a clear movement toward liberal capitalism and away from early or pure capitalism.

The Industrial Union

Let us now look at the most important difference between pure and liberal capitalism. It concerns the modern industrial wage. Recalling the introduction to our discussion of that wage, we searched then for a way in which we could determine what would be a fair valuation of contribution and a fair apportionment of reward within the industrial setting. In discussing the Industrial Revolution, we have already noted that it pitted an entrepreneurial figure who was very new to history against an industrial worker who was having his own new form of labor treated as only a commodity. At the least, the worker was paid far less than what many would consider to be a fair "fruits of labor" return.

The "iron law of wages" concerns of economist David Ricardo over such wages were real enough, but they were largely understood only at a level of intellectual discourse. It was not until later in the nineteenth century that modern labor-oriented organizations began to take hold within most industrialized nations and challenge entrepreneurs over the industrial wage.

Consider one thing about the collective organization of labor right from the beginning. In great part, the degree of prominence that labor organizations may have within a country is determined by the extent to which the social and political orientations of that country are accustomed to a notion of collective work and collective responsibility for that work. In some ways, the range of this individualistic-to-collective orientation is not terribly different from the continuum of human nature viewpoints that ranges from competitive to cooperative. The United States, for example, is considered to be an individualistic nation; that is, its citizens consider themselves to be self-reliant and independent, providing for their own needs. The deep cultural impact of the American frontier, its aloofness from other country's difficulties, and even its separation from the Mother Country of England have led to this deep devotion to individualism.

As a result, Americans tend to believe that individual Americans work for themselves and that they should continue to do so. In the United States, therefore, the labor union as a worker's organization has never been as well received as it has been in some industrial settings in other parts of the world; here, for example, unions have never accounted for more than 24 percent of the work force, whereas in most other industrial nations the percentage has always been higher.

In contrast to the United States, unions have a long history in Germany, based on the Germans' abiding belief in *guilds* or collective trade organizations that reach well back into the feudal period. Apprenticeships brought the sons of journeymen and master workers into the trade of their fathers, and the guilds then went on to foster not only the well-being of their own members, but that of their families and dependents as well. They did this through various beneficial and protective societies that provided early forms of casualty insurance, old-age protection, care for the handicapped, and so forth. There was thus a more naturally communal notion of society, work, and group benevolence. When industrialization came to Germany, it was understandable that the industrial workers would ban together into what we now call unions.

This process of banning together to bargain for wages and benefits has, of course, often been a key to the improvement of the individual worker's condition. It made use of a concept called "collective bargaining," in which the industrial worker attempted to redress what he considered to be an unfair bargaining situation. Why is it that bargaining as a group is better for the worker than is bargaining as individuals? The answer is quite simple for just as the worker was often restricted to working at the only factory in a town and for a wage that was at or near subsistence, the instrument of collective bargaining made the employer deal with labor as part of an exclusive working group. Collective bargaining, in short, prevented the occurrence of other pools of potential factory workers from standing in line outside the factory door. You as a worker could no longer be brushed aside for a cheaper worker if you refused a subsistence wage. Recently, union membership has declined even below the 24% figure. Some of the reasons for this decline involve a movement away from industrial labor into so called "white-collar" employment.

Yet some of the decline is due to the notion of class within America's political history or because class "solidarity" never formed within the mind of the American worker. As a consequence, many of the unions that were formed in Europe were not formed in the United States until late in the century, and union membership was not only low but political resistance to the unions was very strong. Nonetheless, within what remains as a fair-sized industrial segment and, perhaps even within some of the lesser skilled of the white-collar clerkship or secretarial jobs, the union is still an important instrument for the maintenance of wage minimums and other worker benefits. Let me share one story of such resistance with you, one that was quite typical of unionizing activity and beyond that of the traditional craft unions in the late nineteenth century.

The early days of the union movement were often marred by violence, the Haymarket Affair and the Pullman strike being only two of the incidents in which union and union organizing activity were met with strong resistance by business interests and an often business-dominated government. In the Pullman strike, railway labor union leader Eugene V. Debs was thrown into jail after stopping trains that were carrying Pullman Palace Car Company cars south of Chicago. The cars were manufactured in the town of Pullman, a company town built by George Pullman that had its own grocery stores and other facilities. The structure of the wage, however, compared with the structure of rents and prices in the stores (where bills were paid with company script), was such that the worker was never able to pay the entire debt. As the singer Ernie Ford once put it in a song, the worker always "owed [his] soul to the company store."

After great effort, labor leader Debs organized the workers and called for a strike against the Pullman Company, eventually barricading the tracks near the railroad yards. The federal government, against the pleas of Illinois Governor John Peter Altgeld, who was sympathetic to the workers, but with the encouragement of former railroad attorney and then federal Attorney General Richard Olney, entered the confrontation against the workers. Although Debs had consented to permit the U.S. Mail cars to cross the picket lines, the railroad companies refused to disconnect these cars and thus the strike was held to interfere with the mails. Predictably, the strike was broken and Debs was sent to jail.

This one story is typical of what happened to non-craft union activity throughout the United States. From an employer's perspective, unions represented an unfair attempt to overreward an industrial laborer for his work through the device of having the employer negotiate with all of the workers rather than with each of them. From the worker's perspective, unions only represented a justified attempt to redress the sometimes large differences of bargaining power that existed between an employer and the individual worker.

Yet, beyond occasional violent attempts to control unions, in what other ways did owners oppose unions? There were many legal ways to stifle worker organizations, but the primary method was the weapon of the *injunction*, a court order that was used to prevent workers from forming unions or, if workers succeeded in the formation of a union, it was used to prevent the use of the one powerful weapon that a union possessed. What is the union's most powerful weapon? It is the strike, the cessation of work by all the employees of a particular enterprise, and it is this action that leaves the employer with no other means of sustaining business. Of course, union members also make a substantial sacrifice by putting themselves out of work. Indeed, they are often more ill prepared financially to remain unemployed for any length of time.

Yet workers do sometimes feel it necessary to strike, doing so to improve their long-range financial condition. Until the 1930s, unions risked legal action for the injunction whenever they chose to strike. But in 1932, after the crash of the Great Depression, the U.S. government passed the Norris-LaGuardia or the Anti-injunction Act and thus prohibited injunctions against unions and union leaders. The right to strike without being dragged into court or to jail was essential to the union movement, and the Act, again, assured the unions of this right.

Management, of course, was not happy with the loss of the injunction, and in the years immediately following, many companies made their employees sign what was known as a "yellow-dog" contract in a final attempt to restrict unions. The yellow-dog contract stated that the employee, as a precondition of employment, would never join a union. Finally, in 1935, two years after the election of Franklin Roosevelt to the presidency, the Wagner Act that forbade the use of the yellow-dog contract as a condition of employment was passed. It specifically provided for the union shop, which meant that once a majority of workers indicated their desire to join a union, the company had to deal with that union in wage and working condition contracts. Although a later change in that law, the Taft-Hartley Act, permitted individual states to exempt themselves from the Wagner Act, the legislation of the 1930s generally put the United States in line with the rest of the industrial nations who had for some time recognized the right of the industrial worker to deal with an employer as a group. The acceptance of this idea by liberal or modern capitalism, the second major ideology that we are examining, was one of the milestones that had somewhat lowered the distributional pyramid from that of early capitalism and diminished the difference in reward between the employer and the employee (see Figure 3–2).

FIGURE 3–2.
Distribution in liberal capitalism and pure capitalism.

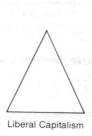
Liberal Capitalism

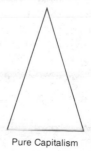
Pure Capitalism

The Problem of Cycles

As we have seen, the criticism of early or harsh capitalism was largely a criticism of the distribution of wealth or the height of the pyramid. You have been asked to consider both the question of worker protection or safety, and the question of collective worker bargaining as issues that dealt with the flattening of the pyramid of distribution between worker and owner. The other problem of early capitalism that also gained attention is as important as the distribution question. It has to do with *cycles* of a pure capitalism system for, from the very beginnings of capitalism, there was evidence that this novel economic system was prone to what we now often call the "boom-bust" cycle.

What is the boom-bust cycle? Ricardo had some hint of it when he wrote about the problems of the industrial era. Yet we know a good deal more about booms and busts now because we have continued to witness cycles even within modern, liberal capitalism. Since Ricardo's writings, more radical critics predicted that capitalism would suffer one gigantic collapse because of what were frequently called the "contradictions" of capitalism. Karl Marx, for example, thought that the cycles of capitalism would become more and more severe. Even in the United States, there were many who believed that the depression of the 1930s signaled the end of all forms of capitalism.

These cycles are best understood through the workings of what is called the *Phillips curve*, which shows that when unemployment drops substantially, the prices of commodities start to inch upward. This inflationary pressure eventually slows down the buying that people do, and thus leads to a reduction in the need for productivity and an eventual increase in unemployment.

Historically, throughout the eighteenth and nineteenth centuries, increasingly larger segments of the economy seemed to be captured by the boom-bust cycle, and the depths of the "busts" seemed to grow deeper. Again, the 1930s depression, which in many ways affected the entire industrialized world, led many to think that the end of capitalism was near, but it was during this very difficult time that a suggested solution to the boom-bust problem presented itself.

This solution should be understood, within the context of modern-day liberal or state capitalism, for it necessitated a rather considerable compromise of the notion of pure capitalism. To permit government involvement in the great cycles of capital investment, economic productivity, and the maintenance of high employment levels and the like was, indeed, a great change from the pure doctrines of capitalism. Yet, even in an individualistic society such as America, most citizens have accepted these changes, particularly the idea that the boom-bust cycles can be smoothed out by governmental action.

To understand what anticyclical actions modern governments can take, we should take a look at the specifics of an economic boom. Remember that a boom occurs when the economy is doing well and spending by citizens for housing, appliances, automobiles, and so on is at high levels. Capital investment by entrepreneurs in new factories, machinery, tooling, and so forth also runs at a high pace. Yet as the price of cars and appliances edges upward, a peak is reached and a maximum of purchasing and investment is reached as well. Hence, markets become overpriced, and there is, again, a slowdown in spending after this point is reached. The cutting back at this point by purchasers and suppliers cools the economy, although it is often cooled in a dramatically exaggerated way.

What, if anything, can a government do, regardless of whether it is within a capitalist country or within any other kind of system, to reverse such a failure of the economy? More specifically, liberal capitalism asks what it is that government can do that still does not disrupt the notion of private ownership of production under an essentially capitalistic economy. The answer to this question was understood best, perhaps, by John Maynard Keynes, an English economist who realized that to get a depressed economy back on its feet, the government might temporarily have to do the things that private businesses had temporarily stopping doing (see Figure 3–3).

FIGURE 3–3.
Pre-Keynesian capitalist cycles and the Keynesian solution.

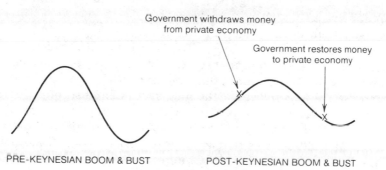

If there was a drop in investment in the private sector, that is, if businesses did not proceed with plans for a new plant or product, then maybe the solution was for the government to encourage such activity by pumping its own money into the national economy. Where would the government get the money to do this supplementary investing? Normally, the government's budget would not have additional money to invest in the economy as a whole. But the government could get that money by borrowing, that is, by going into debt for a while and *priming the pump* of investment back into the economy. That was the core of the Keynesian idea. The other half of the same notion was that when the economy later regained its strength, the government would then pay off the public debt by raising taxes and cooling down what might become an overheated economy.

Once more, the idea of countercyclical activity was for the government to do what the private sector had not done. It would borrow money and restart the economy, thus flattening the "bust" at the bottom of the cycle. When the period for the "boom" arrived, either enough additional tax revenue would be generated to pay off the debt or the government would increase taxes during the boom and keep the peak of buying and selling, once again, from surpassing levels that would not be sustainable.

In all, the Keynesian countercyclical investment and tax strategies sounded like a reasonable plan, and, to some extent, all economies that still depend upon private decision making in consumer and business investment use it today. There are problems with this technique, of course. The pump-priming or "start-up" portion of the cycle seems to respond less well each time it is attempted, and it seems difficult for governments to raise taxes or cut expenditures voluntarily during times when the "booms" of the cycle are overheating and when a cooling down is called for. As the United States has clearly seen, even within very recent times, it is too tempting during times of a rising economy to stop continuing to prime the pump by raising taxes.

Nonetheless, most people still have at least some degree of faith in Professor Keynes's theory. To a greater or lesser degree, they believe that the government should boost the economy in bad times and moderately discourage the economy during times that are prosperous. These policies of debt and governmental surplus, incidentally, are referred to as *fiscal policies*, and, are increasingly accompanied by what are called *monetary policies*, those being governmental policies that attempt to raise or lower the supply of money by raising or lowering interest rates or the cost of money to people who invest. Like fiscal policy, monetary policy has its adherents and its detractors, but the larger point is that pure capitalism has long ago modified not only the height of its pyramid but also its original notion of keeping government away from economic judgments. The stability of the economy is perceived to be in everyone's interest, and virtually all citizens and policymakers of modern, liberal capitalism now consent to having the government play at least some role in maintaining that stability.

CONCLUSION

You should now feel that you have an idea of some of the compromises that were made by early or pure capitalism. Other adjustments were also made, of course, but what has been done to improve the conditions of the worker, improve the worker's bargaining position for wages, and moderate the deep boom and bust cycles of pure capitalism make up the core of how early, pure capitalism has grown into moderate, liberal capitalism. If you can place yourself alternatively in the role of a wage-earning worker and then in the role of entrepreneur, and if you can place yourself in the role of any member of a citizenry that has expectations about an economy's ability to sustain itself, you might agree that the compromises of the modern brand of capitalism are necessary. Again, remember that modern, liberal capitalism is the second of the four basic ideologies that we are considering. The two remaining ideologies have gone farther in their criticism of early capitalism than has liberal capitalism. Correspondingly, they have asked for a greater degree of change than the wage, safety and stability adjustments that we have just reviewed.

Glossary

TERMS

pure capitalism

liberal capitalism

democratic socialism

communism

laissez-faire

labor supply

labor demand

the Enclosures

iron law of wages

labor embodied

labor commanded

the unholy trio

workmen's compensation

guilds

Pullman

injunction

Depression

Norris-LaGuardia

yellow-dog contract

Wagner Act

Taft-Hartley Act

cycles

Phillips curve

prime the pump

fiscal policy

monetary policy

NAMES

David Ricardo

Thomas Malthus

Eugene V. Debs

John Peter Altgeld

Richard Olney

Franklin Roosevelt

Karl Marx

John Maynard Keynes

CHAPTER 4
THE SOCIALISMS

The next political ideology on the broad spectrum of human nature assumptions and distributional heights is the ideology of democratic socialism. From the outset, you should distinguish democratic socialism from Marxist socialism or communism. Although socialism did act as the seedbed from which Marxist socialism or communism eventually grew, the two ideologies are very different. If liberal capitalism is based upon a slightly less competitive notion of human nature than pure capitalism, so socialism still maintains a slightly more competitive view of human nature than does communism. Liberal capitalism already acknowledged that pure economic competition and an attempt to get all that one could out of someone else's labor was not a formula for a just society. For socialists to come to their ideological position, they have gone farther and have openly embraced noneconomic values. With socialism, in other words, the pulling away from a purely economic morality along with a further redistribution in the valuations of economic contribution continues beyond liberal capitalism.

THE EMERGENCE OF SOCIALISM

Do you know of the Broadway musical (later made into a movie) about a London flower girl who was taken in hand by an upper-class English gentleman? The flower girl was, in effect, trained to be a "lady" of the better classes. The movie and Broadway musical were called *My Fair Lady*, but the story originated as a play written by the noted Irish playwright and socialist, George Bernard Shaw. That original work was entitled *Pygmalion*, and as with so many of the works of Shaw, it carried a distinct political message. Other than a playwright, Shaw was also a founding member of what was known as the Fabian Society, a group whose members believed very deeply in both socialist ideology and specific socialist reforms of the industrial system.

The Fabian Society was made up largely of intellectuals and artists, people who, at the end of the last century, decided that capitalism could no longer be reformed. Their answer to both the immediate unfairness of the industrial system and the more broadly based social discrimination of the English class system was state ownership of the large industrial institutions. To be sure, the Fabian Society was hardly the beginning of socialism, for on the continent of Europe, thinkers of a socialist bent had already questioned whether any form of private ownership would permit a moderation of capitalism's injustices.

We should remember that the English, and certainly the continental Europeans, fostered a rather strict social separation within their societies. This social separation during early capitalism led politically to very large distributional differences. Moreover, the ability to "move up" both socially and economically in such societies was severely restricted. The vehicles of public education, and the like that Americans have taken for granted were not available to the young English or European citizens who were not born of the "right" family.

How did these differences make socialism more possible in Britain and in Europe? As Shaw and his associates in the Fabian Society were quick to point out, one of the great underpinnings for the continuation of pure capitalism was a doctrine that argued that some people were made of "better stuff" than were others. The "survival of the fittest" doctrine claimed that a harshly competitive society was really just the essence of nature's plan.

Consider Charles Darwin and his work *The Origin of the Species*, which suggested that a theory of evolution among the animals of the world had permitted the surviving species of animals to refine and improve their condition. The Darwinists argued that humankind was the ultimate product of that evolution, and that very assertion made the entire theory highly controversial because it collided with traditional religious teachings. Yet the arguments of philosopher Herbert Spencer concerning the biological theory of evolution became even more controversial, for he applied the essence of evolutionary survival of the fittest to the area of political and economic thought.

What exactly did Spencer do with Darwinism? He claimed that survival of the fittest went on *within* all species, not just *between* species. He also argued that the stronger individuals within humankind were properly winning out in the new industrial age. From what we have discussed, you should be able to recognize that a thinker whose view of society is one of "survival of the fittest," would be opposed by those like Bernard Shaw, who had a more humanitarian and noncompetitive view of human existence. The view of the Fabian socialists was deeply committed to the notion of the perfectability of all human beings or at least to the great improvement of all people. Some of such thinking, of course, was manifested in terms of moral improvement, concentrating on how people could triumph over their sins of drink, sloth, licentiousness, and the like. But a good part of it also had to do with the improvement of humankind's capacities, and that is the element that brings us to *My Fair Lady* and the London flower girl, Eliza Doolittle.

You remember the story. Eliza, with a Cockney, lower-class accent, is taken in as a kind of experiment by a London gentleman, Henry Higgins. Eliza's "rine in spine" is converted to an upper-class "rain in Spain," while her manners, dress, and social affectations are also upgraded in accordance with the finest of London society. In the final act of the play, Eliza attends a fashionable horse race or "darby," and hobnobs comfortably with all the best of London society. Shaw's point is simply that everyone is potentially as good as everyone else and that anyone's manners and mind can be improved for the better. These, of course, are the basic assumptions of socialism.

Two additional points need to be briefly examined concerning the assumptions of socialism before we review socialism's specific prescriptions for society. The first concerns the nature of the industrial enterprise itself, along with what should be the enterprise's relationship to the government or state. In the early days of capitalism, with what seemed to be the ending of the mercantilist involvement of government in business, the role of government in the economic life of the nation was very limited. Modern, liberal capitalism brought the safety, wage, and business cycle kinds of things into the arena of public consideration in Europe and America. All but the most hardy of capitalists today would agree that these concerns are now legitimately shared by the public and private sectors.

The socialists, however, have argued that what they would call halfway remedies would never be sufficient to ensure justice for the industrial worker. The true socialist argues that the entire society bears responsibility for the economic well-being of its citizens. Indeed, a socialist takes the broad view of government's role in elevating the poor, feeding the hungry, caring for the sick and elderly, and undertaking a variety of other welfare services. Of course, even liberal capitalists grant some role for the government in these areas, but the true socialist will argue that the public sector, or the government, must own the means of productivity of the country and thus guarantee the welfare of all citizens. Specifically, a socialist at the turn of the twentieth century was likely to argue that there would never be sufficient motivation for capitalism to reform itself unless the citizenry, working through the government, clearly wrenched ownership of private economic institutions from the industrial capitalist.

Economic conditions have changed throughout the Western world in many ways, and consequently, the position of the modern socialist is more moderate now than it was 100 years ago. Today, a socialist is more likely to argue that huge, modern corporations should be brought under government supervision, not ownership. A socialist will also argue that the modern sales markets for commodities that are dominated by a few firms, and thus do not always engage in full, vigorous competition, should also be closely supervised by a wary government. Socialists claim that the entrepreneurs who presently control such productivity are contented with their rewards, and that they thus prefer to rest upon their laurels. These entrepreneurs, according to contemporary socialist thought, do not risk the kind of competition in which their truly capitalist predecessors engaged. Thus, the socialist governmental role within modern industry is to direct industry toward the public interest. Modern socialism may accept a certain amount of private ownership, but only under what is deemed to be necessary regulation. We will soon examine where specific socialist remedies have been most accepted, but there is one final component of the socialist ideology that we should examine before we proceed to its applications.

The Motivation for Work

One of the major assumptions of socialism concerns why it is that people work. Why do you think people work? In the early days of industrialization, the battle to survive in a crowded, urban work environment was reason enough to get out of bed each morning. But in later times, many, including prominent socialist thinkers, have asked about other kinds of motivations for why people take on the employment that they do. We have already mentioned that some people work more for material reward and that some are more interested in something else. In this regard, you should recall the difference between *extrinsic* and *intrinsic* work valuation. Put simply, the extrinsic worker tends to work more for the material (economic) rewards of labor or for the status or the prestige of the job; the intrinsic worker, on the other hand, works more for the enjoyment of the job or for the satisfaction of producing something for the well-being of the entire society.

Within socialist writings, the intrinsic value of work comes into full flower, with work being a part of the larger living of life. It is something to be shared with others, and the rewards for such labor and common work experience are ultimately held to be internal or more personally rewarding than is the economic kind of reward. The intrinsic valuation of work becomes more prominent as one moves to the nonindividualistic, noneconomic side of the human nature and political ideology continuum (see Figure 4–1). Predictably, the modern discussion of the intrinsic value of work was begun largely by prominent socialist thinkers like Saint-Simon, Fourier, and others who were concerned with life beyond the working hours as well as with the internal satisfaction of the work that a worker performed on the job.

With this review of work and its motivations, we should now have an idea of the visions of human nature and work and reward within socialist ideology. These visions are optimistic, perhaps even idealistic, about humankind and human nature and they believe in the essential goodness of people. They also believe that much of humankind's poverty and despair can be remedied by wise governments that can create more humane arrangements for economic productivity and distribution.

How has socialism fared as a political doctrine? It is particularly necessary here to differentiate socialism from communism, for

FIGURE 4–1.
Distributions for pure capitalism and socialism.

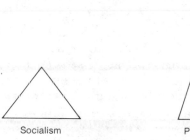

Socialism

Pure Capitalism

socialism has tended to exist in countries that have maintained democratic political procedures, whereas communism has thrived only in nations where the traditions of democratic process have never been strong. Israel may well be the best example of a democratic socialist nation, with some Western European nations, including Sweden, for example, embracing a much milder variant of democratic socialism. In most Western European nations, the transportation systems, the power companies, and, in some instances, the mines and even certain basic industries may be government owned. What is most interesting and important for our analysis as well, is that these nations have almost always been able to embrace this touch of socialism at the same time that they have rejected Marxist socialism. They have, in other words, maintained their democratic political processes while making adjustments in their economic arrangements.

Politically, the essence of the election of a socialist government within the Western European nations has been, at least within certain large industries, to remove the question of productivity and management from private consideration and to place it into the care of the newly elected political leaders. Importantly, however, the removal of these industries from private management has not meant that a socialist government has brought change in the democratic process of that government. Again, the full range of democratic processes, including the political parties' ability to campaign, the holding of free elections, open candidacies, and the like are still embraced. The very parties and candidates that oppose having major industries under government control continue to contest the nationalization of industry, and if they should win the next election, these industries may and frequently do return to private control. The fact that many countries within Western Europe today swing back and forth between mildly socialistic and liberal capitalistic governments has been a testament to the strength of their democratic processes. Perhaps more important is the fact that only a few enterprises switch back and forth from capitalism to socialism—a testament to the reconciliation of democratic socialism with the life and politics of these countries.

Again, the United States has never embraced socialism, largely because a class-oriented social and economic structure never existed here. Its young history, the fact that so many of its citizens came here to escape the restrictions of the European class system, and its very considerable economic achievements have all provided a full reservoir of support for capitalism in America. Various local governments such as those in Milwaukee, Wisconsin, Cincinnati, Ohio, and Bridgeport, Connecticut, have had socialist city governments, but the 6 percent vote for Eugene Debs in the 1912 presidential election was the highwater mark for American socialism on the national level.

COMMUNISM: SURPLUS VALUE

Again, it is essential to keep socialism, the form of ideology that believes in public control of the major industries within an economy, separated from communism, which is an altogether different ideology. Whereas socialism maintains all the democratic political forms, communism is so certain of the correctness of its ideology that it finds traditional democratic processes to be a betrayal of the purpose of government. Communism begins with a very definite view of the origins of human valuation. Even more important, however, it grows out of an unusually cooperative notion of human nature, one so cooperative, in fact, that its principal advocate, Marx, predicted that government of all kinds would some day no longer be necessary. In that and in many other ways, communism is fully at the other end of the human nature and distributional continuum from pure capitalism.

In specifics, pure communism almost totally denies any role for the economic market, whereas, you remember, pure capitalism was almost totally beholden to the market method of valuation. Consequently, communism, more than any other political ideology, fully embraces the rationalistic notion of valuation (skill, risk, etc.), arguing that the real workings of the market, contrary to Smith's predictions, do not approximate the rationalistic method of valuation. In consideration of the height of the pyramid, you should not think that communism endorses absolutely no differentiation between the contribution and the reward of, say, a physician and a street sweeper. Yet pure communism would tend not to look at the differences in skill, risk, training, and so on between a physician and a street sweeper. Hence, the ratio of valuation for communism would most likely be 2 to 1 rather than 10 to 1 (see Figure 4–2).

Beyond economic valuation, however, a location at the other end of the ideological continuum has also had an effect on what we previously discussed in the engineer–psychiatric social worker contrast. Again, we must ask what kind of work it is that a political system values, along with what kind of personal incentives are available for the worker. We know that capitalism, at one end of the human nature continuum, believes that individuals engage in their own self-interest. Communism, on the other end, regards

FIGURE 4–2.
Distribution for pure capitalism and communism.

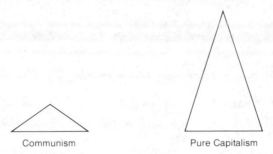

individualism as ultimately dangerous for the good of the entire society.

As you can imagine, the incentives for work are very different within a communist system than within a capitalistic system. Communism argues that everyone should work exclusively for the good of the whole and should be content with a large portion of nonmaterialistic, that is, intrinsic, reward. The pure communist, in reality, argues that everyone should work for a sense of accomplishment, pesonal enjoyment, and common purpose even more than does a democratic socialist.

Where do the ideas for such a reward system come from? And who made the principal arguments for this communist ordcr? Again, these ideas came largely from Karl Marx who was a German by birth but who lived much of his adult life in London. At one time, Marx worked as a London correspondent for Horace Greeley's New York *Tribune*. Yet Marx was undoubtably the severest critic of the new industrial capitalist distributions and, as a consequence, he was largely responsible for the separation of communism from the milder forms of democratic and utopian socialism that flourished during the nineteenth century.

Why was Marxist socialism so different from other socialisms? Like the others, it argued that the industrial worker was not being adequately compensated. Also, borrowing from David Ricardo's notion of *labor embodied*, he argued that the value of an individual worker could be rationally determined at a certain level of productive valuation. Let us say that you, as a steel worker, contributed your skill, took the risks, and underwent the training that allowed you to contribute 10 units of value to the steel mill that employed you. Marx argued that something happened to your 10 units of valuation between the time that you contributed it and the time that you received your reward. Do you remember our discussion of what happened to work during the industrial and in what many now call the postindustrial era? The worker was no longer the owner of what he or she was working on, and indeed, the worker was not even the possessor of the tools of production. After the Industrial Revolution, the worker entered into a place of work along with a number of fellow workers and stood before an assemblage of tools and products, adding to the value of the manufactured product. Then, after adding that value to the product, the worker would pass it along to the next person in the process or to the employer who, again, had owned the object throughout the process.

The entire process that Marx argued for was very simple. He suggested that the new capitalist system of pricing labor as a commodity, much like any other factor of the economic product, violated the notion of a labor theory of value. It violated the idea that the value of anything is a result of the labor that has gone into it in and that it permitted an employer to pay a worker less than that full 10 units of value that the laborer had put into the manufactured object. The labor theory of value had been around for a long time, with even John Locke and David Ricardo advocating that things should have their value judged by the work that had gone into them. With Marx, however, the challenge was more severe, and he labeled that difference between the true value of what someone labored for and the value that the laborer actually received as *surplus value*.

Surplus value is simply the difference between the 10 units worth of productivty a worker truly earned and the 5 units of payment that the worker received, with the other 5 units going to the employer. As Marx put it, the employer had "exploited" the other 5 units of value. Surplus value is the key to Marxist analysis. Volumes have been written on it, but if you can simply remember it as the end product of a view of human nature, a view of incentive toward work, and a view of who creates true productivity, all of which are at the other end of the continuum from pure capitalism, you will understand the essence of the theory. Marx's fundamental economic argument, based upon the notion of surplus value, is the essence of Marxist or communist ideology.

Dialectical Materialism

To complete your understanding of communism, concentrate upon the view of history that Marx advocated very strongly. Think of this view of history partly because it will help toward a full understanding of our final ideology. Also think of this view because it introduces another figure and another concept that we will encounter again later in the development of our political model. The figure is the German philosopher G. W. F. Hegel, believed by many to have been the greatest of the modern thinkers about politics. Marx, for reasons unlike those of other admirers, thought well of Hegel's writings, but he admired Hegel principally because he saw an opportunity to use Hegel's thinking about the evolution of history for his own ideological purposes.

Hegel was known as an *idealist*, a believer who argues that the "ideas" in people's heads, that is, their visions of the world, represent the beginnings of change in the world. Hegel argued, in other words, that we think of things first, that is, that we have an idea or an ideal of what the world should be like, and then, later, we act in such a way that we try to bring our ideal to reality.

The opposing view of history is called *materialism*. It argues that the real world is the original element of reality and that our ideas about that reality follow along behind. The idealist versus the materialist difference, in short, is a matter of what comes first, the idea or the reality. Hegel argued that the idea came first, and Marx, very importantly for our discussion, turned it around and argued that reality came first. In arguing as he did, Marx modified Hegel's thought to assist his (Marx's) political ideology.

To understand Marx's ideology, we must first understand Hegel's view of history more clearly. Idealism was not a notion purely original to Hegel, for even the Greeks had talked about it. Nonetheless, it was Hegel who developed a modern and very sophisticated notion of what is called the *dialect*—one of the most profound concepts in all of philosophy.

What is the dialectic? To keep your understanding of it simple, remember that Hegel, the idealist, believed that an idea comes before the reality. From there, notice that the word begins with the prefix *di*, a splitting of something into two parts. From a position of idealism, Hegel reasoned that at any time in history, there was a prevailing framework or a general approach of the human mind that people adapted to understand their world. That framework, or way of looking at things, was called a *thesis*, that is, an underlying rationale of how the human perception understood the world. What Hegel did with this thesis was to show that before history progressed through its various phases, humankind, at each of these phases, began to see things that were different or that did not fit into the old way of thinking. What this led to, eventually, was a different or modified way of thinking about the world. Remember again that for Hegel, thinking about the real world always came before the real world itself.

What was this new way of thinking called? Hegel called it *antithesis* or "anti-thesis," to reflect the competing way of thinking about something. Again, he argued that it became important when people began to realize that the thesis was falling short of explanations for what was going on in the real world. By "falling short of explanations" we mean that once people became increasingly aware of new things that were happening, that is, as things seemed to fall outside of the patterns of the thesis, they began to turn to new explanations. For a while, perhaps, people would attempt to argue against the importance of the few things that didn't fit into the old thesis.

Eventually, however, there would be such an increase of unexplained events, that a true idealist would use his or her mind and vision to invent a new and more sophisticated model for the understanding of the world. For a while, that more sophisticated framework, the antithesis, would fight against the old orthodoxy of the thesis until something very extraordinary would happen: the intellectual combat existing between the thesis and the antithesis would reach a crescendo wherein the best portions of both ideas would merge. The resulting new set of ideas would become the *synthesis*, the most sophisticated of explanations for what the world was all about. It served not only as the reconciled combination of the two previously competing world views, but also as a way in which humankind could move to the next stage of real history. It suggested that humankind could move to the next historic stage with an ability to understand and, to some degree, even control what stage the world was passing through. Finally, this synthesis would eventually become the new thesis and the entire dialectical process would repeat itself throughout history.

The dialectic, of course, has had an extraordinary impact upon how we look at history. Hegel suggested that the essence of history was in the human mind. Marx took the notion of the dialectic and adapted it to his own view of politics and history. He was deeply concerned with the injustices of the capitalistic economic system rather than with the stretching of human understanding, and he believed that the root of all political systems lay in the hands of those who own the means of economic productivity. Marx's materialism or his reality, in other words, was economics, and he clearly set it off against Hegel's philosophical idealism. Further, instead of viewing the stages of history as represented by different and improving levels of human understanding, Marx believed they were represented by the way in which economic productivity was organized in political societies.

There were several historic stages in Marx's analysis of who controlled economic productivity. These stages all reflected what the arrangement of work was at that point of history, or how humankind provided for itself at different stages of historical development. The first stage and the one that Marx felt best revealed the communal nature of humankind was the period of hunting and gathering of various foodstuffs. This stage encompassed a kind of collective sense of well-being and a mutual protection among families or small tribes. The second stage was a stage in which slavery dominated, with dominant peoples or tribes such as the Romans creating large empires and subjecting captured peoples to the performance of difficult labor. The third stage was the feudal period when relatively small estates dotted the European countryside with lords and serfs locked in a highly static economic relationship.

Although the condition of the serf was clearly better than that of the slave, the means of production was just as clearly in the hands of an ownership class. According to Marx, the communal nature of humankind and the communal routines of work were violated by these arrangements, and he argued that this unnatural state continued into the capitalist fourth phase. Here, ownership was private as the factory system took hold, and Marx hoped that capitalism too would be only a phase in the movement back to communal ownership of work. The two final stages in Marx's scheme were socialism and communism, with the first substituting state ownership of modern enterprise for capitalism's private ownership, and the second removing the heavy hand of the state in a hoped-for return to communal work and ownership. In short, what Marx hoped to see was a full-cycle return to the assumptions of human nature and work incentive that correspond to a low pyramid of distribution. History, he predicted, would eventually return to those kinds of arrangements and assumptions.

Again, what Marx essentially took from the dialectic was the idea that there was an inevitability to historical movement as it progressed from a period when the produce of the land was shared by all back to a final stage wherein all would again share in common ownership. The intermediate stages of slave economies and feudal ownership through capitalist and then state-owned or socialist ownership would all pass away. Marx believed that once this occurred, the state could also "wither away."

Marx's predictions have not been realized, although modern-day Marxists still argue that the "contradictions" of capitalism will one day work out to communism's favor. Certainly, the states that roughly follow the Marxist notions in the world today have not seen their governments wither away, although their leaders usually blame international political and military tensions. Of course, the Soviet Union is the principal Marxist nation in the world, and it considers itself the leader of the communist bloc. The Soviet Union also intends to uphold the Marxist ideal, both by protecting a block of lesser nations, and by attempting to uphold the Marxist notions of productivity and distribution within its own nation.

One short story might illustrate the Soviet attempt at establishing true Marxism, a story that concerns the cherished Soviet workers' *Stakhanovite medal*. This medal is a productivity award that recollects Stakhanovitch, a burly Russian coal miner who, many years ago, broke all records for the mining of coal under the post-revolutionary Soviet system. The new Bolshevik government, knowing that it needed to encourage work, chose this tale of the great coal miner, reporting that Stakhanovitch had done his work not for personal gain but for the betterment of the Soviet state. Again, it was a matter of the right work incentives for Marxism, and the Soviets, and the Soviet Union still attempts to make that state-oriented incentive serve for all Soviet workers.

The years since the 1917 Revolution have passed quickly, and it is clear that these incentives have not worked well. The Soviets have increasingly found that they needed to permit some degree of personally profitable incentive to enter the worker's own equation for labor. Thus, perhaps, the human nature assumptions of the pure communist end of the continuum have been shown to be insufficient just as the assumptions underlying pure capitalism have also not always functioned well. In the case of communism, many have noted that even Soviet leaders have begun to reward themselves substantially for what they do, even though these rewards are often hidden in Black Sea dachas and in shopping privileges at secluded, luxury-filled stores.

To return to our central theme, one of the tenets of Marxist ideology is that capitalism was doomed to failure because the pyramid of distribution would become too high and the *proletariat* or the exploited workers would rebel as members of a supressed economic class. Marx argued, in other words, that *class consciousness* would develop among the workers and that they would confront the bourgeoisie or the exploitive capitalist class and eventually triumph over it. Of course, this sense of confrontation, sometimes called "class warfare," is very different from a democratic socialist's belief in a reconciliation of the classes. Unlike Shaw's notions

of education and understanding, the Marxist sense of class identification with the proletariat has been an important factor in the
slow development of entrepreneurial skills in many Marxist countries. The pure ideology of Marxism, like the pure ideology of capitalism, seems to have had difficulty in the real world.

CONCLUSION ━━━━━━━━━━━━━

The last two chapters have built upon the distributional and valuational pyramid model that we began in the first chapters. With
a brief review of recent economic history, we have described a
continuum of four political ideologies. This continuum has been
presented in the context of an economic model that asks you to
think of rationalistic versus market methods for determining the
value contributed. You have also been asked to consider where it
is that these ideologies fit within assumptions concerning human
nature and orientations toward work. The thinking of Ricardo,
Hegel, Marx, and Smith should have been helpful to your understanding of these ideologies. Nonetheless, your sense of how these
ideologies relate to basic political values is more important than
anything you have learned from significant thinkers. The question
of what is a fair wage within an early industrial or a contemporary
work setting is similar to asking what is a fair return from the
desert island that you shared with someone in the first chapter.
The different stages of economic enterprise that have grown from
simple hunting and gathering to farming, the factory, and now into
a novel kind of service and technological economy that many call
the postindustrial economy, certainly make the analysis of a fair
return for work more difficult. Politically however, the same essential question of determining how much value you have contributed to the general well-being and how much reward you should
thus receive for that contribution is still the central issue.

Glossary

TERMS
Pygmalion
Fabian Society

The Origin of the Species
surplus value
idealist

materialist
dialectic
Stakhanovite medal
1917 Revolution
class consciousness
bourgoisie
proletariat

NAMES

George Bernard Shaw
Charles Darwin
Herbert Spencer
G. W. F. Hegel

CHAPTER 5
THE MODERN
VALUATIONAL DEBATE

So far, what we have done is have you think of the value question. What we are now prepared to do is add the essence of politics, that is, the structure of the very argument over valuation itself, to what has so far been an ideologically based model of contribution. You should now understand the essence of the value question. You should also know which viewpoints have traditionally argued for a greater or lesser differentiation of reward within the industrial economic systems. You should be ready to understand the politics of it all, because if you understand *what* it is that the argument is all about, you can also understand how political procedures and institutions decide upon who gets what from the general well-being of the society.

THE CONCEPT OF EQUILIBRIUM

Just as our best understanding of ideology was described as a *continuum*, so too should our new question of politics and political structure be understood as part of a continuum. Now, familiarize yourself with the term *equilibrium*, the notion that forces exist within continuums or ranges that tend to move things away from the extremes toward the middle or moderate position. The Greek word for the middle position was *méson*, and in politics, the *méson* would be the place where the best compromise between competing claims of different theories rested.

From the ideologies that we have just reviewed, we know that many thinkers and political advocates have taken different positions along the continuum of the valuational argument. As we examine how specific governmental mechanics create the everyday public policies of government, we should remember that the economic distribution model has dominated government for a long time. Moreover, how you feel about the rationalistic or the market orientation of determining the differentiations of work has a great deal to do with how you feel about that distribution.

What we should understand now is that the rationalistic versus market-oriented method of determining relative economic valuation is related to how well political structures define those valuations. Clearly, if we adopt a purely market-oriented approach to economic valuation, the public has almost no role to play in the determination of reward. We say "almost" because the citizenry at least has the ability to either support or not support a political system whose government altogether disregards the question of economic valuation. Clearly, after the early days of capitalism, the equilibrium notion had an effect upon the continuum of distribution in capitalist counties, and as we have seen with the Soviet Union, it is apparently having a considerable effect in the Marxist bloc as well. As we turn to a discussion of the very idea of government or to that political process that acts as a "broker" between the elements of a society, we will see how the distributional matter is handled.

The Governmental Role

We know what makes up the continuum of ideology. Generally, it is made up of capitalism, liberal capitalism, democratic socialism, and communist ideologies. In terms of governmental role, however, what do each of these ideologies prescribe? Think of each of the ideologies and of how much of government and what kind of government is included within each of them. With capitalism, that is, pure capitalism, how much government is involved in the distribution of value? We know that pure capitalism incorporates the market method of valuation for products and labor, and we therefore know that the role of government in pure capitalism is minimal. The market alone decides valuation. We could say that for a purely capitalist society, the meaning of democracy has a very clear orientation toward supporting a particular distributional result. Democracy, for them, has a rather definite valuational plan.

At the other end of the continuum, we know that pure communism attempts to exclude fully the market in valuation. It attempts to reinstate a preindustrial notion of rationalistic valuation based upon what a society, in some aggregate sense, believes products and labor are worth. Although Marx dreamed of an eventual "withering away" of the state, he also regarded the valuational role of the community as fundamental to a fair return for labor. Clearly, government, at least in the sense of an enforceable group decision on valuation, would play a dominant role in the valuational scheme of Marxism. Citizens who believe in this distributional goal would also have a clear result orientation, although their result orientation would assume a much flatter pyramid. They too, however, would see democracy as a result, even if it is a very different result from what the pure capitalist would prefer.

Moving toward the center, more than likely under the influence of pressure for equilibrium in the real world, the reformed or liberal capitalist model still permits a great deal of market valuation. At the same time, however, liberal capitalism moderates that method of valuation with a degree of governmental protection for its less fortunate citizens. Meanwhile, the democratic socialists, moving farther along the continuum, believe basically in the rationalistic mode of valuation, although they often permit the market to operate within broad price and wage guidelines. Let us understand, therefore, that the question of the role of government, or more precisely, the question of democracy as it relates to the process of valuation, can be placed upon a continuum with its equilibrium influences reflecting the mixture of market valuations as opposed to rationalistic valuations. Strict market valuations require less government or democracy as a result with a capitalistic flavor. Rationalistic valuations require more government or democracy as a result with a Marxist flavor. (see Figure 5–1).

Please remember that we are moving toward a definition of democracy. We are searching for a definition of democracy that will

FIGURE 5–1.
Result orientations of democracy.

Democracy as
Result—
Communism

Democracy as
Result—
Early Capitalism

necessarily include notions of how political structures actually work. Soon we will discuss the structures of government and the actual processes that various governmental structures use in deciding policy. We shall also discuss an intermediate point on the continuum of democracy, a place where democracy includes different views of how tall the pyramid should be and permits these views to be discussed as a part of a democratic process. Yet before we proceed, we must consider one intermediate step in the analysis; the step that defines what we mean by public policy and explains how public policy grows from governmental activity. To do this, we need also consider the role of law, for law is the vehicle by which a public order is both stated and enforced.

The Natural Law

Historically, we know that as the political institutions of feudalism crumbled, the act of rising from one's ancestors' position in the feudal order became both more acceptable and more possible. During the Middle Ages, the understanding of the Western world and of humankind's relationship to the divinity was guided almost exclusively by concepts of a *natural law* of existence, that is, the law that explains the physical and moral orders of the universe.

The physical discoveries of Newton on gravity and motion, and the discoveries of Copernicus and Galileo concerning the planets and the stars were revelations of the natural law. More central to our analysis is the idea that humankind can learn more about its own existence by observation and the application of reason. This largely intellectual matter, that is, the matter of observing and thinking about things, is important because it permitted people to understand their world in a way different from relying only on faith. It is also important because, beyond believing in something about the existence of the universe and how that universe was created, there was now the real chance of observing the physical laws of the universe in the real world. Some also thought it would be possible to observe the laws of how a political society should be formed.

As you can imagine, the challenge or the growing acceptability of *observed truth*, together with the development of an invention like the *printing press* that spread information more widely than it ever had been spread before, had a profound effect on the entire range of modern political issues. These new ideas concerning observation also had a profound effect on the way in which various thinkers were to view the world in which they lived.

The Contribution of John Locke

Near the close of the seventeenth century, the political philosopher John Locke was deeply intrigued by the new notions of observation. His interest had an effect on how he felt about law and government, for Locke was particularly taken with the idea of the natural law's application to the rights of the individual. This notion of an individualistic natural law was not original with Locke. There had been others before him who wrote on the natural law's protection of personal or natural rights, such as Thomas Hooker and Samuel von Pufendorf. Yet Locke contributed to reducing the emphasis placed on the group of society, in favor of an emphasis upon the rights of an individual. His writings added to the evolving real-world position of an individualistic merchant class within England. They also helped to support the notion that what is natural about many things, including even distributional valuations, could be accomplished by individual judgments rather than by the aggregate judgment of the larger society. The new mercantile economic grouping within England clearly challenged the traditional aristocratic or landed order of an earlier England.

Locke's own political and personal business orientation clearly favored the new mercantile policies that were emerging in late seventeenth-century English politics. The new direction of his views condemned the traditional privileges of the titled aristocracy and the church as economically unproductive and approved of this emerging individualistic entrepreneurial class's new-found influence.

For our purposes, these historical changes also meant that law and the evolution of democracy were to be greatly affected by individualism. Locke's thinking greatly supported the passing of a milestone in the evolution of democracy known as the Glorious Revolution, a moment in English history when the Parliament established its right to exist as an independent body free of the king's power. This democratic revolution was a watershed in English history because it greatly diminished the role of the Crown and helped to bring about the modern order of democratic government or the development of law by individual legislators and their Parliament. It was a time in which history was beginning to permit democracy as a process to have citizens with different views argue over such things as the distributional pyramid and the balance of economic and noneconomic valuation.

Locke is known as one of the first modern political thinkers because of his political writings on democracy as a process. His writings grapple with a crucial conflict that is still found within virtually all the current writings on public policy and democracy. To understand this conflict, we must also understand Locke's dilemma. On the one hand, he wanted the idea of modern law or law decided on by participating individuals, and the idea of democracy as a process to grow at the expense of the prerogatives of the Crown, the aristocracy, and the church. Yet, at the same time, Locke did not want the process of democracy to grow too far so as to embrace a more purely procedural democratic law. In other words, he did not want law or public policy to be completely determined by an emerging popular will.

What was it that frightened Locke about the prospect of democracy and popular input into an issue such as the distributional issue? To understand Locke's ambivalence toward democracy and popularly created law, we should return to the pyramids of distribution and consider the impact of democracy as a process upon the height of the pyramids. Where on a pyramid of distribution are most people located? The fact is that throughout history, the greatest number of people have been located on the lower end of the distributional pyramid, that is, the poor have nearly always outnumbered the rich. Although no one in Locke's time considered having substantial numbers of citizens participate in the government in a modern sense, Locke visualized a time when government, through an openly elected legislature that would write laws for the society, could alter the distribution toward an increasingly flatter pyramid (see Figure 5–2). Even though Locke was writing before the coming of the Industrial Revolution, he still anticipated the pull of those who might want democracy as a result at the more

FIGURE 5–2.
Perceptions of the impact of democratic institutions upon the pyramid of distribution.

Locke and Madison.
Fear of Democratic
Impact upon Distribution

Locke and Madison.
Perception of
Appropriate Triangle

egalitarian end of the continuum or democracy with a very flat pyramid. To counter this anticipated flattening of the pyramid under a process that would permit distributional restructuring, Locke wrote a good deal about the importance of private property and, indeed, stressed that the protection of property would be the primary task of the newly vigorous English parliament. Remember again that Locke was very concerned with the protection of individual rights. His notions of life, liberty, and property were central to his principle of what should be protected in any civilized society. Yet, when it came to his fear of the very legislature that he so strongly endorsed as a source of democracy as process, he emphasized property, and vigorously denied the legislature's right to disrupt a very private notion of property. In other words, he was concerned that too much democracy would lower the height of the pyramid.

The American Experience

Was that fear of the lowering of the pyramid a fear that only John Locke and the English merchants held? Moving ahead in history almost one hundred years, we see that Locke's concerns were being echoed by drafters and advocates of the 1787 American Constitution. James Madison, writing in the *Federalist #10*, made it clear that the newly created political institutions of the American Constitution should never be so democratic that unpropertied citizens would radically alter the valuations of property. For their time, Madison's views were reasonable, for they at least purported to follow the rules of contribution by which everyone was entitled to the fruits of his or her labor. Locke and Madison's views of law and property coincided with the earlier notions of proportionate contribution and reward as they had been handed down from Aristotle and Justinian. But Madison also advocated something that would bring the earlier notions of a natural order of the universe or a natural law into an everyday law that governed people in their daily lives.

Let us consider if the use of natural law as a protector of property squares well with the idea that increasingly democratic governments create day-to-day law and public policy. To answer this question, we must again define the natural law as a grand representation of the design of the physical and ethical world. As do all ideas that carry such completeness, it is steeped in principle. Unfortunately, however, it is short of specificity and detail. Consequently, the natural law is not well adapted to the guidance of day-to-day governmental policy within a modern political society, and a different kind of law is needed to perform that role.

Positive Law

Historically, as the modern world and its law and public policy needed specification, it began to develop a modern concept that we call *positive law*, namely, day-to-day or specific law. It has nearly always accompanied various natural law notions of ancient and medieval societies, but in England, the step to a modern positive law was made by a deeply rooted set of principles that had existed since the Middle Ages. The English positive law of specific day-to-day relationships was known as the *common law*. It had developed from traditional controversies over buying and selling and a number of other agricultural, business, and trade dealings. The ancient English "writs" stood as early embodiments of "rights" and established a deep sense within the English population of a private person-to-person set of duties and obligations that were protected by the force of law.

By the seventeenth century, modern positive law in the English experience was beginning to come from statutory as well as common law sources. It was growing out of the increasingly vigorous English Parliament that was, in turn, beginning to exercise democracy as a process. Although Parliament's role was expanding and the English middle class was also growing in its political influence, a fundamental question remained concerning the emerging English positive law. How, it was asked, should that positive law square with the traditional natural law? How should different result orientations toward distribution be included within the process of democracy?

To answer those questions, even as we examine their implications for the modern world and for the issue of distribution, it is necessary to understand that positive law or state-created law will have the biases within it of those who are influential in the law-making process. The process of democracy will include the result orientations of citizen participants, and it should be clear to you that those who have influence with the government will be those whose biases will be reflected in law and public policy. Modern positive law, therefore, is the product of the various interests' efforts to get what they each would like from the public policy of the government. Hence, positive law is the result of what different groups in the society think the natural order of that society should be.

What we should now understand is that natural law or, better, the perception of what is right and wrong about any number of questions, including the question of distribution, can vary substantially. Differences over how a society should be constituted or even how tall the pyramid of distribution should be are all basically part of a perception of someone's view of what is the best natural society. If you understand this, you will now be ready to focus upon something very specific concerning the relationship of natural law to positive law. You will be ready to concentrate on what the different result orientations of determining valuation are as they relate to law and public policy.

Natural Law, Positive Law, and Valuation

What specific concepts of natural law were linked to the different views over distribution or the height of the pyramid? You should be able to answer that question, and you should also be able to link that answer to our discussion of law. The link is a simple one, really, because it comes from an understanding of the political method that is used to determine how personal contributions are valued. Let us review the two major methods of valuation or result orientations and see how they were both closely linked to the concept of natural law.

Remember that in the market method of valuation Adam Smith believed that prices would be determined by the "natural" price or the "natural" value. This idea, of course, harkens back to natural law. Smith's valuation mechanism for the labor market was designed to arrive at what natural law would estimate for the valuation of work.

Let us consider the other end of the continuum. What was it that Marx claimed for his ideology or for the radical view of socialism that we call communism? Remember that Marx also relied upon an interpretation of natural law. The very concept of surplus value came from a rationalistic notion of the value contributed by a worker and of how the industrialist allegedly had stolen some of that value. What you discovered about natural law and valuation is that, at both ends of the poles of political ideology and valuation, there is a linkage to at least one vision of the natural law. Those different concepts of natural value and natural law that make up the valuational argument are what directly concern the arguments over day-to-day law. Indeed, your feelings concerning the height of the pyramid today, and the means of determining the economic value of individual work is very much a part of which "natural" notion of valuation you prefer.

Simply, the crucial issues of public policy and law, including the political question of how high the distributional pyramid should be, relates back to how citizens feel differently about the valuation question. As we have seen, different visions of a nonphysical natural law or of a law of the social and political world may stand at or near the poles of a continuum. The positive law, though it is rarely at dead center between these poles, does inevitably represent some compromise of these positions. The positive law, or what we have defined as the specific day-to-day law that governments create, exists somewhere between the two extremes of the continuum (see Figure 5–3), because the positive law is the result of the competition among interests in a community that support different notions of what a political society should be. The positive law, in short, is very much a compromise over the different views of natural law. Although pressure within all systems may sometimes pull something like the valuational pyramid toward one extreme or the other, the positive law of political societies that permits democratic process should never stray far from the moderate center point. No modern system of valuation or ideology, neither rationalistic nor market, has ever worked exclusively as a pure system. The principles of equilibrium—the movement toward some compromise near the center of the ideological continuum—have never allowed the positive law to embrace either pure capitalism or pure communism. The modern positive law of distribution, in other words, has never been able to embrace fully the Adam Smith or Karl Marx view of natural value without some compromise. All modern law reflects these compromises to some degree, and even democracy, which we should now understand as a mixture of different result orientations within a framework of democratic process, has also had to accept these compromises.

FIGURE 5–3.
View of valuation. Natural law, positive law, and ideology.

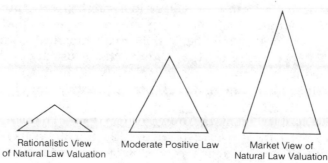

Rationalistic View   Moderate Positive Law   Market View of
of Natural Law Valuation   Natural Law Valuation

DEMOCRACY AND THE LAW:
TWO DEFINITIONS

At this point in our analysis, our understanding of the word "democracy" should be expanding with our understanding of law. We have seen through John Locke and James Madison that the time in history that saw the introduction of democratic legislatures into modern government also witnessed the emergence of modern conceptions of private property and modern patterns of contribution and reward. The movement away from the traditional feudal notion of how wealth was distributed opened the question of contribution and reward to more and different kinds of influences. The distribution question itself thus became one of the principle concerns of an emerging democratic government.

Yet, as the issue of distribution became more debatable, even before substantial progress was made toward what by modern standards we would call democratic government, the emerging method of market valuation was already being opposed by some. Others, particularly those among the new merchant class, strongly endorsed the market method of valuation. If we understand how the two pure notions of natural law and distribution stand near the two poles of belief, and how the positive law ranges within the center position as it responds to both result orientations, then we can proceed to a more precise understanding of what we mean by democracy. Again, concentrate on the *two* definitions for democracy. You should realize that these two definitions are often still argued over in a discussion of politics. The first definition considers democracy to be a *process*; the second definition considers democracy to be a *result*.

Democracy as Process

If we now understand what the origins of democracy as process and democracy as result are, let us look more closely into what these two definitions of democracy mean. The elements of democracy as process should be familiar to all Americans. They include that openness of political activity that is usually evidenced by (1) having more than one political party, (2) having open candidacies for public offices, and (3) permitting freedom of speech, freedom of the press, freedom of assembly, and all the other freedoms that lead to a full debate over political issues. The democratic process (see Figure 5–4) has evolved over the last 300 years in most Western nations. The gradual extension of the franchise (the vote)

FIGURE 5–4.
View of valuation. Democratic result, democratic process, and ideology.

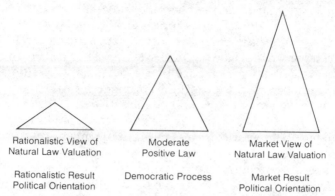

Rationalistic View of Natural Law Valuation	Moderate Positive Law	Market View of Natural Law Valuation
Rationalistic Result Political Orientation	Democratic Process	Market Result Political Orientation

and the gradual replacement of absolutist monarchies with increasingly representative parliamentary bodies are two of the evolutionary changes that have occurred. Coincident with such an evolution, there has also been a growing sense that the natural law that we have spoken of is supportive of a number of fundamental political liberties. In the English experience, the writings of Thomas Hooker, John Locke, and Edward Coke were most influential in establishing basic liberties, and the English Bill of Rights of 1689 secured the basic rights of the modern British System.

The American Revolution was based upon what the colonists perceived as a denial of their basic rights as Englishmen. The Declaration of Independence and the Bill of Rights that were attached to the Constitution clearly drew upon the ideas of Locke and the English Bill of Rights. Even in Europe, where individual rights did not always have the same force as they did with the English and the colonies, the influence of Locke, particularly as he was interpreted by Voltaire, along with the influence of the American Tom Paine, unquestionably played a major role in the French Revolution. The guarantee of free speech, free press, and eventually, the extension of the right to vote still make up the essence of democratic process in modern democratic states.

Democracy as Result: Anticapitalism

Of course, not all who discuss democratic theory agree with the procedural definition. Many political theorists, as well as a number of real-world political systems, feel that leaving matters to the competition of elections, parties, candidates, and the general hubbub of a democratic process is not sufficient to ensure real democracy. Let us examine how those who argue this way feel about a democracy that is defined as mere process. In most instances, those who find democracy as process to be incomplete argue that attention to only the process of democracy ignores certain fundamental issues that plague political systems. They believe that much of what makes up the essence of a good society does not receive consideration within the workings of modern democratic process.

But who, you may ask, would not be satisfied with government's openness to democratic process? Those who would most strongly curtail pure democratic process fall into two major categories. The anticapitalist view argues that democratic process is only a mask that hides how economic elites actually dominate a nation's politics. Those who hold this view have a definite idea of what they consider to be the best society. They also feel strongly about how the economic contribution and valuational question should be handled. The citizens who perceive democracy as process as too partial to dominant economic interests are the citizens who are unhappy with the result that market valuation offers. The holders of this view are wary of the valuations that come from capitalism, and they argue for the restriction of market valuation in the debate over how valuation should be accomplished. In its extreme, the anticapitalist position may be a Marxist position, for it does not fully trust democratic process. Instead, it wishes to have the government undertake a purely rationalistic view of the value of personal labor. Again, the advocates of this position would believe in a government that is deeply involved with the valuation process, and would want that process to be accomplished in a rationalistic way.

Democracy as Result: Procapitalism

If governmental enforcement of rationalistic valuation makes up one form of democracy as a result, what would be the other view of democracy as a result? This view is also linked to a definite perspective on the question of valuation. Instead of favoring a purely rationalistic valuation of economic contribution, it insists upon a purely market valuation of economic contribution. Its preference for democracy as a result is based on what a purely free economic market can give to a society. The advocates of this position are suspicious of pure democracy as process, just as the anticapitalist advocates are equally suspicious of pure democracy as process.

Yet this second view of democracy as result strictly limits the government's role to such matters as external or national security matters and the internal policing of the society. The role of government beyond these limited functions, particularly in the area of economic valuation, is clearly restricted. Perhaps the best example of someone who held this view was John Locke, whose "night watchman" vision of government greatly feared the involvement of citizens in the valuation process. This second restrictive view of democracy as a result should be placed at the other end of the continuum from the view that argues for rationalistic valuation methods.

We should keep in mind that democracy as a process lies somewhere between these two result orientations. In fact, just as the two views of natural law and, specifically, the naturalistic views of both market and rationalistic economic valuation are the starting points for the daily compromises of positive law, so too are the beliefs about the roles of government in favor of one valuation method or the other the starting point for democratic process. The continuum of thought on valuation is subject to the forces of equilibrium. To greater or lesser degrees, many governments today permit at least some degree of process. They also permit at least some degree of discussion of both the market and rationalistic methods of valuation. It is clear, however, that a considerable range from (1) democracy as a rationalistic result through (2) democracy as process to (3) democracy as a market-oriented result, exists within the nations of the world. We shall soon explore that range in greater detail.

THE QUEST FOR PUBLIC POLICY

We have now reached another plateau. If you understand the difference between democracy as a process and democracy as either of the two results, you should be prepared to weave these understandings into the larger general model of human nature, economic distribution, and public policy. If you have understood the model so far, you should be ready to ask yourself which definition of democracy, either process or the two results, is more closely linked to the definition of day-to-day positive law.

Would the definition of democracy embrace the view of law that has a constant and restricted notion of how economic valuation should be accomplished? Probably not. A definition of democracy of that kind would be closer to a single and restrictive definition of natural law. The definition that is closer to the political give-and-take that leads to flexibility in day-to-day or positive law is linked to a concept of democracy as a process.

To remember this, recall what it was that we agreed was the core of positive law. It is the everyday law that comes from the political structure. It is subject to change, and often (though not always) marks the broad middle of our legal spectrum because it responds, within a democratic system, to a wide range of political forces that make up any polity. Conceptually, at least, democracy as a process has certain clear characteristics within government. It does not depend upon a single notion of fair valuation, nor does it tend to concern itself with human nature, either competitive or cooperative. Rather, it depends for its acceptability on the idea that there will be a flexible movement or argument over the very question of what will be the public policy of the political system.

We have placed the two forms of democracy as a result away from the center of the model. These notions of democracy are better placed toward the sides of the model, or near to the purer notions of natural law. We have also divided democracy as a result into two schools; the first is concerned with mantaining a high economic pyramid and market valuation, and the second is interested in maintaining a rationalistic mode of economic valuation and a low distributional pyramid. The result orientations, in turn, refer back to two very different and pure notions of human nature. One of these views believes that humankind is essentially competitive; the other argues that humankind is essentially cooperative. In other words, democracy, may cover all positions of the continuum of our model. As notions about legal categories range from natural law to positive law and back to a different notion of natural law, so too do notions about democracy range, again, from democracy as a result through democracy as a process and back to a different idea about democracy as a result.

THE EQUILIBRIUM OF PUBLIC POLICY ━━━━━━

How then do actual governments create public policy? Let us begin our search by asking about your own biases and viewpoints. Do you have an idea or at least some general notion of how a political and economic society should be structured? Do you have a sense of not only what a proper distribution of wealth should be, but what a society's laws should be as well? Do you also have a sense of what public institutions should be doing to create proper distribution? Everyone has a sense of what makes up the society in which they would like to live. As overwhelming as it may sound, each of us has a sense of the natural law. Each of us also has a kind of *result* orientation.

Let us now consider a question that will lead to a better understanding of both the legal and political continuum. Ask yourself which people with a particular orientation will be more willing to live in a society that also listens to other people's orientations. Would it be the people near the extremes of the result-process-result continuum, or would it be those whose views are more toward the center? Of course, it would be the people at the center of the continuum because they better tolerate other views. Those whose political views are near the poles of the continuum are usually less willing to engage in a democratic process that moves public policy back and forth according to different points of view. Just as the pure capitalists want valuation to take place only through the market, and pure communists want no inclusion of the market at all, so pure result-orientation persons can never tolerate a process that involves other considerations. Such citizens wish to have a government that holds their kinds of biases, and at the same time, they wish that the political system would limit the process to the execution of their ideas exclusively. They do not want a public policy formed by a debate including all citizens.

And what, then, of the law? Again, it is the strict view of the orders of the existence, a rigid view of natural law, that sits at both sides of the continuum. Positive law may merely reflect those narrow views, but within a democratic government positive law has been argued over by various interests and is less likely to represent an extreme view of public policy. Clearly, if there is an openness in the discussion of public issues, it is likely that the law will be more moderate in its ideological flavor.

We are again at a plateau of understanding. Your original notions concerning human nature and the division of work and reward on our mythical island, together with your understanding of the four principal ideologies concerning distribution should now have grown into a sound sense of what a political system is. You should also have a sense that political systems that incorporate a generous share of democracy as process and permit its positive law to reflect the views of a wide range of result orientations are primarily moderate systems. They are systems that have permitted the public positions of various individuals and groups within the society to

argue for their own interests before the interests of public institutions. Such systems will tend toward an equilibrium or a moderation of actual public policy. What we mean by an equilibrium
of public policy is that the set of legislated laws, administrative
decisions, judicial decisions, and the like that make up the public
policy of a particular system will reflect something close to the
"fairest" set of laws that the system could create. Again, consider
that there is an equilibrium for public policy present within democratic political systems. There is a place, or perhaps a range of
places on a continuum, where the laws of a system seem at least
reasonably fair to a majority of citizens. It is at that point that the
system is said to be fair.

One more point is relevant here: even though a system that is
in equilibrium might be considered to be fair, the public policy or
the laws of that system never remain stationary. Competition among
individuals or groups for a public policy that is favorable to them
will always exist. Remember that although political equilibrium
is important, it is still largely a theoretical concept. It stands for a
point or range of points where a number of competing pressures
and interests come together to make public policy. Equilibrium,
at least as it exists within politics, is a place that is always being
argued over and, consequently, is never fully at rest.

To understand this movement of equilibrium, remember your
own feeling about the difference between a physician's and a street
sweeper's contribution to society. You had a ratio for those contributions of, say, 2 to 1 or 10 to 1, but the political argument over
valution was based upon the idea that someone else had a ratio
that was either higher or lower than your own.

When it comes to legislation and public policy, that is, to the
making of what we now understand as positive law, people have
different notions about valuational pyramids and all other types of
policies. Whether the legislation is concerned with tax laws, educational aid, or the building of hospitals, the proposal for public
policy will almost invariably be supported by some and opposed
by others. As a result, tension will often develop in the equilibrium.

Let us keep our understanding simple by not concentrating here
on any one specific area of public policy. Let us instead concentrate
on the height of the distributional pyramid and use that pyramid
as our principal point of debate. In a general sense, one result
orientation of democracy, that is, the one that emerges from a
particular view of natural order, wants a clearly *stratified* pyramid
of contribution and reward. On the other side, however, there is a
preference for a more *egalitarian* and thus less differentiated or

FIGURE 5–5.
Public policy impact upon distribution.

Raising the
Estate Tax Exemption

Supporting Construction
of Public Hospitals

stratified reward structure. These differences, of course, ought to bring us back to our discussion of ideologies. Now it can be seen that the two general views are constantly in tension as they try to pull the height of the distributional pyramid either upward or downward.

For example, let us say that you endorse your government's raising of taxes so that a public hospital can be built to take care of those who are not able to pay for medical care. In a small way, you favor a change in the distributional pyramid. In which direction are you asking for the pyramid to be exhanged? That should be clear to you. You wish to help the poorer citizens of the society, and therefore you are in favor of a flattening of the pyramid of distributional valuation. (see Figure 5–5).

But let us also suggest that you are in favor of raising the figure in which the estate of a deceased citizen does not have to pay an estate tax. The previous law within the United States held that all estates valued at over $60,000 had to pay an estate tax. Yet, you believe wealth should be handed down from generation to generation without tax. You might believe that everything up to $600,000 (an actual tax law change of 1981) would be fairer. Does this raise or flatten the height of the pyramid? Of course, it raises the height of the pyramid, placing you as one who tends to believe in the physician making a good deal more than the street sweeper. You are not an egalitarian. You believe in some real differentiation or stratification of wealth within political societies.

Now, I want to help you to consider two rather simple words—*liberal* and *conservative*—that denote a belief, or perhaps a constellation of beliefs, in a particular ideology. (In Europe, the terms *Left* and *Right* are more frequently used, but they mean much the same thing there, although perhaps with a slightly greater intensity and range.) Until recently, there was not much of a sense that Americans held views beyond those that would promote their personal or group well-being. More recent evidence, however, reveals that American ideological consciousness is growing, and many

Americans now embrace liberal or conservative positions quite knowledgeably.

What then do these terms mean? What is the difference between a liberal and a conservative, between the Left and the Right? In a general sense, the position of the conservative view has favored the more competitive vision of human nature. It has advocated greater differences between the rewards that different contributors receive for their contribution. Conservatives tend to like the high-stakes poker game, and they consequently believe that economic incentives are crucial to a political system. They are also less willing to share what they feel that they alone have produced.

Liberals, on the other hand, tend to prefer the low-stakes poker game, and they argue for a more even share of rewards among different contributors within the society. Their view of human nature is less competitive, and they advocate a lesser distinction between the distributions of the society's productivity. Let us again consider the differences in contributions between the engineer and the phsychiatric social worker that had to do with varying kinds of contribution. We cannot say that conservatives place no value on the bonding associations of a society. However, they generally value the associative or bonding value of a social worker's contribution somewhat less than do the liberals.

We know, historically, that conservatives have tended to defend older arrangements within society; that is, they have preferred those status understandings that have maintained a place of social or economic dominance for certain members of a populace. Also, particularly within the last 200 years, conservatives have generally endorsed the market method of valuation and have argued for capitalistic ideologies. Liberals, however, have tended to be the champions of the less fortunate within the society, and have argued against pure capitalism.

THE ELEMENTS OF IDEOLOGICAL STRUGGLE

With these new understandings of the ideological range of policy preference, we can return to our model of politics and investigate how it is that various groups, or those who hold various ideological positions within political society attempt to achieve their goals within a political system. In other words, how do people get what they want within the models of law, politics, and ideology?

We need first to know what sources have politically influenced the conservative and liberal positions. What, for example, do the conservatives possess that permits them to get what they want from government? What is their greatest resource? Remember, again, that the pyramid of distribution, at least traditionally, has been a real pyramid, with fewer people at the top than at the bottom. The conservatives, traditionally, have rarely been able to organize large numbers of people for political strength because, in almost every political circumstance, they have been outnumbered by the less wealthy members of the society.

What, then, do they have on their side? Principally, the conservatives have had *wealth*. They have had the fruits of their economic contribution to the society, and they have traditionally used some portion of their economic strength, that is, their money, to encourage the very public policies that would permit them to keep the pyramid of distribution higher than others might want it. They have also tended to be better *organized* so that the coordination of their efforts for a high pyramid has been stronger than it has been on the liberal side.

What have the liberals traditionally used as their greatest political weapon? You already have the answer, do you not, for the base of the pyramid is nearly always larger than the tip? For the Left side of the continuum, it is *numbers* that have typically been significant. The greater numbers of citizens at the lower end of the pyramid have been the core of liberal support. Indeed, particularly since the Industrial Revolution, the greatest single goal for the liberal side of the political argument has been to include more citizens in the political debate. The inclusion of more people has generally led to more support for the political position of the liberal side, and the extension of the franchise, that is, the right to vote, has been the great political rearrangement of the nineteenth and twentieth centuries in the Western industrial states. Over time, certainly with great interruptions and not without a fair degree of strife and even bloodshed, more and more citizens of at least the principal Western industrial nations have been allowed to participate in the democratic processes of government.

I again use the term "democratic process" deliberately here because the model we are building is an equilibrium model, with the elements of process at the center acting as a kind of broker for the relatively rigid result orientations that exist at the poles. As time passes, both sides continue pulling to one side or the other, hoping that their government will create the kind of positive law through political processes that will help their position the most.

If you now have a sound idea of the structure of the ideological battle between the traditional liberal and conservative positions, you should also have a sense of what it is that these sides are fighting over and how the battle is fought. Let us focus now on this last point, for how the battle is fought constitutes the approaching step in the construction of our model. We should move toward this next step of the model within the context of defining a relatively stable political system. Later we will consider unstable political systems and why political instability exists.

THE STRUCTURE OF THE IDEOLOGICAL STRUGGLE

In most stable political systems, democratic processes are relatively open, although some undemocratic systems do maintain a degree of stability over short periods of time. Again, what are the characteristics of open political processes? Generally, we have said that processes are open when there is more than one political party, when individuals are free to run as candidates, and when such protections as the right to vote, freedom of speech, freedom of the press, freedom of assembly, and the like all facilitate a full discussion of public issues. Also, in stable political systems, the calls for change that are made from most participants, and particularly from the two ideological sides of Left and Right, are relatively moderate. To put it another way, although the liberal side would typically ask for a revision in the structure of the contribution pyramid that would flatten the pyramid, it would not argue for a very deep flattening of the pyramid. The conservative position, on the other hand, would pull on the equilibrium to give the pyramid a taller structure, but, within stable, moderate systems, they would not ask for an overly heightened structure.

What, then, is the sequence of the debate, or what is it that typifies the moderate struggle between the Left and Right political philosophies? The pulling and hauling of the two sides creates a moderate shifting back and forth of political favor, or an alternation to one side and then the other in the direction of governmental policy. For a while, the law of taxation or public hospital building may be favorable to the conservatives, and then, at another time, it may be favorable to the liberals. Again, however, the key point is that the policy preferences shift back and forth from the liberal to the conservative side without either side of the continuum dominating public policy for too long.

How does this moderated pulling and hauling work? There are various configurations of ideological positions and interest groupings within any political society. We will talk more about who these groups are and what methods they use to try to gain what they want from government soon. Yet if we talk now about the configurations that make up the Right and Left in a general way, we should know that they each generally argue for public policies that are favorable to their side of the political continuum.

Let us say ,for example, that conservatives are in the ascendancy for a while or that their policies have been winning lately in the democratic process. We know that as a result of this ascendancy, the line of policy would therefore move to the Right. Yet, in a stable system, it would move only to a certain point and the pyramid would rise only to a certain height before pressures from the other side would pull policy back toward the center. What pulls policy back toward the center? Let us be clear about this, for there are what we call *cumulative* and *anticumulative* forces within any equilibrium. When the conservatives are in power, they will legislate positive law that benefits them, as a tax relief proposal would do, for example. Such policies will help the conservatives and, for a while, the height of the pyramid will proceed to a higher level.

Although only a small percentage of any population contributes money or becomes involved in political campaigns, the people who will benefit by these conservative policies will almost invariably be the citizens who will support the continuation of those policies. Their support, most likely in the form of financial contributions to personal campaigns but also including party support and even support for various ideologically based movements in a few instances, will be cumulative because it will attempt to continue the pattern of improvement of the conservative position or the heightening of the pyramid. At the same time, such policies will inevitably leave some portion, perhaps even a large portion, of the citizenry behind. These other citizens will eventually see that conservative policies, as in the tax break for the wealthy, are not beneficial to them. The less well-off may need to pay more taxes themselves. Yet, with the pyramid getting taller and narrower at the top, those few who are active in politics will gather to act as an anticumulative force (see Figure 5–6). They will attempt to pull public policy back toward what they consider to be the equilibrium point that they perceive as fair. Of course, the same process also happens on the other side of the equilibrium, with the liberals sometimes being in the ascendancy until anticumulative conservative forces gather themselves to bring policy back to the center.

This cumulative versus anticumulative force notion is only part

FIGURE 5–6.
Ideological flow of policy in stable systems.

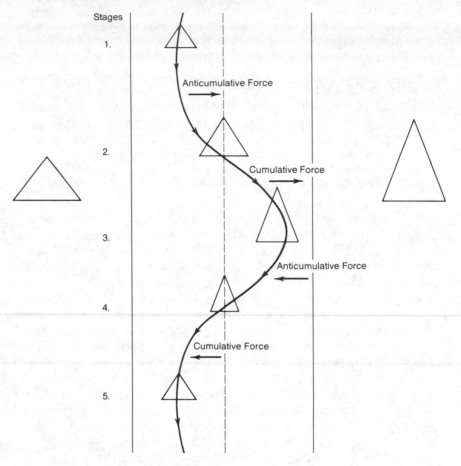

of a model. No nation's public policy record represents this ideal perfectly. Yet, within mature democracies, there is only a moderate swing of policies from Left to Right, that being a function of a reasonable equality between conservative and liberal forces. The United States, for example, ended a conservative, pro-business political period that had lasted since just after the Civil War by embracing the liberal New Deal policies of Franklin Roosevelt in 1932. By the 1970s, a conservative tide, perhaps culminating in the election of Ronald Reagan as president in 1980, may have started to restructure the pyramid in an upwardly direction again.

THE MODERATE STATE ━━━━━━━━━━━━━━━━━━━━━

The United States, as a mature and stable democracy, has not permitted a set of policies to swing too far toward either extreme. Yet, there is another feature that usually typifies stable democracies; the swings of policy from Left to Right and back again are gradual, occurring over many years without the violent short-term shifts that typify unstable political systems.

Unstable political systems usually have strong result orientations but do not have a strong sense of political process. As a result, it is more difficult to keep the cumulative forces of one orientation from pushing toward an extreme public policy and, instead of moving through gradual phases of positive law that emerge from different natural views of how the pyramid should be structured, the Left or Right ascendancy is marked by sudden and often violent changes. What are the manifestations of these changes that go beyond the rules of democratic process? You have read of them in the newspapers, I am sure, and they include assassinations, coups d'état, revolutions, and the like. These are the kinds of cumulative and anticumulative policy methods that mature systems are usually able to avoid.

CONCLUSION ━━━━━━━━━━━━━━━━━━━━━━━━━━━

We will consider why some systems undergo such rapid and violent methods of change when we examine political structure and the preconditions for structure in the following chapter. Let us now conclude our discussion of law, democracy, and the evolution of public policy with a review of the essential elements described thus far. We began to form our model with a discussion of the distribution of work and reward on a mythical island. We then discussed the differences in the kinds of value for which different citizens would work. (You should by now understand the matter of the height of the pyramid, and the relative views about human nature that underlie the range of ideologies or preferences for the height of that pyramid.) We then divided the principal ideologies since the Industrial Revolution into four broad categories, and with our discussion of each of them, we demonstrated how these ideologies constituted a continuum of belief about the pyramid. We also examined the equilibrium notion that worked alongside that continuum during the last 200 years. (You should understand by now why pure capitalism and pure communism never seemed to "take.") As we began to learn about democracy and its three definitions of result, process, and a different kind of result, you should have understood how democracy itself was also best described as a continuum with something working toward the center.

You should now be able to describe the fears of John Locke and James Madison concerning the adequate protection of property as we entered the democratic age. You should also be able to refer to the pyramids and understand that the position that Locke took, that is, that the principal purpose of government is to protect property, and the position that Madison took against popular "factions" and the power of a majority, would both maintain a steep distributional pyramid. Both Locke and Madison were concerned with the protection of the economic records of emerging commercial interests and both feared that large numbers at the base of the pyramid would work against the new interests.

Finally, you should understand that the post–Industrial Revolution valuational methods of Adam Smith (the pure market) and Karl Marx (the purely rationalistic model) made up the two poles of a continuum that argued over what should constitute day-to-day positive law within political systems. You should now be able to recognize that the gentle balance of Left and Right forces, and the smooth alternation between conservative and liberal public policy, are the hallmarks of stable democratic systems.

The political systems of the United States and Great Britain have been very fortunate in the development of their democratic processes during the simultaneous development of their industrial economies. Other nations in Western Europe have done more or less well, whereas those in, say, Latin America, where two distinct economic classes have traditionally mistrusted and mistreated each other, have had little success with democratic process. They have suffered radical swings of policy over short periods of time.

As you begin to understand how these various elements of a political society come together, you should increasingly be able to understand the outline of a unified contribution and reward model. What you have learned so far began with the value portion of the overall political model, and you have used this as a way of determining how a political system assigns value to what someone contributes. Politics is an integrated whole, and although we have not completed the model by any means, the value portion of the model that responds to the question of what it is that we are fighting over in politics should now be clear. We can now proceed to that part of the model that has to do with the actual structures of a political system.

Glossary

TERMS

continuum

equilibrium

natural law

observed truth

printing press

Glorious Revolution

private property

Federalist #10

fruits of their labor

parliament

positive law

common law

democracy as process

democracy as result

English Bill of Rights

American Bill of Rights

French Revolution

egalitarian

liberal

conservative

Left

Right

stratified

wealth

organization

numbers

cumulative forces

anticumulative forces

NAMES

Issac Newton

Copernicus

Galileo

Thomas Hooker

Lord Edward Coke

Thomas Jefferson

Voltaire

Tom Paine

CHAPTER 6
THE BUILDING BLOCKS
OF STRUCTURE

You should now be prepared to study the actual structures of modern government. The study of structure is fundamental to politics for many reasons, the most important being that different structures are capable of bringing about varying results among public policy choices. Nearly as important is the notion that the very structure of government is itself a product of what are generally known as "prepolitical" considerations. Prepolitical considerations include the culture of a nation, its history, its myths, and the stories about important political figures, all of which make up the citizenry's notion of their public institutions.

There are many ways of describing the principal characteristics of a political culture. The one that is the most telling, however, describes the degree of *cohesion* of a political society. For example, when Aristotle spoke of political identifications and the degree to which individuals identify with the *polis*, he spoke of three levels of identification. The first was the *family*, the second was the *village*, and the third was the larger *polis* or the collection of villages that made up the entire political unit.

The intensity of personal identification is not the same at all levels of identification; obviously, identification is much stronger at the level of the family. Similarly, the intensity of identification is moderately strong at the level of a single village, and is least strong at the level of the entire political society or the collection of villages. At the latter level there is less natural political cohesion because there is less personal affinity among a citizenry that does not know or identify as closely with one another.

As we introduce the subject of political structure, then, we need to discuss the levels of cohesion within various political systems. We know that we will never again be at a stage in history where a collection of villages makes up the dominant political unit. We are well along now into the period of the nation-state, and nearly all of the peoples of the world are part of an expansion beyond

Aristotle's third level of identification. Also, in most instances, these nation-states cover considerable areas of the globe, certainly larger than ancient Greece. They also contain, in most instances, several million people within each nation-state. Before we talk in greater detail about the structure of these various national governments, we should understand how the citizens of these nation-states relate to their government and to each other.

THE SOCIAL COHESION MODEL ━━━━━

What do we mean by social cohesion? Social cohesion means the degree to which citizens see themselves as either close to or far from their fellow citizens. We shall borrow a part of the model of a Canadian sociologist to introduce the various levels of social and political cohesion. Gerard DeGré devised five principal classifications of social cohesion as being part of a single continuum.[1] He labeled them (1) *atomistic,* (2) *multipartite,* (3) *pluralistic,* (4) *elitist,* and (5) *totalitarian.* (see Figures 6–1 and 6–2). We will take them one at a time with the idea that each classification represents

FIGURE 6–1.
DeGré's five principal classifications of cohesion. [Adapted from Gerard DeGré, "Freedom and Social Structure," *American Sociological Review,* Vol. 11 (October 1946), pp. 529–536, with permission of the author and the American Sociological Association.]

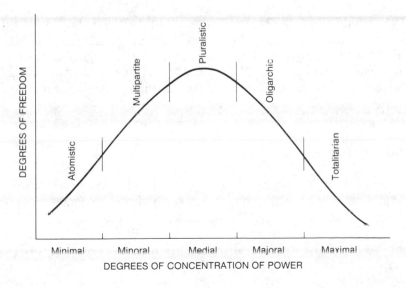

an increasing degree of social and political cohesion among the citizenry and governmental structure.

Atomistic Cohesion

What is an atomistic level of social and political cohesion? Did you ever, when you were younger, play a game called "King of the Mountain"? On what principle was it based? It was a struggle, was it not, for dominance on a hill in your neighborhood? Also important to the game was that there were no alliances between any of you. There were no groups or individual friendships with one another in any form. All the contestants fought only for themselves, and, even in triumph, they recognized no alliances or friendships. Realistically, can you envision a society in which there are no friendships, not even among members of a family? Of course, this would be difficult to imagine, but, remember, we are still at one end of a theoretical continuum.

In the real world, if such a pattern of cohesion ever existed, it probably did not last long. Yet the political philosopher Thomas Hobbes worried about a state of the world where "all against all" would become the true state of social cohesion. Hobbes believed that life on this earth was wretched and unhappy, and he wondered whether friendships or even alliances within a political system might be so fragile that a political system would ever survive if only such alliances were to hold it together. Society, in short, was seen by Hobbes as an almost empty shell, with only separated individuals inside. At best, a leader might survive for a short time, but the leadership would always be insecure, much like in the King of the Mountain game. Hobbes's work *Leviathan* argued for a strict and overpowering political structure for an atomistic society, for he thought that such a structure was all that could hold a political system together in such a world.

Multipartite Cohesion

Moving toward the center from the most individualistic or atomistic pole of the continuum, the next condition of social and political cohesion is what DeGré called the multipartite state. It recognizes small collections of friendships, alliances, and, of course, family groups within the social and political society, and it recognizes some bonding among peoples as existing naturally within human social organizations. It also acknowledges that small groups may work together for political goals. Nonetheless, the size of the groupings in the multipartite state are small and the social cohesion is still very fluid. Conceptually, the shell of the multipartite political society contains slightly larger modules than the single individual of the atomistic model. Yet these larger models still do not coalesce well with other models. Perhaps the best political example of such a structure would be the traditional structures of the American Indian alliance, particularly within the Iroquois Nation. There were many tribes within the Iroquois Nation, most of which had a loose social and political organization.

Pluralistic Cohesion

The third and, for DeGré, the middle level of political cohesion is labeled pluralistic cohesion. This classification deserves a great deal more of our attention than do the two previous categories (we will devote additional time to pluralism later in the chapter.)

To begin our discussion, you should understand that pluralism substantially continues the trend of increasing cohesion that we have already described. We know that the multipartite system contains a large number of very small friendship circles and alliances. Within the pluralistic system, however, there exists a smaller number of larger alliances or interests. This configuration is in fact close to the reality of some modern, industrial nations.

Again, Aristotle's three levels of personal identification—the family, the village, and *polis*—may be helpful to your understanding of pluralism. In multipartite systems, only personal indentifications that extend a small distance away from each citizen can exist. Each individual and family interacts and extends an identification only with a somewhat larger grouping such as a tribe or village. But identification beyond a small group or tribe is absolutely necessary within modern society, for it is there that the groups that make up modern national identification can and do flourish.

You have heard of such business groups as the National Association of Manufacturers, the Motor Vehicle Manufacturers Association, and so on. You have also heard of labor groups such as the AFL–CIO and individual unions like the Teamsters and the Machinists, all of which are politically active within the United States. You also know of the American Medical Association, whose membership is doctors, and the American Bar Association, whose membership is lawyers. Putting all these groups together creates a true pluralistic structure. Conceptually, a pluralistic system has larger and fewer components than the multipartite model. It would still, however, have more of the superstructure elements than appear in the following DeGré classification.

Elitist Cohesion

The elitist system, which in democratic nations has existed more frequently in Western Europe and to some degree in modern Japan, moves toward even broader circles of identification. An elitist social system has fewer groups of political identification than does the pluralist model. It may, in extreme cases, have only one truly important political grouping such as a caste, a particular ruling family or a ruling economic elite. In most instances, however, there will be at least a configuration of social and political groupings known as the counterelite, a grouping or a politically relevant cohesion that opposes the dominant configuration. Also, there will be one more identifying characteristic of the elitist society that sets it off from pluralism. Sociologists call this element *stratification*, a term we have already used to describe economic differentiation. In the language of political science, what we visualize is a series of lines that separate categories of rank or class and that exist beyond the leadership group throughout society.

Classes are forms of allocations of privilege. Usually, they present very steep barriers to "moving up" into an occupation or a position of greater responsibility. Thus, elitism generally means that fewer and more stratified groupings are part of the element of cohesion. Consider our discussion of feudalism and the allocation or the return from a feudal economic arrangement that depended upon a person's station in life. Although with far less intensity today, the European social system still exhibits vestiges of that earlier feudal arrangement.

Most of the forebearers of the current generation of North Americans (at least in the United States and Canada) came to these shores specifically out of frustration with the very stratification of the European feudal orders which had continued into later centuries. The American experience generated a more pluralistic model because the Americans, unlike the Europeans, attempted to restrict new social stratifications from forming. American pluralism, at least in theory, fought against anything that might keep citizens from rising to their level of potential. Hence, a greater degree of social cohesion surrounding whole classes of citizens, and the ranking that accompanies large social groupings of an elitist model, have been resisted by the American people.

Totalitarian Cohesion

To complete the DeGré continuum, the final condition within the model of social cohesion is called the totalitarian condition. In one sense, it is the opposite of the atomistic state of social cohesion because it represents an almost total meshing of the elements of the society into a highly unified and purposive whole. What also typifies the totalitarian pole is that only one leader, or a very small clique of leaders, clearly dominates the totalitarian state. The King of the Mountain game, in effect, has been declared ended. One person or, again, a very small group has taken charge and seems determined to remain there for the foreseeable future. As you can imagine, the temper of the form of leadership is rarely very open or democratic within a totalitarian structure. It is certainly not tolerant of competing potential leadership alliances within that political society. Unlike the elitism of today's Western European nations, no alternative leadership group exists that can represent different notions of the natural order. Within totalitarianism, no group competes over how the system should legislate and administer a broad set of laws.

Also, within a totalitarian configuration, little credence is given to the various classes or stations that might give an alternative personal identification to that system's citizens. Part of the burden of totalitarianism is that all internal groupings of citizens have been either obscured or taken over by the leader and only an undifferentiated mass of citizens is permitted to stand before that leader. If there is a balancing of viewpoints within the totalitarian system, it exists only because the succession of totalitarian lead-

FIGURE 6–2.
The continuum of social cohesion.

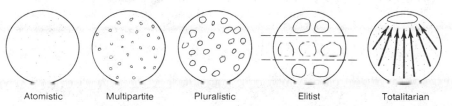

| Atomistic | Multipartite | Pluralistic | Elitist | Totalitarian |

ership is almost always unstable. The death of a totalitarian leader usually brings great upheaval to the state, particularly if a set of bureaucratic or party institutions has not been developed within the political community.

THE SIMILARITY OF THE POLES ━━━━━━━

We have now completed our review of DeGré's continuum. As you can see from Figure 6–1, however, DeGré recognizes that neither extreme on the continuum, neither the atomistic nor the totalitarian condition, represents a significant degree of political freedom. What DeGré might have mentioned is that the two sides are not only sitting on two poles of a continuum, they are also very close to one another in several ways.

What happens to the totalitarian structure when the autocratic ruler dies? What happens when the ruler is overthrown, assassinated, or driven into exile? Look closely again at the absence of intermediate groupings within the two extremes. Think also about the effects upon the atomistic model when one "king of the mountain" manages to remain for a time at the top. Finally, consider for a moment the real similarities between the internal social cohesion of the atomistic and totalitarian models. Aren't they both very loose and nonaligned within the circle? Aren't they also linked only to the top in a very precarious way?

One might say that there is a great deal of similarity between the two extremes. One might even say that the continuum is not just a single line and that perhaps it is really a circle. Again, from the perspective of the inside of the polity, both the atomistic and totalitarian models maintain the citizenry in a solitary condition. Perhaps the only real difference between these states is the somewhat more permanent existence of the totalitarian leader.

THE OTHER SIDE OF THE CIRCLE ━━━━━━━

If the social cohesion model is in reality a circle, and if the atomistic condition and the totalitarian condition are really very similar, then what can we expect from the other side of the circle? Many observers claim that the pluralist condition is the perfect opposite of the atomistic-totalitarian side of the circle. They reason that pluralism represents the ideal level of social cohesion, although others argue that modern-day elitism is a better representation of the ideal social and political cohesion level.

What is it about pluralism that is attractive to its adherents? In part, it is the degree of social cohesion itself, a factor that pluralism's adherents consider to be at the right level for stable and effective government. Pluralism exhibits a degree of togetherness in society, and a sense of identification with groupings and structures. At the same time, however, there is no severe rigidity within the social pattern of pluralism, as there is in other societies with clear class or caste social structures.

Curiously, in the early days of the United States, a Frenchman, Alexis de Tocqueville, visited this country and, in his two-volume work *Democracy in America*, he discussed the openness of the American social system as compared with European social institutions. He noted that there were no preordained statuses in this new country and that, because of this, new American citizens were able to rise to their own level of ability. De Tocqueville observed further that citizens were not expected to identify solely with the family or class that one was born to, but could voluntarily form their own social and occupational groupings. Finally, de Tocqueville noticed that a far larger number of groupings existed within America than existed within Europe. He called these groupings *voluntary associations*, and he found that they represented practically all the diverse interests and groupings that existed within the emerging American society.

Pluralist Stability

Beyond de Tocqueville's reflections on America, a number of other aspects of a pluralistic social system have been helpful to both the maintenance of democratic political processes and a fair mix of different natural values within the positive law. Many of these have to do with the relationship of various social and economic groupings to what is now known as a pluralistic structure of government. We will soon describe the structures of government that relate to the DeGré model of social cohesion. Let us concentrate now on the importance of the *stability* of a political order. It should be clear to you that instability will exist in the atomistic and totalitarian models of social cohesion, as well as in the types of government they generate. Pluralism's supporters claim that it is the most stable of all systems because there are more possible combinations of alliances or *coalitions* among the groupings of a pluralist society.

Let us examine what we mean by "coalitions." Imagine that there are only two important economic groupings in a society, and that these groupings are competing over the distribution question, that is, the height of the pyramid, as well as some other matter in the political system. Over time, with only these two groupings in existence, relations between these groups would be severely strained. (Remember, in this example, that every issue, be it tax reform or aid to hospitals or some other, the same sides line up together because there are only two principal groupings in society. The same people, in other words, always find themselves arguing against the same opponents.)

In the real world of politics, where might we find examples of such continued fissures in society? Perhaps the best example is in Latin America where, as we noted earlier, the schism between the rich and the poor, that is, between the economic classes, is very great. Where a polity has two very distinct classes, one made up of a large body of the very poor and politically frustrated, and the other made up of the very wealthy and politically powerful, the degree of animosity between these groupings can be substantial. This animosity results in a bitterness toward virtually all political conflicts within deeply divided countries. Governments in Latin America often change leadership because of assassinations, coups, or revolutions and counterrevolutions. The fact is that normal patterns of doing public business, as well as normal patterns of changing from one direction of policy to another, as we saw with the cumulative and anticumulative public policy model, are difficult to sustain within a deeply divided social environment.

Pluralist Cross-Pressures

For reasons that you can now understand, stable social systems and stable governmental institutions have the benefit of a free interplay among many major social groupings. Such an interplay is healthy because it allows government to manage disputes in a smooth and less conflictual way. One observer who has studied the moderate kinds of political confrontations that occur when there are many social groupings is Seymour Martin Lipset, who has developed a concept that he labels *cross-pressures*. According to Lipset, because pluralistic social and political systems contain a great number of cross-pressures, the deep and sometimes permanent schisms of more divisive systems are less likely to develop.[2]

What is the essence of Lipset's cross-pressures? By way of explanation, think of a number of ways that you would classify your interests or identifications as a citizen. In other words, how do you identify with a political subgrouping to get what you expect from the political system? First, what about your economic standing? Do you consider yourself to be well-off or not so well-off? Do you identify with a wealthy dominant class or grouping, or do you identify with a poorer, economically deprived class? It is true that the United States and pluralist systems generally have been able to prevent economic standing from deeply dividing its citizens. This is true in part because we are the most middle class of all nations, with great numbers of neither terribly wealthy nor seriously poverty-stricken citizens within the population. But the United States does have some economic divisions among its citizens, and it avoids severe political divisions along lines of economic class in great part because the entire matter of economic standing is not the only identification that citizens have within the American policy.

Along with an economic identification, what other kinds of identifications are prominent within a pluralist society? Think again about your own group memberships. What about your religious affiliation? Are you a Protestant, a Catholic, a Jew, a member of another religion, or even an atheist? What region of the country are you from? Are you a Northerner or a Southerner, or do you identify with the West, the Midwest, or a major metropolitan area? What about your race? This has certainly been an important identification in the civil rights issues of recent years. Are you black or white or maybe Oriental or Native American? Does that identification make a difference to you? Finally, what about your sex? More recently, many political issues have revolved around equal treatment of the sexes. This identification too would certainly be a relevant classification in a pluralistic system. If we spent more time, we could probably think of other classifications, but the identities of (1) economic standing, (2) religion, (3) region, (4) race, and (5) sex should give us a good start on the understanding of the impact of cross-pressures.

Cross-Pressures: An Example

Let us now examine a political issue, specifically, the controversy over the public funding of private schools. This issue has been vigorously contested over the years, and strong feelings exist on both sides of the argument. Yet, if the debate has been a serious one, we should ask why it is that it has not deeply divided the

American citizenry. Why has it not caused the divisions that exist within a place such as Latin America?

The United States has not suffered severe political repercussions from the school-financing argument because, considering the varied classifications of identifications, none of the other subgroupings feels unanimously one way or the other about the topic. Most wealthy Americans may favor the funding of private schools only because they anticipate that their own children may attend such schools. Most poor Americans may be opposed to their tax dollars being used toward the funding of schools that their children will not be able to attend. But let us also consider the difference between blacks and whites on the issue of private school financing. Many blacks regard private schools as a haven for only the wealthier citizens of the society. But some, including blacks who are not well-off, may feel that access to good private schools would grant their children the same kind of educational and occupational mobility that the wealthy have enjoyed. In this example, economic divisions may continue as racial groupings are crossed, and thus racial hostility in the society is kept to a minimum (see Figure 6–3).

It is clear that wealthier citizens, black and white, as well as poorer citizens, black and white, have the option of banding together so that the differences between being black or being white are obscured. Perhaps, the economic class to which one belongs, again negating differences in race, is the most significant factor in

FIGURE 6–3.
Cross-pressures.

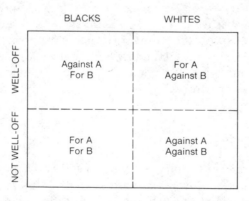

Issue A: Aid to Parochial Schools
Issue B: Civil Rights Legislation

the controversy over private school funding. But race is not the only division within a political society, and therefore the issue is not a dangerous one.

The key to cross-pressures is that people's identifications are so varied that the alliance they form with people on one issue will not be the same alliance they form on the next issue. Wealthy whites and poor blacks may group together on the issue of aid to private schools. Yet whites, generally speaking, may oppose blacks when an issue such as the renewal of the Voting Rights Act is being contested. Legislation that is particularly designed to help black registration and voting in areas where discrimination has been practiced in the past, may be contested by some whites but supported by blacks. The division on this particular issue would be a racial rather than an economic one, and the point, again, is that the alliances are never the same. With cross-pressures, no division ever permanently divides the society and makes political divisions rigid or bitter.

As you can see, the cross-pressure idea rests well with the pluralist structure of social and political cohesion. It would not fit in as well, however, with elitism or, with any of the other models. The multiplicity of group memberships and identifications of which de Tocqueville spoke and which the American culture has certainly continued to generate are the proper kind of seedbed for the cross-pressure benefits of pluralism.

The Element of Trust

There is one more aspect of pluralism that many people find attractive. This aspect was discussed by an American professor of sociology, Talcott Parsons, who found himself deeply concerned with the question of how intense political competition among groups could afford not to disturb the fabric of a political society.[3] Parsons sensed, as others have also done, that the key to the stability of any political society is that the citizenry must not be in constant fear of political calamities.

Parsons used the analogy of bank deposits to describe this sense of security. Let us consider for a moment that you have deposited $500 in a checking or savings account at the beginning of the school year. Is the $500 you deposited still sitting inside the deposit window where you left it with the clerk? You know, of course, that it isn't, and you know that it has been mingled with all the other deposits that have been made. You know also that the bank has gone ahead and done something with that money to make its own profit. Now, what if you and everyone else with an account at this bank were to go to the bank to withdraw the money that each of you had deposited? Could the bank pay you your money? You know that it could not. We should focus on why it is that you don't go down to your bank and withdraw that money. The simple answer is that you trust your bank, for you know that if you really needed your money, the $500 would be given to you. Thus, you are willing to let the bank use your $500 as it wishes.

Again, trust is the key to your willingness, and much the same kind of thing happens in a stable, or trusting, political system. As a citizen you are a member of the larger society of political depositors, as well as a member of many individual groups. You do not feel that because your political group recently lost a battle over something that you will also lose all other political battles. You trust the system, and believe that you will in most cases be given at least a reasonable political return. You are content, therefore, to vote, to give money to a political candidate, or perhaps even to be involved with a political campaign. In other words, you are content to participate politically at a level of politics that is somewhat routine and that essentially trusts how the political system is run.

What is the alternative to such trust? What does the insecure, untrusting citizen, that is, the citizen who feels that the system never responds to justified needs, do as a result of such mistrust? The majority of mistrusting citizens will resent the political system so deeply that some portion of that untrusting population will participate in a much more intense level of politics. Perhaps the reduced level of trust is such that protest in the streets, organizing massive economic and political strikes and slowdowns, or, at an even higher level of disaffection, engaging in assassinations, coups, or revolutions, are from this perspective considered justified. You have heard of a "run" on the bank. You know that in times of financial crisis when everyone's $500 seems insecure, depositors rush to be first in line at the bank to get their $500 before everyone else gets theirs. They no longer trust that their money will be there when they need it, and they will do whatever is necessary to withdraw it.

Again, the political analogy of that withdrawal is a kind of political bank run. It may range in intensity from serious political agitation to the fullest levels of renunciation of political process that come with assassinations and revolution. Clearly, Parsons was a pluralist and his analogy of money deposited with a high degree of trust corresponds with Lipset's notion that political flexibility and stability come from a multiplicity of political groupings. We all would like to be comfortable with our right to vote and our participation in a few trusting and low-key political activities. We hope that there will be sufficient political justice within the political notions of contribution and reward just as we trust that our personal money will be in the bank when we need it. As you do not need to be at the front of the bank line every morning to make sure that the money is there, so too you do not need to engage in extraordinary political activities to protect your political rights when the element of trust is present.

POLITICAL STRUCTURES

Let us pause for a moment and reflect upon what we have added to our model. You are being asked to think about the kinds of political structures that correspond to particular levels of social cohesion. Just as it was necessary to discuss the contribution portion of the model before we could discuss law, public policy, and democratic process, we also had to discuss fundamental prepolitical considerations before we could move to the essence of political structure. The DeGré continuum set out a relationship between a citizenry's level of social cohesion or togetherness and the basic political relationships within the system. Lipset's notion of cross-pressures demonstrated how a multiplicity of groups gives a resiliency to the political system of pluralism. Parson's contribution was one of trust, and with it came the absence of the kind of intensity or frustration in political beliefs that made every embattled issue capable of breaking apart the social cohesion and political structure of the system. There are other important prepolitical considerations, of course, and from time to time we will make reference to them. But we have gone far enough along in our discussion of these prepolitical matters to concentrate more specifically on the essence of political structures themselves.

Let me begin by noting that within the modern world, only two forms of structure—the pluralist and the elitist—are seriously considered to be representative of democratic government. We have explained why we find the atomistic and the totalitarian systems to be unacceptable to both democratic principles. DeGré's classification of the multipartite level of cohesion, although important perhaps at one time in history, does not fit well with the prepolitical realities of virtually all modern societies. What we have come to in modern history is a more complicated set of social patterns. The governmental structures that represent these patterns, and the degree of cohesion within them, are necessarily going to be more complicated.

Thus, the range of what are considered to be the dominant pre-political cohesion patterns of democracy within the late twentieth century has fallen between that part of the larger DeGré range that encompasses the pluralist and elitist structures. As we have noted, the pluralist structure is often represented as being at the center of the accepted range. To be sure, pluralism does possess certain structural benefits for a political system. Yet, for reasons that we should now begin to examine, the advocates of the modern elitist view, that is, an elitism that is free from many of the traditional abuses of nobility and privileged aristocracy, claim now to be equally democratic.

Where is the elitist structure the dominant mode today? Generally, it is dominant within the countries of Western Europe. It is there that even a much weakened residue of the traditional elitist social structure supports forms of government that still more clearly acknowledge a vertical differentiation among the status of its people. To some degree, the contrast in political structure that we will focus on to complete our model is, at least in part, a comparison of the political structure of the United States and the Western European democracies. Yet there is another comparison that you should think about first and, as you do, keep an open mind about your own preferences for the elitist or the pluralist model.

As an aid to an unbiased analysis, it might help you to continue to think of the pluralist-elitist contrast within actual governments as being very much on a continuum like the prepolitical social cohesion continuum of Gerard DeGré. Simply put, there is not a purely pluralist system in the democratic world nor does there exist a purely elitist system. There are only degrees of more pluralism or more elitism, these being real-world examples of certain aspects of each model. To understand the comparative merits of the two systems in greater detail, however, think of the two classical Greek scholars who were the most profound in their discussion of politics, Plato and his student Aristotle of that momentous Grecian era when modern notions of democracy were born.

PLATO AND ARISTOTLE

How did Plato and Aristotle each think of democracy? Clearly their views, although within the range of what many would consider to be democratic for that time in history, were very different from each other. Aristotle argued that there was less inherent social cohesion in society than did Plato. Aristotle was thus concerned that the competitive rules of political advocacy be well defined and that the competition between individuals and groups in society be peaceful and constructive. In one sense, Aristotle was more of an egalitarian in his views of people's relative capabilities. Within the guidelines of the Greek culture (though, again, women, slaves, and non-Athenians were clearly excluded), Aristotle did advocate a full and democratic procedural participation on the part of Athenian citizens.

Plato, in contrast, had a very different view of politics and political participation. Starting from a more elitist perspective, Plato argued for what he believed to be important differences in the capabilities of different citizens. He described these differences in a variety of ways, using as one defining structure the ladder of gold, silver, and bronze citizens. According to Plato, some citizens in any society were perceived as inherently more capable of political leadership than were others. A few citizens, in effect, were held to be natural leaders, and others were more or less bound to respond to the wisdom of those leaders. Plato felt deeply about this notion and argued that any society that did not acknowledge its natural leaders and place such people in positions of responsibility would only threaten harm to the entire polity. Perhaps, from an American perspective, the Platonic view threatens to place too much authority into the hands of only a few leaders. We should point out, however, that Plato placed very clear restraints on how those rulers would be chosen and how they would be allowed to govern.

Plato, for example, referred to his principal political leaders as philosopher kings, saying that such citizens should be of the utmost moral character and possess a better vision of what is good for the entire political society. Further, the life of a philosopher king was to be divorced from material or economic satisfactions, with clear prohibitions upon property ownership being one of the burdens of leadership in the Platonic state. Important also, the Platonic vision possessed the two key linkages within the society that accounted for both high levels of social cohesion and political unity. The first included a deep sense of obligation among all the rankings or statuses within the *polis*. The city-state leadership, including the philosopher king and the guardians who were the second-level administrators, all were held to have a deep sense of commitment to the Platonic citizenry. Further, the Platonic community held that the citizens of the political community would have a deeply interdependent relationship with one another. This view, sometimes known as the organic view of society, certainly relied, again, upon a more compact notion of social and political cohesion.

Now, again, return to a contrast between the pluralist and elitist models. The differences between the generally more American and the more European visions of politics, apart from the more prominent existence of social classes in Europe, is that Europeans accept the Platonic notion of the natural differences in people's abilities somewhat more than do American. Americans, as a rule, are more willing to argue that people are more equal in their natural capabilities. Americans are also more comfortable with a political structure that allows for competition among near equals rather than an automatic elevation of the most capable leaders. Although Americans may often privately believe in such gradations of ability, they rarely emphasize such things as intellectual superiority or in-depth familiarity with a public office in their selection of public leaders. Typically, Americans have believed that many citizens are capable of assuming positions of public leadership. This view reflects de Tocqueville's observation of the often mediocre level of American leadership. Again, do not take either of these two prepolitical positions as being fully separated from each other. They both rest upon a continuum, but they are generally valid as tendencies that typify the American pluralist and the European elitist views.

THE POLICY AND THE STRUCTURES

It is tempting now to begin a more detailed discussion of the various structural aspects of pluralist and elitist governments. However, in the remaining sections of this chapter, you should do more than simply learn the details of these two models of democratic government. You should also be able to compare and contrast the two governmental models in terms of the relatively favorable governing attitudes of each as well as the governing difficulties that the two models suffer from.

Let us start with a brief extension of what we have just said about human capabilities. If we have said that the assumptions about relative human capabilities, that is, the views of Plato as opposed to the views of Aristotle, have a great deal to do with elitism and pluralism, then what we have already discussed about the definitions of democracy also has a good deal to do with the preference for elitism or pluralism. You will recall that we defined an equilibrium of public policy, court decisions, and the like as representing a "fair" or "equitable" set of decisions on public policy questions. We know that there will be cumulative and anticumulative forces that push away from and push back toward that center point on both the conservative and liberal sides of the distribution argument. What we should now realize is that there is also a continuum that is very relevant for the understanding of pluralism and elitism. It deals with how democratic institutions will be structured. As a general notion, the pluralist political structures will be more diffuse, that is, more decentralized, as they reflect the pluralistic level of social cohesion in their societies. Elitist political structures, in contrast, will tend to be more concentrated, that is, more centralized, as they reflect the elitist level of social cohesion. Also, pluralist systems are slightly more ready to define the mix of process and result in democratic public policy in favor of the market method of economic valuation. Elitist systems, again in contrast, are prone to consider the mix of process and result in democracy as being in favor of the rationalist valuational view.

As is the case with all analyses based upon a continuum, there are no pure types of either alternative. Democracy, as we have so far defined it, has process at the center. Democracy as process does not take pure result orientations of what the world should be like and convert them directly into public policy. As we have said, the positive law that democratic systems create should be a full and fair mix of varied natural law views, such as the two views of market valuation or rationalistic valuation in the matter of the pyramid. With reference to the model that we have built so far, process, again, should be represented in the center. It should be approximately where the different claims of various result orientations are about equally considered.

But let us now remember the question of governmental role. That is the question that throws light upon the equilibrium between result-process-result in democracy. It also throws new light on the equilibrium view of natural law on one side, positive law in the middle, and another natural law view on the other side. Think again about the market method of economic valuation and the rationalistic method of valuation in terms of one important element. Think of whether the amount of government needed to achieve market valuation and the amount of government needed to achieve rationalistic valuation are the same level of government. Put another way, does market valuation and rationalistic valuation need government itself to exist to the same degree?

The answer is clear, is it not? The market method of valuation requires less government than does the rationalistic method of government because rationalism requires some measure of publicly aggregating people's views about what risk, skill, training, and the like are worth. Now think about this same issue with respect to the question of what Plato and Aristotle argued over. Did not one of these philosophers argue more for allowing the competition of elements decide what should constitute public policy, while the other argued that people of high qualifications should make the determinations that constitute the society's public policy? Of course, there is a difference, with Aristotle believing more in the competition of individuals and groups that are more or less equal, while Plato believed more in the inherently good judgment of those who lead.

Do you see a pattern developing here? What we have learned with regard to process and policy should now merge into a new understanding of the kinds of politicial structures that will grow out of different assumptions about competition, cohesion, and the like. The DeGré model's equilibrium may have theoretically landed upon pluralism as the center. Yet, when our analysis merges into the realities of determining valuation and structuring governments to engage in such valuations, we should see that market-oriented valuation systems will tend to be more pluralist in their structure, and rationalistic systems will tend to be more elitist. Put another way, the real balance among democratic systems, although it at first seems to be where there is the most pluralism, is instead at some mid-point between pluralism and elitism. The equilibrium is at a point where there is still a good deal of process such as free elections, free speech, and so on, but it is also at a point where one system permits groups to maintain more of a market orientation in valuation. The other system deals more clearly with rationalistic valuation within the distribution argument.

To be very clear about this coalescence of structure and policy, think about Aristotle and Plato as though they were creators of modern, constitutional, and democratic systems. What would the structures of their government look like? An updated version of Aristotle's structure might very well look like today's American system. All elements would compete for what they get from government and private society, and it would be difficult for the government to interfere too greatly with a liberal capitalism's market determination of valuation. Plato's structure would more likely derive public notions of what is good for the society from some public set of elite institutions or from the ideas of wise leaders rather than from open competition among all groups. It would maintain an active involvement in ensuring some determination of value based upon a rationalistic sense of the risk, skill, training, and so on of those who produced something for the society.

Let us now look more closely at why pluralism has more market valuation and less government in its democracy, and why elitism flourishes with more government and a bit more rationalism in its valuation. Of course, the reason has much to do with the level of social cohesion, a fact that relates directly to DeGré's model. Part of the reason also has to do with cross-pressures in a system. The fact is that the looser the social cohesion of a system, that is, the more different groups there are, the better the chance is that there will be fluid, floating coalitions of identification among those groups. These tendencies within pluralism mean that the demands that citizens make upon the government will not bring a clear or consistent ideological ring with them. Put another way, the citizens of a pluralistic system seem to want their system to respond to individual and particular needs, rather than to comprehensive programs or philosophies.

To be sure, with an elitist system, there are groups and individuals who wish for certain things from their government. Yet, as we have said, there are generally fewer particular groupings as well as stronger unifying themes that tend to give the politics of these countries a more ideological tone. What are these unifying themes? In Europe, the single most important unifying theme has historically been the division of the classes, that is, the feudally-based conflict between the landed aristocracy and the peasant, or in the nineteenth century, between the entrepreneur and the industrial worker. In other countries, race, region, or some other division within the populace may be paramount, but in those nations, the dominance of one group over another has accounted for a kind of politics that, in extreme cases, has not allowed for much democratic process. In the Western European countries, however, there has tended to be a good deal of democratic process, although politics has still often revolved around the economic divisions between workers and owners.

Within an elitist government procedural openness is still important to a considerable degree. Yet, with elitism, the degree of trust that comes from having open democratic processes within pluralism comes slightly more from an acceptance or a nonacceptance of the public policy that the elitist system generates. More important, the very fact that public policy has had a class-based and ideological history within elitism has meant that the very discussion of fair wages was more likely to be a public discussion. Further, that discussion is far more likely to include actual mention of the kinds of considerations, (skill, risk, scarcity, and so on) than it would within a pluralist system. For this reason, elitist governments are more likely to use a rationalistic method of valuation than a market method.

With this analysis of how different political structures tend to deal with the question of valuation, we should be able to understand why it is that the burden of satisfying the citizenry has historically been slightly greater for the elitist rather than for the pluralist system. Historically, in societies that have had major class divisions, the citizenry has pulled more toward the result orientation of their preferences. At certain times, their requests from the government have been somewhat more adamant and their view of government more distrustful. However, it may be that this difference was more true historically than it is now. It may be that within the decline of social and economic class barriers in Europe, this aspect of elitist salience, competition, and conflict is less significant.

As we proceed in our analysis, we will see a number of other attributes of the pluralist and elitist systems that may lead to advantages for one system in some respects and advantages for the other in other respects. Yet, before we continue to compare these models in detail, you should understand exactly how it is that political systems deal with the differences of opinion that citizens have over public policy. As noted earlier, elitist systems may have traditionally had a more difficult time satisfying citizen wants. Now you should concentrate on the nature of these difficulties among citizens and the effect that such difficulties have upon a nation's politics.

What I suggest we do, therefore, is build a continuum that reveals not only what the intensity of disagreement is among citizens but that also shows that that intensity relates to the manner in which political controversy is manifested. To begin, let me suggest that there are three major gradations of controversy. Each represents a different level of intensity over the disagreements of a political system. Let us try to identify them simply as levels of controversy and then let us apply them to political action itself.

First, consider the American paratrooper jumps that occurred just before D-day in France during World War II. The standing order to all units was to assemble themselves as a unit quickly and quietly after they had been dropped over occupied France. The key to these paratroopers' ability to find each other, however, was their clear understanding before the drop of what is known as *saliency*, the idea that what is inside your mind is pretty much what is inside somebody else's mind. In other words you and another person know that each of you is thinking the same thing.

The American paratroopers in France were told that after the drop, they were to look for the nearest point that would be visible to all of them for a long distance. They were even told what that salient point might be. In most cases it was the small-town church steeple, something that could be seen from virtually everywhere in the countryside. As you can guess, the percentage of American paratroopers who found each other and organized as an effective unit was very high in this crucial pre–D-day period.

I ask you to familiarize yourselves with this concept of saliency because it represents one pole of another continuum of understanding that is very important for politics. Remember, in our example, that the paratroopers all wanted the same thing, to meet up with each other. Their goals were identical, but consider within how much of politics public goals are identical. Of course, there are few instance of total salience in politics, and, as you would expect, those instances are passed through the political system quickly and without difficulty. Much like the condition of one person residing on the island, if there are many people in a population but they all feel basically the same way about what public policy should be doing, the politics of that society should be very simple.

In the larger world, as we saw with the argument over valuation, there are many disagreements over public issues. The continuum we want to consider is one that starts with one mythical pole of full agreement or salience and ends at the other pole of total discord or conflict. We should now ask ourselves, "What would constitute the conditions of conflict?" You can think about conflict by thinking of a polity with no common goals or interests among the population. Living in such a society would be a constant struggle, would it not, with each citizen knowing that no one else believed in what he or she held to be important? Now, of course, the chances of there being total conflict or discord in a political society is every bit as small as the chances of there being the kind of total salience of interests as there was in the case of the paratroopers. Under the pressure of equilibrium, the continuum tends toward the middle where there are appropriate degrees of each of (1) *salience*, (2) *competition*, or (3) *conflict* (see Figure 6–4).

Let us define these terms. (1) Political salience is a very strong overlap or agreement among the members of a political society on the questions of valuation and other political questions. (2) Con-

FIGURE 6–4.
Salience, competition, and conflict.

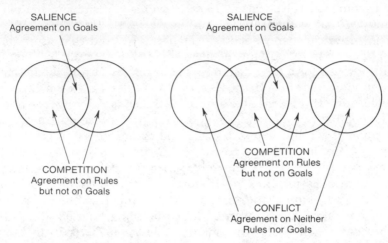

flicts toward the other extreme, are represented by those disagreements among a citizenry that push the society beyond the peaceful and routine rules for solving political disputes. (3) Competition is in the middle of this continuum, for competition occurs where there are disagreements over valuation and other policy questions but where there are also rules that take care of how those differences are peacefully resolved.

We know, of course, that politics does not always have such rules and sometimes that it is not even capable of enforcing the rules of competition that it has. We also know that an occasional contestant in a political game, just as in sports, will choose not to abide by the existing rules. Such a nonrule-observing situation brings about conflict, and conflict, of course, is a more serious state of political activity. Conflict causes both a greater degree of disruption in the political argument along with a greater degree of danger to the citizenry. Such conflict, again, generally stems from a substantial lack of overlapping values and identifications including, more importantly, the value of playing by the rules.

Once more, what the salience, competition, and conflict continuum represents is the real-world continuum or spectrum of agreement and disagreement within a political society. Theoretically, the continuum ranges from a position of near unanimity of both the goals of the system and the rules of the game (salience), through the place where goals are different but the rules are agreed to (competition), to a place where neither the goals are agreed to and there is also no argument over the rules of the political contest (conflict).

Let us use this salience-competition-conflict continuum now and see what it means in real-world political situations (see Figure 6–5). First, let us keep in mind that in the real world of politics, most political situations fall somewhere near the center of our saliency-competition-conflict continuum. There are very few situations of only saliency or only conflict. Second, within almost all political situations, there exists some degree of saliency, some degree of competition, and also some degree of conflict. Within all political constituencies, even perhaps during difficult situations like a civil war, there is some mixture of agreement on goals and agreement on method of argument. Unfortunately, however, disagreements that go beyond the rules of competition do continue to exist.

How then can we best understand how this continuum works? How can we place this continuum into the model of political understanding that we have already begun to build?

To examine how saliency, competition, and conflict work, let us identify some real political examples of each. In a general sense, all organized political systems have a degree of saliency within them when something like the economic prosperity of that system is at issue. We know that the distribution of the wealth of a system or the value kinds of questions that we have talked about are examples of real political competition. But in all political systems, there is a given amount of wealth available, and virtually everyone

FIGURE 6–5.
The political behavior of salience, competition, and conflict.

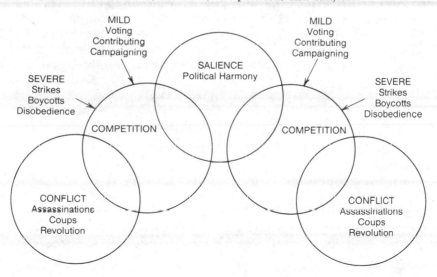

would agree that creating a growing pool of national wealth is far better than facing national poverty. National economic well-being, therefore, may be something that has almost total saliency. Perhaps even a better example of saliency comes about with regard to foreign policy. Again, although there may be substantial differences over the international posture of a nation, all citizens tend to be concerned with the essential physical security of their own peoples.

If we now understand how salience may manifest itself, let us move on to competition. We should begin with relatively moderate forms of competition, or with the kinds of rules that systems use to work out the differences among people's beliefs. Can you think of a number of moderately competitive political methods? By now this should be an easy question for you. These competitive political methods are the kinds of procedural methods that typify democratic processes. They are the procedures that are near the center of the result-process-result continuum of democratically determined public policy.

What are the central elements of any competitive democratic process? We have already mentioned such things as voting, running for political office, working in campaigns, and things of that kind. These are the milder forms of competition, and again, those activities occur within the center of the democratic continuum. Of course, there is also a good deal of result orientation in democracy. The different views of what the political system should be doing are why it is that people wish to be politically active. But the commitment to process is normal only with moderate kinds of competitive political activity.

But move a little farther along the salience-competition-conflict continuum and you will find that what happens is different from process-oriented competition. When competition becomes more strident, the result orientation overwhelms whatever respect there might have been for the rules of process. What kinds of political activities usually fall under such strident competitive activities? Think, if you will, of groups in society that are more highly dissatisfied with their political situation and you may recall that political strikes or economic boycotts, marches, demonstrations, and the like typified what these groups often did to redress their grievances.

Are these kinds of activities within the range of democratic process? Yes, such activities as strikes and boycotts still fall within the limits of legitimate political competition. If they are entered into peacefully, they are permitted and even encouraged in truly democratic political systems. Nonetheless, they do represent a level of strain within a political society as well as a lack of full trust, as Parsons would understand it. If they occur frequently, however, and if some level of reconciliation between protestors and the political rulers does not take place, it is possible that such strained political competition may spill over into conflict. Again, where should we place such strident competition on the continuum of saliency-competition and conflict? It is clearly closer to conflict than it is to salience and, on the democratic result-process-result continuum, strident result orientations of this kind clearly strain democratic processes.

Before we explore various examples of political conflict, we should understand that the movement from competition to conflict almost always occurs when the belief in the rightness of one's position or cause outweighs a belief in the established competitive process that achieves that believer's goals. Think again about both democratic process and the impact on process of strident result orientations, and satisfy yourself that a belief in political goals, without a belief in process, nearly always brings about political violence and upheaval. At the end of the salience-competition-conflict continuum, political conflict is something that implies the assassinations, coup d'états, or revolutions that we have spoken of elsewhere. All too frequently, the resort to this kind of allegedly "principled" activity leads to similar kinds of political activity. Can you think of an area where these kinds of activities occur frequently? Unfortunately, Latin America again seems to provide many examples of conflict. In Central and South America, fair elections or even moderate political protest are often the exception. Assassinations, military coups, and revolutions and counterrevolution too often make up the accepted pattern of politics.

Recall what we have said of the fabric of the Latin American political society. Often the wide differences of wealth between economic classes have meant that there is little trust in the political system among those who perceive that their interests are ignored by the government. Also, as we have mentioned, the differences between these economic classes are such that all fissures of a political difficulty lineup on the schism of economic or class difference. We now know that political conflict occurs much more frequently when there are no cross-pressures. We also know that the continuum of saliency, competition, and conflict is really a part of the larger model that places the pressures of political result orientation upon democratic processes. The differences over valuation preferences, or over any public policy, are reflected in that model of democracy. They are also reflected in the proportions of salience, competition, and conflict with which all political systems live.

As we approach our specific discussion of political structures, recall (1) that all political systems live with some degree of salience, sometimes called political unity or harmony, and that all systems experience some conflict, and (2) that certain attributes of a political society affect how it can deal with the most difficult question that it faces without a great deal of conflict. You should realize now that the questions of cross-pressures or trust in a system are both related to the tension that comes from an individual political issue or political system and how well it is tolerated within that system. There are many causes of political tension, of course, and there are many devices for keeping tension under control. Generally speaking, however, the absence of traditional respect for both just law and democratic process is highly responsible for political conflict.

LEGITIMACY, AUTHORITY, AND POWER ——————

Eventually, we will be asking some important questions concerning the kinds of political structures that best accommodate democratic process and best avoid political conflict. Yet, as we approach a discussion of political institutions, you should understand one additional set of concepts that will help you to learn how political institutions work. There is a specific set of notions that relates to how the citizens of a polity relate to its institutions. There are three more terms to familiarize yourself with that describe that relationship; think of these concepts as deeply tied to one another and to the workings of political institutions. The terms are (1) *legitimacy*, (2) *authority*, and (3) *power* (see Figure 6–6). Let us first be clear about what we mean by each term.

What do we mean by the word "legitimacy"? If we think of the term outside of the context of politics, we might agree that something is legitimate if we accept its existence and the role it plays within whatever it does. A family structure and the position of a mother and a father, for example, are legitimate when children perceive that their parents have their best interest at heart and that they are using their positions as parents in a spirit of helpfulness and guidance. A family that is mutually supportive and that promotes the well-being of all its members will have a kind of legitimacy in the minds of each member. In politics, we say that a

FIGURE 6–6.
Legitimacy, authority, and power in stable and unstable political systems.

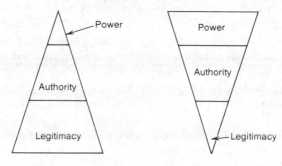

STABLE POLITICAL SYSTEMS   UNSTABLE POLITICAL SYSTEMS

government is legitimate if the citizenry feels that the govern-mental structure is appropriate for that political entity and was developed and offered to the citizenry with either their active or tacit approval. Legitimacy, in other words, is more than simply feeling comfortable about the political decisions that political systems generate. It represents an active sense on the part of the citizenry that the government and those who run it are acceptable.

Also, legitimacy makes other things possible that are very necessary to any political system. Primarily, legitimacy makes *authority* far more respected because the usage of authority is understood and accepted by large numbers of the citizenry. What do we mean by authority? Authority is the idea that certain individuals or, individuals who hold certain positions, are understood to be empowered to make decisions regarding other persons or positions. They do this with an expectation that these decisions will be carried forward. Political authority, in short, simply means the right to make decisions that affect public policy, and what you should think about now is the relationship between authority and legitimacy. When there is legitimacy within any structure, from a social club to a government, the authority of these offices can be exercised with a feeling that it will be respected.

Again, a family may be a good example of authority, for the ease with which parents of children exercise authority is very much a part of the perception of legitimacy that children have of their own parents' disciplinary motives. If a child believes that the reasons behind that parent's setting of bedtimes, regulating of dating, or limiting the intake of sweetened foods, for example, are truly linked to a feeling about the child's well-being, then those decisions may go unquestioned. Conversely, if the legitimacy of a parent's motives are in question, as when the child suspects the family discipline simply makes the parents' task of parenting easier, the authority of that parent will no doubt be questioned.

Finally, the third concept is related to legitimacy and authority: power. Although power is a very important political concept, power is not necessarily something arbitrary or brutal within human or political relationships. Power can be arbitrary or brutal, and throughout history, it often has been. But power can also be nothing more than the utilizing of one's resources on a matter of personal or group interest against the resources of an opponent. Power is used to compete over what public policy should be, or in many political writings, power is described as getting someone to do something that they otherwise would not do. Although I do not find such a definition wrong, it seems to lump together a number of things that are really very different.

Consider a particular piece of legislation, say, a bill to raise taxes. Clearly, the side that wins the battle within the government exercises power. What is significant for politics is the way in which the battle was fought. What were the tactics and the weapons used? What kinds of resources did the two sides gather to aid their positions? Very simply, if the weapons and tactics, along with the marshalling of resources, were used in nonconflictual ways, that is, in ways that use the established rules of democratic process, then that exercise of power would be something that no one should be unhappy about.

CONCLUSION

Democratic process can accommodate the struggle between different viewpoints and different groups. It can also absorb the use of power in various groupings' notions of what they want from government and make their request heard within the democratic process. Finally, of course, if the tactics and resources of the two sides that engage in their power struggle both utilize the roles of modern political competition, then the use of power between these groups does not overflow into conflict. Remember that the uses of power just described mean that the legitimacy of the governmental institutions and the regularized authority of those decisions are not harmed by that power. Procedurally correct or "normal" usages of power serve to fortify government and to bring respect to governmental institutions at the same time they help to make difficult public decisions.

You already know that there have been too many instances in both modern and ancient times when the marshalling of resources to overwhelm the opposition embraced unorthodox and often violent methods of political persuasion. Routine democratic devices of exercising power such as organizing large numbers of people to lobby for a position, spending money for political advertising, and the like may push the equilibrium of public policy substantially to one side or the other. However, anticumulative forces, using their own political power, will at least have the opportunity to return the balance to what they consider to be a moderate range of policy. It is these interests that are either too intent upon getting what they want from government or that are convinced that government will not provide them with what they deserve, who will resort to assassinations, revolutions, coups, and other improper expressions of power.

Finally, we must remember that improper expressions of power do not all come from unhappy groups or individuals. Governments that are insecure about their ability to stay in office through democratic means are prone to engage in the kinds of political repression that include imprisonment, torture, and assassinations of members of the political opposition. As you can see, the tactics of such conflictual and heavily result-oriented politics, again, negates democratic process. It turns competition into conflict and assures that the legitimacy of political institutions and the authority of those institutions' decisions will always be in question. When power is used out of the context of institutional legitimacy and authority it violates the norms of democratic process. Power used within the context of institutional legitimacy and authority, however, reaffirms the democratic process.

Reference Notes

1. Gerard L. DeGré, "Freedom and Social Structure," *American Sociological Review*, Vol. 11 (October 1964), pp. 529–536.
2. Seymour Martin Lipset, *Political Man* (Garden City, N.Y.: Doubleday, 1960), pp. 220–232.
3. Talcott Parsons, "The Monopoly of Force and the 'Power Bank'," in Talcott Parsons, "Some Reflections on the Place of Force in Social Processes." In Harry Eckstein, ed., *Internal War* (New York: The Free Press, 1964), pp. 57–65.

Glossary

TERMS

cohesion
family
village
polis
atomistic
multipartite
pluralistic
elitist
totalitarian
Leviathan
stratification
Democracy in America
voluntary association
stability
coalitions
cross-pressures

Plato
Aristotle
philosopher kings
salience
competition
conflict
legitimacy
authority
power

NAMES

Gerard DeGré
Thomas Hobbes
Alexis de Tocqueville
Seymour Martin Lipset
Talcott Parsons

CHAPTER 7
THE MODERN POLITICAL STRUCTURE

We are at another plateau of understanding where we should review what we have learned thus far and look ahead to building another segment of the political model. We have examined three conceptual settings in relation to political structure. We understand, it is hoped, that these conceptual sets are deeply tied to one another. You should now be able to understand the relationship of (1) the democratic result-process-result continuum, (2) the salience, competition, conflict continuum, and (3) the elements of legitimacy, authority, and power. We have also begun to explore what it is that helps to maintain the location of political systems within the middle of the ranges that all three of these conceptual networks offer. How do you maintain the essence of democratic process within a political system? How do you build upon the common goals of a people and encourage competition not to overflow into conflict? How do you maintain the fundamental legitimacy of political institutions in the public's mind and maintain respect for the just uses of authority and the moderate uses of political power?

Various answers to these questions exist, but to respond to them systematically, let us try to identify certain qualities that are helpful to a stable political structure. Let us begin with a minor point because some writers have argued that the mere existence of abundant national wealth is a guarantee of political stability. The ability to provide certain amenities to a population is certainly helpful for any political system. The reality of human nature, however, is such that a citizenry usually takes the level of economic prosperity they are accustomed to for granted. It is their unrealized expectation to more personal abundance that often causes instability. Surely, a sudden drop in a political society's wealth may well cause political instability, but a relatively constant state of wealth or poverty does not always have an inordinate impact on political well-being.

CONTINUUM AND EQUILIBRIUM ━━━━━━

Let us first recognize a very simple fact within our discussion of structure: all political systems need not be alike. A good deal of day-to-day political argument invariably claims that one form of government is superior to others. The reality is that different political structures serve different political communities. As we look for what may aid a particular political process as well as aid the legitimacy of any political system, let us accentuate those aspects of the prepolitical considerations within which each political structure seems best to survive.

Recall that we began our discussion of structure with the DeGré model of social cohesion. The model argued that different degrees of social cohesiveness were likely to bring about different degrees of cohesiveness within a political structure. The more individualized kinds of social structure, where the elements of cohesion were less evident, were linked to corresponding political structures that were also fragmented in structure. Such fragmented social systems also tended to create governments that were not far reaching in the governmental policies that they created. On the other side of the continuum, social systems that were somewhat more integrated and less fragmented tended to create more far-reaching governmental policies. The natural unity of identification within a citizenry on the more cohesive side of the continuum tended to prefer governmental forms that were both more compact in their structure and more comprehensive about what the government would do for its citizens.

What you should focus on now is a very important category of factors. It exists within all political communities, and in ways that we will discuss, it links the degree of social cohesiveness and the fundamental social norms of a system to the actual political structure. Although there are many linkages that tie social and political structures together, four of them are particularly significant: (1) *political myth*, (2) *political culture*, (3) *political symbol*, and (4) *political socialization*.

MYTH, CULTURE, SYMBOL, AND SOCIALIZATION ━━━━━━

Let us begin with the notion of political myth, and let us examine two American political myths that serve as linkages between the level of American social cohesion and the American political structure. Think for a moment of what you were taught as a child concerning America's political leaders. What stories about such leaders do you remember from your earliest days in school? Surely, you remember the legend of George Washington and the cherry tree. It is a story that represents the personal qualities of honesty and responsibility, for the young George Washington's confession to his father over the fallen cherry tree promotes both individualism and personal trustworthiness. What is perhaps America's second most prominent myth, that of Abraham Lincoln walking many miles to return a nickel to someone he owed, upholds similar kinds of personal values. Both stories, again, emphasize personal responsibility and promote the American political notion of individualism. What we should understand is that such myths also tend to promote a kind of personalism in government, a preference that may lead to fragmented and noncohesive governmental institutions and a limited scope of public authority.

Political culture, as you would expect, fits well with notions of political myth. America's political culture is filled with political ideas that correspond to individual responsiblity. Culture usually depends a great deal upon history, and American history, as you know, is filled with the adventure of pushing out beyond the Eastern shore and confronting a vast frontier. In a sense, our culture was the very adventure of it all, whether the adventure took place in the mud huts of Kansas or on the Oregon Trail. The initiative and hard work that went along with coping with hardship only ratified the American ideals of fragmented governmental structure and restricted government.

The symbols of a country are also important. A flag in the American case represents the existence of the separate American states, and symbols such as monuments and memorials largely commemorate individuals who served the country with personal bravery and fortitude. In America, such symbology, again, clearly represents a rejection of collective structures and a preference for personal leadership over institutional decision making.

Finally, the political socialization of America, like the socialization of all countries, is the vehicle that transmits the myth, culture, and the importance of symbols to the new generation. The idea of socialization is not new, Plato having talked of its importance in *The Republic* nearly 2,500 years ago. All political systems attempt to instill the values of their polity into each succeeding generation, thus hoping to retain the continuity of political allegiances and identifications held by the older generation. A great deal has been written about socialization in the last years, but in brief, the principal socializing institutions have been found to be the *family*, the *school*, the *church*, and the *peer group*. The family, interestingly, still retains its position as the most important socializer of political attitude. Perhaps even more interesting, it is the mother who retains her position as the greatest single force in the formation of political attitudes and orientations.

Once more, what we are looking for is how different kinds of political structures are a function of both underlying prepolitical conditions and the prepolitical linkages that tie these citizens to political structure. Such prepolitical conditions as myth, culture, symbol, and socialization are significant causes of why political systems prefer their kind of governmental structure over others. American prepolitical conditions are quite individualistic, and the linkages of myth, culture, and so forth that we have briefly reviewed reflect that individualistic vein. Other countries, particularly those within Europe, for example, have traditionally respected both more group-oriented prepolitical orientations and a more collectivist set of political linkages.

European history, at least in the last centuries, has permitted little sense of living far from civilization. It has, rather, promoted a sense of the proximity and the interdependence of European peoples. The European culture reflects that history, and its more collective sense of national destiny is reflected in something like the French revolutionary slogan of *liberté, égalité, fraternité*. The myths are based upon the bringing of civilization and the rule of law to others, as the Caesars through Napoleon purported to be doing, rather than on a running away from civilization. European symbols such as the French tricolor stress the unity and the struggles of a whole people rather than the separateness of internal political units. The legend of the fifteenth-century French heroine Joan of Arc, who lead the French armies that had flagged in the Hundred Year attempt to expel the British from their land, is certainly an example of such unity.

The effects of such a different tradition as that of the Europeans is, again, that prepolitical social cohesion and the four dominant political linkages all lead toward greater European collectivism as well as a tendency to support an elitist rather than a pluralist form of government. In an elitist government, remember, the various public institutions are somewhat more closely linked than they are in a pluralist form. There is also a tendency for governmental policy, again, to be more comprehensive in its scope than a government like that of the United States would permit.

FEDERALISM AND UNITARY STATES ━━━━━

If we understand the relationships of both prepolitical social considerations and principal political linkages as they relate to the degree of cohesiveness of a government's structures, we can begin to discuss specific structural arrangements. Each political system has two essential features as the principal elements of its structure. The first is the degree of overlap or cooperation among the principal institutions at the national level of government. The second is the sharing of authority between national and subnational governments. We will discuss the specifics of overlapping when we discuss political parties, legislatures, executives, and the other institutions of national government. For now, however, we need to look at the second major structural characteristic of government, one which describes to what degree the national government and lesser subnational governments share authority within the overall political structure.

Do you know what one of the correct, although rather legalistic, descriptions of the U.S. form of government is? It is *federalism*, a term that means, simply, that citizens of one level of government (in our example, the national government) are also citizens of another level of government (in this case, the subnational or state government). In the United States, these subnational governments, the states, share their powers with the federal government everywhere except within the District of Columbia.

Not all national governments, of course, are federalist. Some governments are *unitary*, that is, all citizens are citizens of only the national sovereign. Again, consider the federalism concept because it is the key to an understanding of a basic structural component of all governments.

Let us introduce two terms that you may already be familiar with: *centrifugal* and *centripetal*. Centrifugal forces, in a physical sense, are forces that pull out from the center; centripetal forces are forces that pull back in toward the center. Let us say that you have a rock on a string and you are swinging that rock around your head. Centrifugal forces are pulling it away from your finger because of the momentum of the rock. Centripetal forces, which are contained in the string (as long as it does not break) pull it back toward the center. The length of the string, in this example, keeps the rock at a particular, constant distance from your finger. Curiously, there are similar distances in politics that dictate the balance between centrifugal or centripetal forces within a federalist or unitary structure of government (see Figure 7–1).

FIGURE 7–1.
Centrifugal and centripetal forces in political structures.

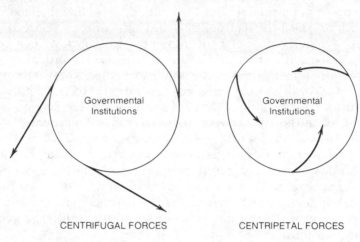

CENTRIFUGAL FORCES   CENTRIPETAL FORCES

Let us examine what causes these structural distances. As we have mentioned, Aristotle recognized that there were different levels of political identity and allegiance, even within the small polity of ancient Greece. Aristotle's three levels of political identity—the family, the village, and the *polis*—acknowledged that human nature made all of us identify more strongly with the level of structure that is closest to us. As we have said, our immediate families are more important to us than the village as a whole, and the village, where you may know all or most of the people, will have a stronger identity for you than will the entire collection of villages of the *polis*.

History has come a long way from villages and the collections of villages that were often only a few miles apart in ancient Greece. We are now at a stage of history where the equilibrium of centrifugal and centripetal forces has given us the nation-state, a far larger and more inclusive political organization than ever existed, even through the feudal period. There are even those who now argue that we have started moving out of the nation-state phase into a period of regional or even worldwide political integration. The historian Barbara Tuchman believes that the nation-state system has substantially broken down and contends that much of the current disorder in the world stems from a progressive movement away from nationalism.[1] Perhaps the period of nationalism, that broad sense of a togetherness of a people that often expresses itself in a common culture, history, language, or even a struggle for recognition itself, is indeed coming to a close.

Nonetheless, what we should concentrate on here is where the distances dictated by centrifugal and centripetal forces fall within various national political structures. What I am suggesting is that, along with understanding the degree of overlap of the various institutions at the national level, we can also understand to what degree a system is a federated system or to what degree there is a concentration of power within a national government. Again, what we are examining is the degree to which the nation-state shares its powers with lesser governments inside its borders. Eventually, we should be able to understand how that degree of concentration or fragmentation within a federated system relates to the preference for pluralistic or elitist forms of government.

Federalism: Prenational

There are three categories of the national political condition that depict the extent to which the centrifugal and centripetal forces within a political structure balance themselves out: (1) *prenational*, (2) *national*, and (3) *supernational*. What they describe, essentially, is where the center of power is within major governments today.

Prenational systems are systems that for one reason or another still maintain a degree of governmental decision making at a level that is either below or, in one example, outside of the national decision level. There are four subcategories of prenational political structures: *colonial prenationalism*, *artificial prenationalism*, *disintegrative prenationalism*, and *evolutionary prenationalism*.

Let us consider colonial prenationalism first, even though it has become a relatively minor category in recent years. Colonial prenationalism is the condition in which a geographical area and a people are still under the control of another state. The best example of this category today is the case of Namibia, or South West Africa as it was called when it was a League of Nations Mandate of South Africa. South Africa has still not relinquished its control over Namibia, and it maintains its position there today largely by military force. There are a few other colonial prenational possessions in the world as well, but virtually all of them today are small, including several islands. As history continues to evolve, most of these seem to be achieving either independence from or accommodation with the colonial powers, although a dispute such as that over the Falkland (or Malvinas) Islands in the South Atlantic shows that emotions can still run high over the colonial issue. Unfortunately, the structures of these prenational states often tends to be underdeveloped, and whatever local government authority there is is usually deeply fragmented.

The second classification of prenationalism is artificial prenationalism. There is still a fair amount of this form of prenationalism in the world today, and it occurs when many different loyalties exist within a national population. Different identifications with language, literature, political myth, culture, and so forth may exist, although perhaps somewhat incompatibly within a single political state. To put it another way, states can be made up of different nationalities, and the recently created states of Central Africa are perhaps the best example of such artificial statehood. These political units were created for the most part after World War II, and the colonial powers, particularly France and Great Britain, clearly drew the new national boundaries to suit their own purposes rather than to delineate the true culture identifications of the Africans. The result of such artificial boundary drawing is that many African states today are made up of groupings that do not have common cultures, myths, languages, or history. Similarly, some of the larger tribes that did share common attributes have been divided between two or more formal nation-states. As you can imagine, the deep divisions that such maladjustments have caused within these nations has harmed both economic development and national political reconciliation. Here, too, the structures of such states often tend to be highly fragmented, with the new national governments still struggling for the legitimacy that will lend respect to their structure's authority.

A third subcategory of prenational structure is called disintegrative nationalism. It is related to, but not quite the same thing as, artificial nationalism. Disintegrative nationalism is a decaying process, as where an already established political state now seems to be coming apart. Portions of that nation that may have appeared to have been well integrated now seem to be preferring their more separate, local identification to the larger national identity. A contributing cause of disintegrative nationalism may be that the citizens of a minority region within the larger state feel that they have not received fair recognition within the larger state for a language, a literature, a history, or even for the culture, myths, or symbology that they hold dear.

Some precipitating act such as drafting a new national constitution or a prescription for the use of a single language in the elementary schools may ignite this dormant, subnational set of identities and set it against the larger national identification. A structural resolution of these tensions sometimes recognizes these different identifications before full disintegration takes place and may, of course, save a prenational system from complete disintegration. Canada may have satisfied its French-speaking Quebec minority sufficiently to prevent Quebec from leaving the Canadian federal republic, although it is clearly possible that centrifugal pressures could rekindle and eventually dissolve the Canadian federation. The Basques in Spain, the Bretons in France, and the Armenians in Turkey are further examples of how such disintegrative nationalism continues to appear, even into the late twentieth century. Here, again, with disintegrative prenationalism, centrifugal forces keep the national government more fragmented than it otherwise would be.

The final subclassification of prenationalism is evolutionary prenationalism, which is represented by a more or less steady but still incomplete movement of political authority toward a national government. The usual reason for the incompleteness of full national authority is the continuation of major, regional, ethnic, or other subidentifications within the national polity. Under these conditions, the political structure thus continues to reflect the existence of the subnational identifications.

The United States is certainly an example of evolutionary prenationalism, for its 50 separate states still jealously insist upon the sovereignty that they formally retained after their original grant of power to the federal government in the Constitution. The institutions of the American government, particularly with regard to the relationship of the national and state government, still reflect that historic condition. Much the same kind of prenational federalism exists in a nation such as the Federal Republic of Germany, although it has been one nation (now divided from the German Democratic Republic) for a shorter time than has the United States and has still achieved a more integrated level of national structural cohesion during this shorter period. Curiously, a certain amount of federalism still exists within the Soviet Union, although the overriding influence of the national Communist party makes such federalism relatively unimportant in most national policy areas.

The Unitary State

With this discussion of four prenational categories within the centrifugal-centripetal equilibrium, we can now discuss the national category. Within this category, you should know that a number of prominent nation-states now exist as what are called unitary states.

France, Sweden, Japan, and other countries are states that do not have subnational political entities or sovereignties. All but purely local political authority resides within the national government alone. Please remember that our central theme reflects upon pluralism versus elitism from the perspective of centrifugal and centripetal structures. As we discuss both the prenational subcategories and the fully national category of political structure, you may notice the reference to a number of historical circumstances. All these circumstances, without question, have an impact upon the degree of national integration that exists in various polities. Remember that the degree of overlap or cohesion within the national unitary institutions of a nation-state is a product of many factors, some of which depend upon such circumstances as the (1) regional, (2) ethnic, or (3) religious makeup of a nation or any of its parts. These separate identities are important to many people, even in unitary systems, although over the long pull of history, there seems to have been a slow and certainly uneven coming together of both larger numbers of people and larger geographical areas into single political units.

Within shorter periods of history, this long-term trend toward integration may often have been halted or even reversed. The subcategories of people within a nation-state or the regional, ethnic, or religious kinds of identifications account for at least a good deal of whether or not there is a centralized or decentralized political structure within the national government. The regionalism within France, for example, is at least part of the reason that the French unitary government is more fragmented than, say, the postwar unitary government of Japan has turned out to be.

One final part of the analysis of these unitary governments requires an analysis of more subjective kinds of orientations toward political cohesion. Here, again, the questions of social cohesion, along with the political culture, political myth, political symbolism, and political socialization that transmit these values all reflect and contribute to the degree of political cohesion that there will be in a polity. We started the discussion of the structure of political institutions with a review of DeGré's model of social cohesion. We used his five categories of social cohesion to demonstrate the full range of extreme independence through extreme cohesion. We then suggested that these levels of social cohesion were reflected in the degree of political cohesion that a political structure and its institutions possessed.

Having discussed two of the three categories of centrifugal and centripetal equilibrium within the structural question of federalism, you should now understand that a number of different components have an impact upon what a national political structure will look like. Again, objective or classificatory variables such as region, race, religion, and so on play a substantial role in that degree of cohesion as do subjective variables such as myth, culture, symbol, and socialization. Importantly, these variables impact on both the degree of cohesion of a government at the national level, which we will discuss shortly, and the degree of federalism in a political system. We focus now on the federalism question that we have been dealing with, for we are now seeing the first beginning within the history of humankind of truly supranational political structures. We are, in short, beginning to witness the beginnings of political allegiance beyond the nation-state.

Supranationalism

Consider the European Economic Community, or the Common Market, the economic union of ten of the principal nations of Western Europe. Starting with the European Steel and Coal Community shortly after World War II and continuing with the addition of both new countries and new economic areas of trade and labor cooperation, the European Economic Community has now become an established political entity as well. In 1979, the EEC held direct, popular elections to its own parliament, a parliament that took the place of a previous structure whose members were selected only by the governments of the individual nation-states. The integration of governments within Europe is far from complete, and certainly a considerable time will pass before significant powers leave the nation-states and pass on to a regional, European government. Yet it is worth noting that the nations we have mentioned, which were either prenational in the sense of having some powers remaining at the subnational level (West Germany) or purely national in the sense of having a unitary form of government (France), have found that these national structures do not interfere with their achieving supranational identification and allegiance.

Certainly such factors as geographical proximity and a high degree of natural economic integration have played significant roles in the newly emergent supranationalism. But other considerations, for example, the desire for cohesiveness within the mildly collective political culture of the Western Europeans as compared with the United States, may have also had something to do with the building of the political structure of the European Community.

NATIONAL INSTITUTIONS ─────────────

Let us pause for a moment. Although the categories are not purely distinct, with race and even religion, for example, containing subjective elements, we have described how objective factors like race, religion, and region as well as subjective factors like culture, myth, and social cohesiveness have had an impact upon the degree of federalism or the degree of sharing of national powers that national governments have permitted.

When we discussed national governments, we also suggested that both objective and subjective factors may have had an impact upon national political institutions. We will soon begin to look at a number of specific institutions of government as well as at how each of these institutions works within different political structures. If we can then take the valuation issue that we spoke of in the early development of our model, and if we can combine that issue with (1) the question of democracy as process or result, (2) the salience competition or conflict continuum, and (3) our understanding of the legitimacy, authority, and power of various political institutions, our discussion of specific institutions should be both thorough and readily understandable. Let us now look at those institutions.

The Interest Group

We have prepared ourselves to talk about specific institutions of national government as well as how these institutions relate to one another. It is tempting to launch directly into political parties, legislatures, bureaucracies, and the like, but it is better for our understanding to begin with a discussion of the interrelationships of various public institutions with the public or citizenry as a whole. In doing so, we will continue to stress the contrast between the pluralistic and the elitist model, and we will periodically include a reference to totalitarian systems as well.

The brief introduction to the pluralistic model that accompanied our description of the five DeGré stages on the continuum of cohesiveness referred us directly to the role of interest groups in the pluralist model. It would not be wholly accurate to say that individuals in a modern, postindustrial political society have no political influence whatsoever. There are always a few individuals who do have a particular access to their government. The reality of modern government, however, is that the primary method of exercising influence within a modern governmental structure is representative of groups of citizens who have interests similar to your own. The history of the United States and its individualistic culture has always made Americans suspicious of both prominent governmental institutions as well as of large social or economic collections of power.

De Tocqueville, as we have mentioned, reported on the very loosely formed American social patterns that strove to support the political structure of the new and expanding nation. But all political systems need some way in which to organize their affairs. They also need the intermediate kinds of identification and loyalty that make the whole society something more than a formal government and a formless mass of citizens. Again, the Europeans have a history and a rich culture that has always assisted with both identification and loyalty. Europeans also have had a sense of place or station, which, though sometimes oppressive to those who wished to better that station, still contributed to an internal stability or cohesiveness for that polity.

The problem for the new America was difficult, but de Tocqueville found that the inventive Americans solved it by creating and then expressing themselves through various popular groups. Remember that he called such groups "voluntary associations," and he found that Americans were comfortable with a vast array of both social groupings and occupationally created groupings.

If you have followed the news in the papers or on television, you certainly have heard of these associations. Here is an exercise that will cement the importance of such groups in your mind. If you ever visit your state capital or travel to Washington, D.C. to visit the federal government, do not begin your tour by visiting the legislature or other governmental buildings. Instead, go to the private office buildings immediately adjacent to the government and look at the building directories in the main lobbies. Examine the directory carefully and see for yourself how many of the offices inside the building are trade associations or what we call "lobbies" for the practice of button-holing legislators in legislative hallways. The situation in terms of voluntary associations in America today is still pretty much the way de Tocqueville described it, although there are many more such groupings than what de Tocqueville ever knew. Each of these interests also directs its lobbying input into a larger and more comprehensive governmental structure. Whereas in most state capitals you can see the names of the interest groups on the directories of perhaps one or a few office buildings, in Washington, D.C., you would need to visit many buildings to grasp the full impact of pluralism at the level of the American national government.

If we now understand why interest groups are so plentiful in the United States, we can move to the question of how these interest groups make their policy preferences known within a pluralistic government (See Figure 7–2). Here is where pluralism and elitism greatly diverge in their governmental styles, for although the European nations have never had the same number of voluntary associations that America has had, they have developed a fair number of associations that do represent various interests. The divergence between European elitism and American pluralism is that within pluralism, the intermediate institutions, that is, those institutions that stand between the interests and the government, are substantially weaker. Within pluralism, structures that would significantly

FIGURE 7–2.
The policy process in pluralist and elitist systems.

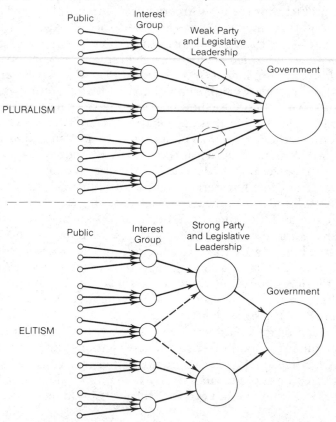

moderate and refine the policy preferences of the associations are not so strong, whereas in Europe and within elitist structures, the interest groups are generally required to have their policy preferences considered as part of a general public policy. In Europe, in short, the requests of interests, at least to a larger degree than in the United States, must be considered along with a number of other, competing public policy preferences and claims.

Of course, all interest groups want what they think they should receive from government, be it a tax loophole or a bill on the deregulation or the protective regulation of an industry. What is different in the pluralist system, again, is that there is little that prevents these interests from involving themselves directly in the decision-making process of government. We will have a chance to talk about political parties at greater length soon, for parties are one of the institutions that elitist systems use to transmit the interest group needs to the policymaking institutions. Concentrate now, however, on the specific linkages of a pluralistic society that tie it to a pluralistic form of government.

Access Points and the Captive Agency

To begin, let us remind ourselves that everyday American pluralist politics is very decentralized. We have already seen that the United States has both a very fragmented government at the national level and a great deal of federalism or shared power between national and state political structures. What you should consider here is that, with a fragmented government like that of the United States, there are many *access points* available to those who wish to influence governmental policy. What is an access point? It is a term that represents the place at which the specific interest group touches the portion of the government that is directly responsible for policy in its area (see Figure 7–3). You may wish to ask another question here. Is not the entire government responsible for all policy? In a sense, the answer is yes, for in times of true national peril, all governments, even that of the United States, can exercise general policy choices that make decisions for the entire system. Nonetheless, during more or less routine periods of history, pluralistic government, in contrast to an elitist structure, permits a greater separation of the institutions themselves, along wtih an absence of a meaningful intermediate buffer betwen the interest group and the government. What this means is that different policies are made at very different points within the government.

What does it mean to have different policies made at different

FIGURE 7–3.
Access points in pluralist and elitist systems.

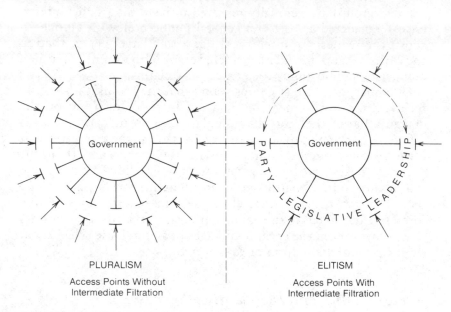

PLURALISM

Access Points Without
Intermediate Filtration

ELITISM

Access Points With
Intermediate Filtration

points within a government? Does such an arrangement lead to inconsistency in policy within pluralistic governments when decisions made at one place do not "square" with decisions that are made someplace else? The answer to that question is yes and the following is an example that should help you to remember how such inconsistencies come about.

The American national government, working with the American Cancer Society (an interest group) as well as with some of its own agencies such as the National Institutes of Health, has spent a great deal of money on both cancer research and treatment. As a general statement, it would be fair to say that the American national government, as a function of its public policy, wishes to fight cancer. Specifically, however, it may be more accurate to say that part of the American government has had the fight against cancer as its policy. On the other hand, consider the American Tobacco Institute, an interest group that represents the cigarette industry before the government or, more specifically, before a body like the Department of Agriculture within the government. What is it that the American Tobacco Institute and the Department of Agriculture do when they combine at an access point in order to influence the government? As you would think, they promote the growth, processing, and sale of tobacco, and they do so under government subsidies just as the ACS/NIH group spends public monies on its research and treatment programs on cancer.

We should understand that the contradiction of these two configurations is not at all unusual for a pluralistic government like that of the United States. Pluralism likes to satisfy as many interest group claimants as possible, even those who logically seem to contest with each other. What is interesting about pluralism is that it usually accomplishes this by providing access to many different interests. Again, it can do so because pluralism provides an extraordinary number of access points for those who approach the government.

We will speak about specific governmental institutions soon, but let us place our understanding of this point into the full pluralistic model. If we can imagine a circle of government and a countless number of spokes running out from that circle, that is essentially how pluralism works. Those spokes reach out from government to touch each of the interest groups that wishes to have an impact upon government. The points at which these interest groups and the government touch are what we are calling access points.

Now familiarize yourself with another term, one that describes the political essence of the access point between the interest and the government within much of the pluralist structure. The term is *captive agency*, and it refers to the "capturing" of the governmental unit by the very interest group that that agency of the government supposedly oversees and regulates. If there were a single policy of government, that is, a central, general policy that marked a direction for public positive law, the representative of the government that intersects with the representative of the interest should represent that policy with that interest (see Figure 7–4). For example, the National Institutes of Health should represent governmental policy when dealing with the American Cancer Society. The Department of Agriculture should represent

FIGURE 7–4.
Normal access point and captive agency access point.

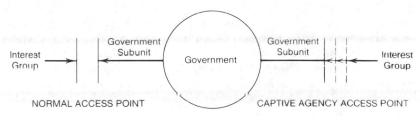

NORMAL ACCESS POINT   CAPTIVE AGENCY ACCESS POINT

governmental policy when it deals with the American Tobacco Institute. But we have already noted that pluralism, with its restricted degree of social cohesion and its highly fragmented governmental structure, has a great number of access points. What happens, apart from the absence of a unified public policy coming from the core of government, is that the people who work on the "government side" of the access points tend to develop a strong identity with the very interest group with which they interact. They tend, in short, almost to favor the interest that they face and, correspondingly, they tend to have a weakened identity with any general governmental policy that may exist.

Let us phrase it another way. Within a pluralistic form of government, the governmental unit that deals with any private interest group, supposedly for the enactment of general governmental policy, tends to develop an identification with that very interest group that may be stronger than the general interest of the government. We use the term captive agency to describe this circumstance, and what you should understand is that there are two rather separate reasons for why the governmental unit or agency becomes captured by the private interest. The first, as we have said, is that the pluralistic government is so decentralized that in the long run the well-being of the unit that deals with a private interest depends for its own budget, indeed perhaps for its own very existence, upon the well-being of the interest that it serves. The health of the served interest may also depend so much upon those who serve it that governmental units or agencies actually become very worried about their own particular "clients" or interest groups' well-being.

But there is also a second reason for the existence of captive agencies. Who do you think works in the agencies of the government? Who works for the public, but who also works with a level of expertise on the subject of that interest group that that agency oversees? In the modern world, so much of public business has become highly specialized and technical. Knowledge of particular subject matters such as tax, energy, exports, and the like have become so complex that the government must often rely upon people who come from the affected interest to work for the agency that oversees governmental policy within that industry. In a way, it makes sense. Where are the best people who might serve on, say, the Interstate Commerce Commission? More than likely, they are people who have worked in the railroad business or the trucking business. Where would the best people to serve on the Federal Power Commission come from? The fact is that they often come from the energy industry itself. Although in recent years there has been some legislation to limit this private-to-public career shift of

occupational role, many of the most influential members of the
very agencies that deal with particular interests continue to be
people who identify with the interest that the government deals
with at an access point. Pluralism, as a rule, is subject to the
creation of the captive agency.

The Iron Triangle

We are now at another plateau of understanding. We have described
the fundamental structure and operation of a pluralist form of government. Now we add one more concept to those that we have
talked about. Taking what we have come to understand about the
decentralization of a pluralist government, we can apply it within
a concept known throughout the study of the American government as the *iron triangle*. What is the iron triangle? It is a notion
created by those who have studied pluralist governments like that
of the United States who believe that the key decision making
within the government is located within the interactions of three
particular institutions.

What are the three institutions? The first is the interest group
itself, that being the institution, again, that is a modern legacy of
the voluntary association that de Tocqueville spoke of in America's
early days. The other two are what many consider to be the two
key access points of the American government. They are the two
places where the interest group links up with key public institutions. Those who have spoken of the iron triangle argue that these
two points are located in (1) the bureaucratic or administrative
agency that has responsibility for an area of policy, and (2) the
segment of the legislature, usually a committee or a subcommittee
in the American Congress, that is responsible for the particular
legislation that would affect that interest group.

Let us reflect on this iron triangle for a moment. In most of what
you have previously learned concerning the American government,
you have no doubt been asked to memorize the three branches of
government as the legislature, the executive, and the judiciary.
Although such institutions are important, we should examine the
government from the inside and look at where decisions are actually made, rather than at some formal positioning of decision-
making units. This is a more accurate way of looking at government. By viewing different models of government, we can see that
the points of decision within pluralism, although still housed within
the three principal structures, are really the active elements of that
structure. Many observers argue that the iron triangle is the real

structure of a pluralist government, for that is where the interest group that encourages government to enact a public policy favorable to them interacts with the very elements of the government that not only serves them but continues to enhance their own bureaucratic and legislative role within the government.

FAIRNESS AND EFFICIENCY: DEFINITIONS

As we close this chapter, keep in mind why it is that the degree of decentralization existing within the operation of pluralism has such a great effect on the way that decisions are made within pluralist governments. Further, as we begin to examine both the formal institutions of power within pluralist and elitist systems, as well as increase our understanding of how elitist systems compare to pluralism, you will be introduced to two standards for the comparative judgment of pluralism and elitism. These are the standards of *fairness* and *efficiency*. Let us begin to understand what these terms mean.

Remember that we are still dealing with the question of the valuation of work or the height of the pyramid when we speak of the fairness of any system. We used the pyramids of distribution to test fairness, but of course a variety of other issues exist that people have argued over politically through the years. We described fairness as a happy compromise among the competing wants of a people. It can also be described as a gentle oscillation of the public policy of a nation near a moderate midpoint, a compromise on the question of distribution and a broad range of other political issues.

The second term, efficiency, is nothing more than the ability of a political system to get done what it needs to accomplish. All systems, of course, need to work well, and we will compare the pluralist, elitist, and, more briefly, the totalitarian systems to judge how well they work. Near the extremes of political ideology, where result orientation is strongest, efficiency may mean the rather ruthless carrying through of every public policy. Nearer the center of ideology's continuum, efficiency will include the ability of government to provide for the economic well-being of a people and to maintain a number of services within an open society that respects citizens' rights and liberties. All public policies will be debated, but moderate states agree that whatever the public sector does should be performed well, at a reasonable cost, and with due respect for the full range of human values.

Toward the close of this work, we will return to the DeGré spectrum and compare pluralism, elitism, and totalitarianism as they are relevant to what we are discussing about governmental systems. But fairness and efficiency will be two prominent standards for comparison, and as we keep these two standards in mind, we should also begin to look at the behavior of some traditional political institutions.

CONCLUSION

Following our discussions of the valuation question, ideology, and the relationship of a variety of prepolitical considerations to the degree of cohesion within a political structure, this chapter introduced you to some specific attributes of modern political structures. Our reviews of myth, culture, symbolism, and socialization should help you to place such important concerns within the context of the larger model that we continue to build. Further, our examinations of federalist and unitary states and, ultimately, of the European supranatural configuration have all spoken of the degree to which political institutions have transcended Aristotle's family, village, and *polis* in identification and loyalty. Our discussions of interest groups, access points, and the captive agency gave you the opportunity to utilize your understanding of cohesiveness within governmental structures. These discussions were meant also to prepare you for a comparative analysis of pluralism and elitism as we consider specific governmental institutions in the following chapter.

Reference Note

1. Barbara Tuchman, *A Distant Mirror: The Calamitous Fourteenth Century* (New York: Alfred A. Knopf, 1979).

Glossary

TERMS

political myth
political culture
political symbol
political socialization
The Republic
family
school
church
peer group
liberté, égalité, fraternité
federalism
unitary state
centrifugal forces
centripetal forces
prenational
national
supranational
colonial prenationalism

artificial prenationalism
disintegrative prenationalism
evolutionary prenationalism
European Economic
  Community
Common Market
lobbies
access point
captive agency
the iron triangle
fairness
efficiency

NAMES

George Washington
Abraham Lincoln
Joan of Arc
Barbara Tuchman

CHAPTER 8
THE PRINCIPAL
INSTITUTIONS

We shall begin our discussion of specific political institutions in a way that dovetails with the principal themes of our model. Before we begin to look at the first institution, the political party, think for a moment about what it is that public institutions do. There are two principal views of what public institutions do. Like so many things we have discussed, neither one is wholly correct and neither one is exclusively, that is, solely, represented in our model in a way that would keep the other from having its impact.

Nonetheless, there is an almost classical disagreement over whether governmental institutions are designed to (1) check various individuals and groups in the society from overwhelming other individuals or groups, or (2) facilitate the entire society in its development and realization of certain public goals. If you consider these two notions, you will see that to a great degree, the notions of checking and preventing one group's inordinate influence upon public policy stems largely from a fearful or even a competitive view of human nature. People who hold this view of human nature tend to feel that government must never permit humankind's essentially hostile disposition from seizing the public reins and trampling citizens' rights.

On the other hand, the notion of a more comprehensive governmental structure, that is, one that is allowed to effectuate public policy in a fairly comprehensive way, is based upon the idea that human nature is not so devilish and that natural cooperation among citizens can lead to effective public policy without trampling citizens' rights. Two good examples of this differentiation come with the American and European styles of government, for in the American government, as described in *The Federalist Papers*, there is a great fear of government and the tyranny that government may bring. James Madison's concerns with potential attacks upon private property, coupled with Hamilton's concern over the maintenance of a very well-defined social and political order, revealed the authors' suspicions concerning humankind's untrustworthy nature. The American goverment's fragmented structure and the estranged relationship of our government's institutions with one another is a result of this view of humanity. The European governments believe in the somewhat greater ability of humankind to cooperate for the general good. The closer and more compact arrangement of their public institutions testifies to that general belief. Let us now look at specific governmental institutions, keeping in mind the continuum of human nature that we have discussed, as well as the DeGré continuum of social and political cohesiveness that we have also examined.

POLITICAL PARTIES: AN OVERVIEW

To begin our examination of political institutions, let us concentrate on the political party. It is an institution that we have briefly mentioned and that, in different ways, plays a major role in all political systems. Totalitarian systems, as you would expect, permit only one political party. This party inevitably represents an orthodoxy that includes one exclusively result-oriented view of the world along with a restriction of the democratic process that might reconcile that view with others.

You might wish to think of fairness and efficiency in the case of totalitarianism with regard to political parties, for this is an easy first case to analyze. Most totalitarian systems are on one side of issues like the height of the pyramid. Indeed, they tend to be quite strongly on one side or the other of the distributional argument, which is one of the reasons they distrust democratic processes. Again, political parties tend to have a specific role in such systems. They reinforce the singular orthodoxy and drape the other political institutions behind a common belief. At first glance, such a role for parties would seem to encourage efficiency, but let us refrain from drawing conclusions on this point for a while.

Moderate political systems, such as pluralism, permit more than one political party. Such systems believe in democratic process by accepting the idea that there is a range of views about the height of distributional pyramids and other issues, and that democratic process itself acts as a broker for these different views. These different parties, with more or less precision, represent different views. Thus the argument that is carried on by the parties is important to maintain a balance among the range of different political orientations.

Yet parties in a pluralistic political system are not separate entities that survive apart from other influences. What do you think the influence of a pluralistic political culture, along with a large set of pluralistic interest groups, has on actual political parties? Are these factors not useful to specific interest groups seeking to influence the two other parts of the iron triangle without party interference to get what they want? Again, we must be careful not to overstate the differences between pluralism and elitism. Much of the difference is a matter of degree, but the fact is that pluralistic political structures do not usually have their political parties intercede between interest groups and the appropriate governmental access points. The ability to receive favorable administrative rulings from administrative agencies that have jurisdiction over them, or to move favorable legislation from committees to the full legislative body is so crucial to the well-being of interests that they often perceive political parties as obstructive to that process.

What would parties tend to do if they became more directly involved in pluralist government? Generally, they might tend to do what political parties have done in elitist systems. In those systems, where the assumption of a polity's preference for cooperation over competition is greater, the parties are more willing to take the interests of the various lobbies or pressure groups and *aggregate* them within some overall policy. What does this aggregation mean? It means that political parties, particularly within nonpluralist systems, attempt to coordinate the requests and needs of various interest groups (such as the American Cancer Society and the American Tobacco Institute) and blend them into a more consistent general party orientation. Again, our analysis is concerned with differences of degree, but within an elitist political structure, there is typically a greater place for the kind of political party that would reconcile the differences between the part of the government that subsidizes tobacco and the part that engages in research and public education on cancer.

As a rule, parties in elitist systems typically hold national conferences to determine what positions they will take on various public issues. Party platforms with some degree of specificity are usually agreed upon, and once in power, the parties feel obligated to transform the series of party promises that make up that general program into a political effort to move the nation in one direction or another. A term that is often used to differentiate elite system parties from pluralist system parties is *responsible party*. Responsible parties are those that run on a fairly specific set of principles or a specific "platform," and when in office, they truly attempt to place that program into policy. The term "responsible" comes from the idea that the public, in its appraisal of a party in power, can decide whether the nation has done well or has not done well during that party's tenure. It can then choose to reelect the same party or give another party's set of policies a chance at solving the nation's problems. The party is responsible in that sense to the people who have voted for its members and to whom the members must later answer for their performance. It should also be noted that higher levels of party responsibility have often caused elitist party systems to be *multiparty* systems, that is, systems in which no one party will gain a majority and control the parliamentary government. Although the *coalition governments* that are formed in multiparty legislatures are often stable, as they have been in Scandinavia, they have sometimes proved to be unstable as well. In countries like Italy, for example, coalitions made up of many parties frequently have come apart and governments have fallen there with great regularity.

CANDIDATES

So far the discussion of political parties has not mentioned the role of the individual candidate who runs for office or the election procedures by which candidates attempt to become officeholders. This was done for two reasons. The first was to let you concentrate on the structure of decision making within governments before concentrating on who it may be that would serve as a decision maker. We have said that the key issue about parties in pluralist systems is that their influence is not usually felt at the various access points of policymaking. The second issue is that the configuration of decision making, represented by the pluralistic iron triangle, suggests that little incentive exists for individuals to become candidates for office within the confines of specific party policy.

Let us look more closely at the relationship between a candidate and a party as well as at the relationship of a candidate to specific policy positions. In an elitist system, and again this is a continuum rather than an absolutely opposite set of principles, a particular candidate tends to be closer to his or her party and to the party's positions on contemporary issues (see Figure 8–1). The selection of a candidate in an elitist system is usually the result of an active search. There is also a closer understanding that the party's candidate will remain faithful to the principles of the party both during the campaign and if the candidate is elected to office. However, this understanding can vary among different nations. Members of parliament in the European nations, for example, are expected to both support the policy initiatives of their prime minister if that party is in power and to back the opposition leadership if that party is in opposition. Party loyalty is symptomatic of policy-oriented parties, and it is generally symptomatic of the kinds of parties that elitist political structures typically possess.

Remember that on the question of parties, as well as with the other political questions, you have been asked to think of the fairness and efficiency of the institutions we are studying. As we look at political parties that are more inclined to have strong *platforms*, as well as at officeholders and candidates that warmly embrace these platforms, we see that both desirable and undesirable events can occur. Supporters of the elitist view of political structure generally cite the closer relationship of the various units of a party, including the party platform's relationship to a candidate or to governmental leadership. They argue that this coordination creates more effective decision making once the party is in power, and that, therefore, efficiency of government is enhanced by an element of cohesiveness within political parties.

The elitist argument concerning the question of fairness is more

FIGURE 8–1.
Identity of candidates with parties and local interest in pluralist and elitist systems.

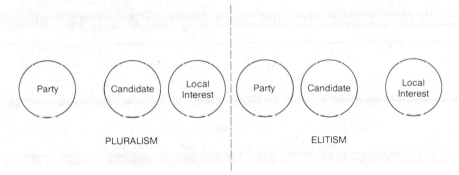

subtle. It claims that definitive points of view are more often represented to the public than are the varied points of view of many interest groups that work hard to promote their ideas before the government. The question comes down to whether it is fair to request an aggregation of interests. Is it fair to ask that all or most interest groups whose ideas would create a heightening or flattening of the pyramid agree to reconcile what they want from government with what others want? Advocates of the elite party model would generally agree to this suggestion. They believe that public interest as a whole is larger than all the private interests, and that therefore, a reconciliation of interests would be beneficial. Note, again, how this evidences a more naturally cooperative view of human nature. Pluralists, generally, would tend not to agree to a reconciliation of interests. They would rather permit each interest to find its own point of governmental influence, and would prefer not to concern themselves with a reconciliation of the policy demands that flow through all access points of a pluralist government. You should note once more how this manifests a more competitive view of natural human interaction.

Shortly, when we have more of the principal institutions of the elitist versus pluralist models in place, we will return to a broader discussion of the questions of fairness and efficiency within each system. Yet, within the context of political parties, the fairness and efficiency questions are not always easy to grapple with. You should be aware of the growing implications of the time-worn argument between a reasonably coordinated and coherent public policy, or a compromised, dispersed public policy. The one side of the argument, the coordinated view, is very close to the cooperative human nature view. Those on the other side of the argument tend to say that coordination limits the ability of competitive individuals to take care of their own needs, and stifles the initiative of private groups and individuals. These latter adherents argue that when decentralization or fragmentation of public decision making is permitted, the government is prevented from making major, comprehensive errors of public judgment. The elitists, however, argue that not being able to make major decisions may be the greatest of all errors. Again, we will continue to develop these issues, but with the introduction of the first major political institution—the political party—you should understand how the elitist-pluralist argument and its human nature assumptions are reflected within the discussion of an important political institution. Finally, you should also understand how the DeGré model of cohesion relates to the actual operation of pluralist and elitist structures.

LEGISLATURES

Let us now consider another key political institution: the legislature. Legislatures exist within virtually every modern political state as well as within virtually all substates of the prenational or federal systems. Legislatures have a long history, and yet, from all those years and across all the varied experiences of nations, the debate on the role of the individual legislator has not changed a great deal.

What does a legislator do? The central task of any legislator is to design and adopt the fundamental public policy of a political system. The legislator usually also designs the very ground rules for the political debate over policy, and we must remember that procedural rules are rarely neutral, nearly always favoring one side of the political argument. Think back, if you will, to the question of democracy as process, drawing from the different orientations toward political result. Do you believe, for example, that within a totalitarian system there will be much doubt over whether process will be broad enough to incorporate a great number of possible policy results? From what you already know of totalitarian structures, and particularly from what you know of the role of totalitarian parties, you should be able to understand how the result-process-result matter affects legislation. Indeed, in most totalitarian states, legislatures tend to pass into law what the totalitarian political party has already declared to be policy.

Both pluralist and elitist systems have more lively legislatures than do totalitarian systems. They are places where ideas truly clash and real decisions over policy can at least be tolerated, if not encouraged. The two elements of democratic legislatures that we should focus upon, therefore, are (1) the means of *selection* of legislative members, and (2) the method of *representation* that exists within the legislature.

Legislative Selection

Let us first examine the means of selection. To do so, we should recall that pluralist and elitist political systems leave a good deal of room within their democratic processes for the consideration of various political orientations. We should also recall that all political structures attempt to maintain a fair degree of political saliency or harmony by establishing legislative rules of fair competition among these orientations. Although there may always be a threat of conflict within political systems, stable polities will attempt to anticipate their potential conflict within all political systems and resolve them within established democratic ground rules. Active legislatures, that is, legislatures with more than one political party, set rules of competition to maintain an orderly democratic process within their structure. Such rules maintain that reservoir of political trust that exists within the culture, myths, and other prepolitical conditions of the democratic nation.

In this sense of trust and maintenance of cultural and political norms, legislatures, perhaps more than any other political institutions, reflect the long-term health or absence of health of a political system. Respect for its role within law-making matters, and the lengthy tenure of many of the people who serve within legislatures, give the public a sense of something stable within their nation's politics. Yet whether that sense of stability leads to a long-term sense of the legitimacy of the system, and a respect for the authority of the laws that it passes, also depends upon other important characteristics. Within pluralist and elitist political systems, those characeristics vary somewhat. To examine this variance we can look to the means of selection of a legislature's members and to the kinds of representation that both an individual legislator and a legislature as a whole give to its people.

In a nation whose populace is diverse, that is, in a nation that has a variety of regions, races, religions, and economic interests, the sense of having each interest well represented is unusually strong. Apart from a pluralist tendency toward political parties that do not aggregate or coordinate interests very strongly, there is a tendency in pluralist systems to refrain from selecting representatives on the basis of an ideological orientation. The means of selection that maintain a local orientation within candidates is very important, for local parties and the jurisdiction of which they are a part will jealously guard the right to nominate and elect the people who represent them in a national or subnational government. Elitist systems must respond to local preferences to some degree as well, and local wishes are thus at least marginally considered in candidate selection. In elitist systems, however, the local nomination processes are often shared with national party organizations, and the voting itself tends to be a statement of preference for a national public policy or ideology.

In pluralist systems, again, the nominating process for political office is jealously guarded by local interests, and to be elected, a candidate must be viewed as representing the interests of the business, ethnic, religious, and other groups that are prominent in the area. We should understand that if such local interest representation is the single most significant cause for a candidate's election to a legislature, this factor alone enhances the degree of fragmentation of the political process. When these local election incentives are combined with, and perhaps contribute to, structural fragmentation within the legislature (such as in a vast committee structure), the number of access points are increased within that legislature and the possibility of captive access points at the committee and subcommittee levels will also increase.

Legislative Representation

As you can see, the issues surrounding the role of both elections and party involvement elections overlap with the issues concerning styles of political representation in legislatures. What are the dominant styles of legislative representation? And how, with regard to elections, do they vary between pluralist and elitist systems? To answer, let us return to a primary theme of our model and question how legislative representation can be affected by a general tendency toward cooperative or competitive assumptions within institutions.

One way that has been used to separate different kinds of representation is the differentiation between *collective* and *dyadic* representation (dyadic means that individual legislators represent individual interests, regions, religious affiliations, and so on, and that, when the political system as a whole is considered, every interest will have its own personal representation).

Collective representation manifests the opposite notion, for its means that although there is no direct relationship between the representative and those that are represented, there is still an assurance that within the overall makeup of a legislative institution such as a parliament, a fair and equitable representation of all the groupings of that society exists. That representation, again, need not be direct. A black citizen in Detroit, for example, might not have a black representative in his or her district, but under a collective notion of representation, that citizen will still be represented by, say, a black representative from Los Angeles. Collective representation, or "virtual" representation as the British philosopher Edmund Burke referred to it, is every bit as concerned with fair representation as it is with direct or dyadic representation. However, there is no sense that a citizen will be better represented by those who are specifically chosen by that citizen. As you can surmise, collective legislatures tend to have more legislative cohesion, often through stronger party systems, whereas dyadic legislatures tend to have more of an individualistic structure. Further, the collective structures are more apt to exist in elitist political structures, whereas the dyadic structure is more likely to occur within pluralist systems.[1]

There is a similar kind of differentiation with regard to representative styles of individual legislators; that is, whether they represent a specific, dyadic interest or a broad collective interest. To explain this, we should introduce two terms that represent the two poles of the representation styles that individual legislators offer: *trustee* and *delegate*. Trustees are representatives who consider their election to signify that the citizens of a district trust them to use their best judgment when debating and voting on public issues. When difficult public issues arise, that trustee will feel an obligation to vote the way that his or her conscience and experience dictate. Surely, if expertise on public matters is what placed the trustee within his or her position of trust, as Edmund Bruke argued, then that expertise is what should be used in acting upon public concerns.

The other view of representative style is the delegate view in which the representative occupies a position within the legislature only as a kind of messenger for the concerns of the local citizenry. Should these citizens visit the capital or petition by mail or by phone, the delegate will insist that the representative is responsible for listening to the petitioners and designing public policy in response to their specific needs and requests.

Now that you understand the contrast between trustee and delegate styles of representation, which style would better accompany the pluralist, and which would better accompany the elitist structure of government? In the first instance, the difference may not seem obvious. The use of one's own standards or the standards of the citizenry that one represents may not appear to relate to either notion of political structure. But contemplate the relationship further. If the standards that trustees use are largely their own, from where do you think these standards grow? In one sense, would not these standards develop out of a general or theoretical notion of what government should be doing, and would not such a trusteeship notion of government be a part of responsible, elitist parties? Representatives who believe in programs and platforms do tend to be in favor of parties that stand for a clear and definite program. Such legislators favor responsible parties, whereas law makers who listen principally to their constituent preferences usually do not have a deep commitment to a specific party program or platform. Hence, these latter representatives tend to be more prominent within a pluralistic governmental mode.

Representative Level

The difference between trustee and delegate styles of representation is closely linked to the difference in the level of constituency that is represented. If you were in the U.S. Congress, either as a representative or a senator, which level of jurisdiction, again thinking in terms of different levels of identification and allegiance, would you feel had a greater claim on your loyalty? In any legislative body, there are tugs of identification that would cause you to either identify with your *local* or subnational interest, or with the larger *national* interest. Although similar to the question of trustee versus delegate constituency style, there is also a continuum in which some of both orientations exists for all representatives. Yet it is still clear that certain representatives prefer one level of identification over the other.

Reflect now upon which orientation, either national or local, would tend to be within the framework of the pluralist structure and which would more likely be found within the elitist structure. Would it not make sense that a national orientation would more confortably exist with the elitist structure, whereas a local orientation would better exist within a pluralist structure? Why is this the reasonable linkage? Again, what we now know about interest groups and about the different places where policy is made should help us to understand this pattern. Local orientations, that is, orientations that protect both local interests and the specific structural notion of local importance in national offices, work better within a pluralist structure because elitist structures do not place the same importance on local interests and issues.

Structure, Staff, and Leadership Loyalty

If we reflect once again on the fundamental social cohesion model of DeGré, you will see how the range of political cohesiveness to political decentralization is presenting itself in so many different places. With representation in legislative bodies, as with parties and other political institutions that we will examine, the social distances between people and institutions remain in significant tension. The struggle between cohesion and fragmentation is constant, and the questions concerning legislative representation reflect that tension within the structure of any legislature.

Which legislative structure, the pluralist or elitist, would tend to create more committees and subcommittees to divide up the work and the policymaking of the legislature? Your answer should draw from our discussion of access points and the iron triangle, as well as from what you now know about legislatures. The local constituency and the interests within them are paramount within a pluralist model of government, and if the delegate style of representative relies upon support for locally important issues, what kind of subdivision structure will such reliance bring to the legislature? Of course, a decentralized structure is deeply broken into many committees and subcommittees. Such a structure is a manifestation of the DeGré model of cohesion within pluralism, and it is a very real element within the pluralist iron triangle.

As an additional exercise, which of the legislative adaptations, the pluralist or the elitist, would permit larger and more personal staffs, and which would have smaller legislative staffs? Also, which structure would require that those staffs answer to party institutions and the leadership of the legislative institutions, and which would prefer that they answer solely to the legislative members? The response to these questions should be clear. Indeed, the U.S. Congress, currently with 535 members, has 23,000 staff members, all of whom are beholden to and protective of the individuality of reelection of "my Congressman" or "my Congresswoman" as the staff often phrases it. In Canada, which has the next highest number of legislative staffers of the major Western nations, there are 3,300 legislative assistants; in Europe, the figures are even lower. Curiously, American staffers like to refer to themselves as the "Congressional staff" or the "Senate staff," but in doing so, they engage in misrepresentation. They are members of the private staff of congressional officeholders, and only very rarely do they have allegiances or responsibility to the entire legislative body.

Before we leave our discussion of legislatures, one more element should be added to our understanding. It has to do with the style of the election of legislative office seekers. In one context, we have already spoken of how styles of elections are influenced by how they in turn influence the pluralist or elitist structure of political systems. From our analysis of responsible or nonresponsible political parties, you know that candidates in a pluralist system prefer not to campaign on highly specific party platforms. From our discussion of pluralistic legislative groupings, you should know that candidates within a pluralistic system will rarely identify themselves with the leadership of the legislature or with comprehensive legislative programs that are debated within the legislative houses.

When elections within pluralist systems are won or lost at the local level, with appeals going directly to the local populace and the interest of the subnational groups that they represent, it should be clear to you that these local interest groupings will wish for the continuation of decentralized access points. It should also be clear that the absence of national party allegiance, and the absence of allegiance to the entire legislative body rather than to decentralized access points within that body, detracts from respect for legislative leadership and party allegiance. Certainly, within the U.S. Congress, candidates for reelection speak little of their loyalty to the Speaker of the House or to the Minority Leader, and loyalty to the Senate and its institutional majority or minority leadership is even less than it is in the House. Clearly, you should see that even the individualistic and competitive assumptions of a pluralistic legislature extend to the style of elections of that legislative body.

Of course, what we have discussed with regard to pluralist legislatures is somewhat different within elitist legislatures. The internal leadership of elitist legislatures plays a more significant political role in elitist systems because it more readily enforces what is called *party discipline* in the matters that come before the legislative house. Committees and subcommittees are fewer as a rule, and, when they do exist, their principal members are loyal to the overall legislative leadership in far greater degree than they are to either their individual voting constituencies or to the interests that might attempt to "access" their committees. Further, campaigns in elitist systems tend to accentuate the broad policy differences within the population, believing that clearer alternatives give direction to comprehensive policy, even though the potential cross-pressures of several different identifications may be surrendered. Finally, a proponent of the elitist view will argue that policy-oriented elections and the relatively disciplined legislative institutions that they foster are both fairer and more efficient.

On the question of fairness, elistists will argue that the clear policy orientation of elitist parties and elections, along with the somewhat more comprehensive scope of government itself, extend from a more rationalistic interpretation of value contributed. They will also stress that policy-oriented parties afford different groups the political opportunity to become part of the valuational debate within the government. The elitist view of efficiency will argue that strong legislative bodies with strong internal party leadership, together with the impact of election campaigns that clearly present issues, help government to coordinate its institutions toward policy goals better than a pluralist structure is able to do.

As we close our discussion of legislatures, do not lose sight of the original DeGré notions of various levels of social cohesion. Also, do not lose sight of the relatively individualistic or collective notions of political myth, culture, symbolism, and socialization. Political structure is important in any polity, but the roots of all systems lie in what we have described as prepolitical elements. The degree of individualism, and the differences in racial, regional, ethnic, and other identifications, as well as the simple momentum of the history of certain styles of politics, greatly influence institutional design and function. The personal loyalty and the ideologically more significant party orientations of the European parliaments contrast to the localist and pluralist orientations of the American Congress for reasons that go much deeper than the actual framework of the political structure itself. What flows through the structure, the policy preferences and the exercise of power in which various interests engage, must fit well with each political structure's prepolitical considerations.

THE INTERNAL EQUILIBRIUM

Before we complete our review of political structure, we should remind ourselves that our references to prepolitical considerations and our continuing review of the specific political institutions embrace a full range of governmental structures within the range of democratic forms. We have used the American and the European structures as examples of pluralism and elitism. You should understand as well that not only is there a great variance along the entire continuum, but there are also substantial variances of ranges even within pluralist and elitist structures. Further, there is a variance over time within each kind of system. The pluralist American government, for example, has seen centripetal and centrifugal periods ebb and flow throughout its history. These forces have pulled and hauled each other, and the loose cohesion of the government, represented by the degree to which the "separation of powers" and "federalism" have been strengthened or weakened, has reflected that pulling and hauling.

Generally, the centrifugal federalism forces and the pre–Civil War weaknesses of the national government were great enough to nearly destroy the American union in the American Civil War. The Canadian government is an interesting mix of pluralism and elitism, for although it is largely pluralistic, it contains a European-style national parliament yet leaves a great deal of control to the individual Canadian provinces. Even within Europe, the ranges within the category of elitism are real. The centralism of the French and British governments contrasts to a more federated West German system, which, as we mentioned earlier, maintains a degree of subnational autonomy within its individual states or *lander*. Germany, however, still lies comfortably within the elitist political model when its parliamentary legislature and its issue-oriented parties are taken into account.

There is, in short, a lesson that you should take from both the full pluralist–elitist range and the pluralist and elitist parties of that range. The lesson is that there is more or less of a natural *internal equilibrium*, or a kind of sympathetic alignment between prepolitical and political factors that is observable within various nations. Everything from the size, diversity, and the history of a nation to its fundamental social cohesion has an impact upon where that nation will fall on the continuum. As we noted earlier, there is no single form of government that is best; the continuum that we have constructed has no single place that is correct for all nations and their governments. The emphasis here is the importance of an internal equilibrium or the compatibility of a nation's governmental structure with the deeper prepolitical attributes of the nation itself. Before we are finished, you will consider one other factor that has an impact upon the range of pluralism or elitism, namely, *external equilibrium* or the impact of the world's emerging equilibriums upon the structure of individual nations. For now, however, let us consider the internal equilibrium of nations and, to complete that analysis, let us look at the remaining institutions and continue to contrast pluralism and elitism.

BUREAUCRACY

The bureaucracy of a political system is what many political commentators as well as active politicians often think of as the "under side" of the public sphere. Bureaucracies and bureaucrats seem to always be unpopular, this unpopularity being the one attribute that is perhaps applicable to totalitarian, elitist, and pluralist political systems alike. In the minds of many, bureaucracies appear to be the segment of government that forces citizens to do things that they would rather not do. In some nation-states, the administrative methods of bureaucrats are indeed rather arbitrary. Also, in some, the rules of bureaucracy and the enforcement of these rules, although very much a part of modern government, often seem unfair.

Democratic systems, however, have developed standards for bureaucratic behavior, and the dual principles of the *notice* of administrative proceedings and the *hearing* of all sides of a dispute, along with the right of appeal into a nation's court system, are virtually universal within democratic structures. Some citizens, however, still question why we have bureaucracies. The answer to this question carries with it an understanding of all modern governments, for the reality of public authority is such that legislatures and the routine enforcement of the laws that they create are simply not able to deal with the volume or the complexity of modern public policy. Let us focus our analysis upon what are the two major functions of bureaucracy: *rule making*, whereby legislatures and executives find that they are willing to step away from the specifics of deciding public policy in a particular area and give that power to an administrative body; and *adjudication*, whereby specific judgements are made to resolve disputes between contesting individuals or interests.

Why does a legislature or an executive engage in what is often called a *delegation of authority*? Legislatures are still the primary rule-making body in all democratic systems. But it is no longer possible for legislatures of broad general authority to handle the quantity of rule making that is presently required, nor do they possess the level of expertise that is necessary with a large number of sophisticated public issue areas. The simple truth is that the technical rules that are made by, say, the Federal Aviation Authority, the Federal Power Commission, or the Federal Communications Commission can only be made by people who follow complex and often rapidly changing areas of concern with a real commitment and competence.

Another reason why bureaucracies are a permanent part of modern governmental structure has to do with the extent to which the political structure is pluralist or elitist. It is conventional wisdom that legislatures use when they create law to make that law as specific as possible. However, although it may be beneficial for all laws to be precise, there are reasons why lawmakers do not always permit laws to be as precise as they could be.

Consider the expression *loose legislation*. Which kind of legislature tends to have strong platforms and strong party leadership, as well as the kind of electoral strategies that link candidates to rather than separate them from their party position? The answer, of course, is the elitist legislature. The pluralist legislature, on the other hand, generally possesses weak leadership, vague party platforms, and an individualistic, localist notion of both electoral strategy and legislative style. What we should next ask ourselves is: Does one kind of legislature tend to legislate less precisely and, as a result, settle for what is now called "loose" legislation? Once again, we are speaking of continuums, and the pluralist legislature, with many highly divergent interests accessing it from varying perspectives, does seem to have a more difficult time arriving at precise and comprehensive legislation.

Indeed, in recent years, the U.S. Congress has been unable to engage in the specifics of a legislative mandate regarding many agencies. To compensate for this, it developed what is known as the *legislative veto*. Under the legislative veto, the executive branch could reorganize or even abolish a bureaucratic agency, and the Congress was given an average of 60 days in which to overrule what the executive branch had done or to let it stand. Theoretically, the legislative veto could apply to a broad range of executive initiatives wherein the legislature could only reject or accept the reality of an executive rule-making initiative. The spread of the legislative veto certainly indicates a weakening of legislative power vis-à-vis the executive branch and, in 1982, the Supreme Court held that the legislative veto was an unconstitutional abandonment of legislative responsibility.

Remember that all legislation, all rule making, is the work of compromise. Politics has often been called "the art of the possible" by many of its most able practitioners. Sam Rayburn, a former Speaker of the House of Representatives, would often say to young representatives, that "to get along, you had better go along." Yet when the members of a majority party in the legislature have not been elected on the basis of a specific policy, and when no deep loyalty to the party or to the party leadership exists, there is less of a chance that legislators will be able to achieve agreement on the specifics of a legislative problem. In other words, when the legislature is comprised of a loose majority and a loose minority, with allegiances and constituency styles stressing the delegate role and local orientation, it may be that the compromises that lead to each piece of legislation "rob" the legislation of any precise meaning. Problems of energy, health, economic productivity, and so on may never achieve a consensus solution from the legislative members, and even the members of a majority party may pass only the most noncontroversial portions of a bill into law.

On the contrary, using our emerging models of the pluralist and elitist forms of structures and institutions, it seems clear that the elitist model achieves a higher degree of consensus among members of the majority party in the legislature. Further, to the extent that rule making is more specific within elitist legislatures, bureaucracies are less likely to have broad rule-making authority. Although all bureaucracies will have some rule-making capability and the ability to make certain decisions that have the force of law, there is usually a difference in the range of the arena of bureaucratic decision making in pluralistic and elitist systems.

ADJUDICATION

Although some observers might agree that a certain amount of rule making within modern bureaucratic structures must inevitably be permitted, others might argue that the ability of these bureaucracies to make judgments concerning particular disputes among parties should be strictly limited. Within many areas of public policy, a dispute that exists, say, between two competing airlines or two competing oil companies about a regulation concerning routes or rates will be settled by an administrative hearing and decision. This is the *adjudicatory function*, the making of decisions when there is a dispute under the rules made by the legislature or the bureaucracy. Haven't we all been taught that judgments are made by judges? Don't courts make all the judicial decisions in a political system? No, courts do not make all adjudicatory decisions, and we should ask why the adjudicatory function now falls within bureaucracies more frequently than it ever had before.

Bureaucracies make so many judgelike decisions, in great part, because the intrusions into the court's adjudicating function may in fact be welcomed by modern courts. Here, again, a more traditional political institution seems willing to delegate some of its authority, for increasingly, the capability of adjudicating within a number of complex, technical areas within bureaucratic settings may be a necessary relief for courts that are overburdened with difficult cases. This problem of overburdened courts has been dealt with in part by creating special court jurisdictions. The Tax Court, the Court of Claims and other specialty courts are long-time institutions within the American judiciary. But specialized courts cannot always serve as the answer to court crowding and the lack of judicial expertise. The bureaucratic agency, with its informal rules of evidence, its lack of jury usage, and its specialized, technically proficient lawyer-advocates who have mastered patent law, antitrust law, and so on, greatly short-circuit the time and difficulty of courts that must observe full legal procedures.

All democratic political structures, of course, have open court systems that mete out fair justice without regard to governmental policy or ideology. They operate publicly, the English-derivative systems of which the United States is one, specifically rejecting the Star Chamber of the Middle Ages that heard secret and usually predecided cases to suppress political opposition. As we have discussed, the larger English and American systems are based upon the common law, a nonstatutory case law method of adjudicating current disputes on the basis of rulings on prior similar controversies. The continental or European system of law, on the other hand, is a written law, and its origins go back through the Napoleonic Code to the time of Roman law.

Although both judicial systems are based to some degree upon what is called the adversarial process, that is, although they are both systems where both sides of the issue are vigorously advocated by the participants themselves, the common law is certainly far more adversarial. Its rules of evidence approach that of a medieval joust, and the role of the trial judge is almost exclusively that of a referee who is placed between the combatants. In the European law, which is called the *civil law*, a judge often actively intercedes as an unbiased or even biased questioner at the time of hearing evidence. Criminal cases are often reviewed by supposedly unbiased, nonadvocative investigators before they are given to advocative prosecutors. Also, as a general proposition, there is much less formal legal combat between private parties within the European court systems.

People in the United States employ nearly 600,000 lawyers to settle their disputes. Indeed, a full 2 percent of the American gross domestic product is taken up with legal adjudication. Consider for a moment whether such an extraordinary level of dispute resolution within the United States, and the lesser level of such need within Europe, are related to such factors as the relative social cohesion within the different national systems. Also, consider why it is that even with all these legal professionals, the more established, judicial segment of the American government, such as the legislative segment, has yielded many of its prerogatives. Whether more of this delegation of authority goes on in a pluralist system than in an elitist system is something that is not always clear, although there is a greater tendency to appeal administrators' adjudicatory rulings to traditional courts in the United States than there is in other nations. Hence, in rule making, and perhaps in adjudication as well, the centrifugal forces of structure, starting again from the original social cohesion patterns, do have an impact on the amount of bureaucratic discretion that any political system permits within its structure.

With this discussion of the rule making of bureaucracies and the adjudicatory nature of both the bureaucracy and the courts, we should now be prepared to proceed to the final principal component of modern government: the *executive*. As we close this chapter, we should be able to understand how executives work within modern governments and how their workings fit into our models of pluralism and elitism.

THE EXECUTIVE

Virtually all modern states have an executive of one kind or another. In the immediately postfeudal era, the era of the birth of nationalism and the modern monarchy, a king, or sometimes a queen, became a powerful institution. Yet within the evolution of democratic governments, the incentive to build institutions that could compete with the power of the Crown grew increasingly strong. Perhaps the most notable exception to the idea that modern states have executives occurred when the early American government, under the Articles of Confederation, attempted to carry on for nearly a decade without the services of an executive. The plan clearly did not work, and for this and other reasons, the new nation eventually yielded to the desire for a reasonably strong executive. Some of the Founding Fathers, you may remember, would even have had George Washington become an American king.

Understanding modern ambivalence over the executive is essential to our view of contemporary government. It is not much of an exaggeration to say that the structures of modern legislatures, courts, and even political parties were in great part conceived of as a protection from the real or anticipated abuses of undemocratic executives. The evolution of government within modern elitist systems was such that the parliament slowly chipped away at the monarch's powers, with a prime minister emerging as a democratic executive replacement for the Crown heads of years ago. Most of those governments have become known as *cabinet governments*, where the executive is comprised of a number of important departments, the heads of which form the entire government under the party banner of either a majority party or a majority party coalition. In reality, many modern critics of the elitist system point to the fact that cabinet officers are effectively excluded from the inner counsels of governments, and that the prime minister makes up the executive office from his or her own staff and advisors.

However you may feel about the parliamentary system, the prime minister in the parliamentary elitist model is closely identified with a legislature, a party, and a platform. Thus that office is said to represent the issue-oriented or programmatic view of government that we have described. If we consider that issue-oriented factor once more within the question of electoral style, we would see that in the elitist system, the prime minister candidate (although he or she does not run for prime minister in the popular election) would more likely campaign on the issues of a platform. He or she would also more likely campaign with and for other members of the party throughout the country. Once elected from the predictably safe district that his or her party has carefully selected, the prime minister is ceremoniously chosen from the party caucus of that winning party, that party having already decided whom it will choose as its prime minister.

Within a pluralist structure such as that of the United States, the presidential election is very different from elitist parliamentary elections. Even the presidential candidate, at least of the two major parties (Republican and Democratic), runs primarily upon his or her personal merits and only secondarily upon party or platform. The comparatively wide party identification swings in American presidential vote, the fact that presidential candidates such as General Eisenhower could decide which party they identified with only shortly before the presidential election contest itself, as well as the often substantial differences between the presidential election turnout and the turnout for local offices all indicate that the president is "running away" from other electoral influences.

In addition, the offices of president and prime minister are very different. An American president is known as a head of state as well as the head of government; that is, he will assume the position that is held either by a monarch (England and Spain) or by a more ceremonial president (West Germany and Italy) in Western European nations. (The prime minister is clearly the head of the governing political party, holding the position at the head of a cabinet of party leaders.) An American president may well have to share party leadership with someone like the Speaker of the House or the Majority or Minority Leader of the Senate, as well, perhaps, as with someone like a large state's governor. Former Democratic

President Jimmy Carter had to share a good deal of party leadership with the popular Senator Edward Kennedy from Massachusetts.

Further, a president is elected by the entire people of a country such as in the United States, even though we still use the electoral college as a kind of buffer between a direct vote for president and the final selection stage. In the parliamentary system, the prime minister is elected to the parliament only by the people of a particular district and is then selected to be the prime minister by the members of the majority party after that party assembles in the parliament. Clearly, the subsequent ability of a prime minister to control the legislature is far greater in the parliamentary system than in the presidential system, as the president has no such authority.

Finally, even apart from the structural separation of the presidency from the Congress under the American notion of separation of powers, the president acting alone plays a number of roles that an elitist system with its history, its aristocratic tradition, and its monarchs often have played by other actors. The very absence of formal class distinctions, or the absence of a history that found sometimes arbitrary leaders among the "chosen" families, finds the American president needing to be more regal and more common than his European prime minister counterpart. The president in America, more than any officer of any major national government, stands alone, and more than any other executive, the American president is expected to lead most vigorously and independently from that position of isolation. The American president must tend to public business within what is perhaps the most fragmented of national political structures, the American pluralist structure.

CONCLUSION

With this chapter we have an understanding of the principal institutions of democratic governments. Our discussion of political parties and candidates stressed the degree of cohesion typically demonstrated by pluralist and elistist systems. The means by which legislative candidates are chosen and the very structure of legislatures themselves also reveal the essential differences that exist between pluralist and elistist systems, as do the differences in the kinds of legislative representation.

In preparation for our discussion of the increased importance of global considerations in the following chapter, we examined how specific institutions of government were originally designed to respond to purely internal or national prepolitical considerations. Our discussion of courts and bureaucracies was meant to alert you to the costs of responding only to such internal considerations, rather than also to some broader notion of how efficient and fair political systems are designed.

Reference Note

1. Robert Weissberg, "Collective versus Dyadic Representation in Congress," *The American Political Science Review*, Vol. 72, no. 2 (June 1978), pp. 535–547.

Glossary

TERMS

aggregated interests

responsible party

multiparty systems

coalition governments

platforms

selection

representation

collective representation

dyadic representation

trustee

delegate

local interest

national interest

party discipline

whips

lander

internal equilibrium

external equilibrium

notice

hearing

rule making

delegation of authority

legislative veto

loose legislation

art of the possible

adjudicatory function

civil law

cabinet government

safe district

NAMES

Edmund Burke

Dwight Eisenhower

Jimmy Carter

Edward Kennedy

CHAPTER 9
PLURALISM AND ELITISM
EVALUATED

By now, you should have a strong sense of the patterns of offices and institutions within pluralist and elitist political structures. You should also have a sound idea of how the principal models we are studying compare with each other. It is now time to test these models within the notions of the salience, competition, and conflict continuum as well as within the standards of legitimacy, authority, and power that we covered. When you can understand these variables as part of our model and then as systems that attempt to balance democracy as process between the varying views of different result orientations, you should feel confident about a basic understanding of political structure. Further, with these understandings, you should have also begun to see how political structure has an effect upon something as fundamental as the valuation questions that we spoke of in the early portion of our model. Let me suggest that apart from the prepolitical considerations and the structural matters that we have already reviewed, some additional considerations are helpful to an evaluation of pluralist and elitist structures.

AN EVALUATION OF PLURALISM AND ELITISM

One of the most basic assumptions that underlies pluralism is that a great deal of what is usually called an ideological *consensus* already exists within the political society of a pluralist nation. What does this consensus span? As you might expect, if a pluralist society exists without one major, deep cleavage within its population, the consensus spans most, if not all, of the broad national goals of the society. It may also span the competitive process by which individual citizens achieve their goals.

168

We know that an elitist society usually gives birth to a political culture that has internal divisions such as those that have separated economic classes. Thus, the elitist view acknowledges the impact of more intense result orientations within the political system. Further, the elitist society usually acknowledges its history of conflict and the lesser degrees of salience that have existed in earlier times. The elitist society, in short, has not always believed that its citizens' public policy goals have a high degree of saliency and are thus only moderately competitive. As we have said, the emerging line of policy within an elitist structure must attempt to deal with its deep separations. It must therefore be able to move back and forth more broadly into various result orientations to at least temporarily satisfy one ideological view. It then must be able to shift rather considerably to satisfy another ideological view, and the structure and authority of that elitist government must be designed so that it can create comprehensive policy orientations in one direction or another. Pluralism, without feeling the pressure of deeper ideological convictions, need not move policy so dramatically to one side or the other, and it can afford not to do that, again, because there is either a real or an assumed consensus underlying policy.

If we have now outlined how the particular institutions of both pluralist and elitist structures work, and if we have reviewed the major specific linkages and/or nonlinkages that occur among those institutions, we should now be able to conclude that the political linkages of elitism are far more cohesive than are the linkages within pluralism. Whereas the term *separation of powers* has been the key phrase within the American national government, the European parliamentary governments have permitted aggregating institutions like political parties and legislative leadership to tie together an executive, a legislature, and even the upper echelons of a sometimes reluctant bureaucracy. These links within elitism are not only a result of a deeper social cohesion or a more group-oriented set of myths or symbols. They are also, quite clearly, an everyday adaptation to the need to create more comprehensive public policy.

THE EMERGING WORLD

We are turning the analysis around just a bit, aren't we? We are suggesting that within elitist governments there is an assumption of some conflict within what is still a cohesive population. We are also suggesting that this very conflict may bring a need for a higher level of cohesion within political institutions in the elitist model. Finally, we are finding that there is a greater need for active government within an elitist structure. The elitist government must be able to reply to the more deeply result-oriented demands of various segments of the citizenry and move policy in a comprehensive way. The elitist government and society meet new challenges and move through history with a broader mandate for the scope of public policy.

In contrast, a pluralist government that assumes a policy consensus within a less cohesive social structure and that feels that it need not move back and forth across the policy continuum will probably not feel that it needs to develop policy in such a comprehensive and active way. Its government and the lesser degree of cohesion of its institutions need not be designed for the movement of public policy that pluralist systems do not see as necessary when they meet new challenges (see Figure 9–1).

But now let us consider something that is simple yet important. It is that the world is changing. In fact, the world and the circumstances of politics seem to be changing more rapidly as history moves toward the close of the twentieth century. Politics and what we know about politics will have to adapt to more and different circumstances than ever before. In part, these circumstances will continue to be brought about by the requests that different groups will place upon governments. Yet new kinds of problems will also impose themselves upon all governments, and they will make the task of government even more demanding than it is now.

The single most important circumstance that typifies the changing world is that the world is coming together in many different ways. The simple reality of tomorrow's politics is that so much of what happens in one place in the world has a marked effect on everyone else throughout the world. This circumstance has brought about what we refer to as the *interdependent world society*. Using Aristotle's term, we are moving toward a new level of polity.

If you recall our discussion of centripetal and centrifugal forces, we said that in Western Europe real suprapolitical structures were already growing out of national and even prenational governments. Even more important than the growth of political supranationalism, however, is the development of an increasingly worldwide economic order, that is, a kind of economic supranationalism of the industrial states, if not the entire world.

We cannot fully discuss the vast changes that have occurred within the world economic system since World War II or even since the early 1970s. Yet, surely you remember the Arab oil em-

FIGURE 9–1.
The breadth of policy in pluralist and elitist systems.

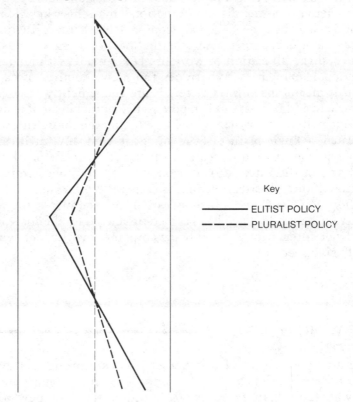

Key

——— ELITIST POLICY

– – – PLURALIST POLICY

bargo of 1973. You also know that oil is now truly a world product that tends very much toward a worldwide price. What you should also understand is that a number of other products, particularly important industrial metals such as bauxite, chrome, copper, and the like, are also "world" products, with prices controlled by worldwide markets. Further, it should not surprise you to realize that although labor prices are not fully determined on world markets, the wages within individual states are increasingly affected by worldwide economic competition among the laborers of different nation-states. Finally, and perhaps even more important than the world prices of raw materials or even growing competition of national labor prices, there has been a dramatic increase in the worldwide flow of *investment capital* over the last few years.

What is investment capital? Why has it become such an important concept in recent years? Investment capital is the money that people loan to other people or to enterprises with an expectation that the loan will bring a profitable return to the lender. The fact that modern investment is an international matter is a key element in the growth of a new, global economy. Now, more than ever before, major decisions concerning the location of new industrial plants and the allocation of work are being made without regard to national boundaries. What does this new mobility of capital mean? It means that if raw materials are conveniently discovered somewhere and if labor or even potentially trainable labor is available somewhere other than where an existing economic enterprise is located, a single plant or even an entire company might move out of one country and relocate to this more favorable place. This trend within the international economy has been accelerated by the growth of an institution that is called the *multinational corporation* (MNC). There is little question that the increasing complexity of the modern age has been compounded by the increasing worldwide integration of worldwide corporate institutions within a truly *global economy*.

THE WORLD IMPACT

We must now inquire as to whether this continuing worldwide economic integration has had an impact upon national political policy and political structures. Without question, the new world economy does have such an impact, and the way in which the global economy affects all national systems is something we must now begin to understand. Nations have competed politically and even militarily for a long time. In many ways, they have also competed economically, at least since the postfeudal mercantile period when modern states were coming into being. But in the past, and this is an important distinction, the nation-state competed almost exclusively as an economically independent nation-state. Nations may have battled one another, literally as well as figuratively, for land, raw materials, or markets, but they battled almost entirely with the economic interests of their nation securely controlled within the country's borders. All nations, in short, securely held their own investment capital that built new business and industry, and virtually all of the decisions concerning investment capital were made within a purely national context.

Yet within the last few years, the basic economic unit as well as the relationship of that unit to the nation-state has begun to change dramatically. Even our original model of valuation and distribution, which we had assumed to be within one national polity, is now very much subject to distributional influences outside that single polity. Our task is to understand how the dramatic change that is global economics affects the well-being and the stability of nation-states and their people. To accomplish that understanding, we will have to continue our comparison of elitist and pluralist systems and then introduce the new global economic variables into that analysis.

THE PUBLIC AND THE PRIVATE SECTOR

We have already discussed how the prepolitical considerations of a nation-state should be in a state of equilibrium with the structure of the nation's government. These are what we have called the internal elements of a national equilibrium. But what happens when the elements of global and economic considerations begin to have an impact on the overall national structure as well? The answer should be clear to you, for beyond bearing the impact of internal equilibriums, we now see that nation-states are receiving the impact of an emerging external equilibrium.

Up until recently, if one nation-state organized its productivity better than did other states, the impact of the difference in productivity, although important, was not immediate and direct. The manufacturing of products within national boundaries was still largely for local, that is, national, consumption. Although some states were more productive than others, differences were not achieved by global capital movement. The international competition that existed was of such a nature that nation-states could provide for a good number of their own needs and do well within at least one line of foreign trade. However, with capital currently moving across national borders at a quickened pace, the very structure of the way in which a nation-state organizes its productivity will have a dramatic impact upon the attractiveness of many of its products and the lure of new and important investment.

If one nation-state organizes its productivity better than does another nation-state, or if the labor price in that first nation-state is lower than it is somewhere else, then surely that state will become more attractive for something as important as the international investment of capital. The advantages of one nation-state, again, will be very real within the new global economic competition.

When economic investment competition is global, surely what each state can do to prepare itself for this new form of competition is highly important. But what can each nation do? You will recall that over the last sections of our inquiry, we looked at the kinds of political institutions that were most likely to exist within various patterns of social cohesion. We also discussed the degree of integration of various public institutions. We found that the United States with its federalist notion of state and national power, along with its separation of powers between the national legislature, the executive, and even the bureaucracy, is firmly at one end of the democratic continuum. We also found some of the nations of Western Europe, say, Great Britain with its absence of federalism and very little separation of powers, to be near the other end of the continuum.

Now we must consider the degree of integration between the public or political structures of which we have been speaking on the one hand, and the economic institutions of a nation on the other. In other words, we must turn our attention from the degree of integration of various public institutions (legislatures, parties, etc.), to the idea of the degree of integration between those public structures and the various productive or economic structures that exist within each country.

You will recall that in the early stages of our discussion, we reviewed the histories and the underlying beliefs of the four basic political ideologies. These ideologies were (1) pure capitalism, (2) liberal or state capitalism, (3) democratic socialism, and (4) Marxist socialism or communism. You were asked to learn from that continuum how various systems solved the problem of *distribution* of their national wealth. Again, the traditional nineteenth-century political ideologies that we have talked about were predominantly concerned with the question of how the wealth of a nation should be divided up, and that issue was called the valuational or distributional issue.

That valuational issue is still with us, of course. But the distributional matter has always been accompanied by another vital economic matter—*productivity*—for national political systems are always concerned about how much economic wealth they are going to be able to produce.

Without question, the productivity issue is just as important today as it ever was. At the time of our discussion of the distributional question, whether you were a socialist or a communist or whether you were a capitalist or a modern liberal capitalist had to do with how you felt about the state or the government's role in altering the early distributional results of capitalism. But today, there is a new term being used to discuss the economic policy of nation-states: *neo-mercantilism*. It refers, in part, to the time before the Industrial Revolution and industrial wage labor when governments and their businesses stood in a cooperative relationship to produce more wealth for the entire polity.

Under mercantilism, government franchises to productive manufacturers, subsidies to shippers, and even monopolies to favored artisans were commonplace methods for achieving maximum national productivity. That system, as it continued until roughly the middle of the eighteenth century, was known as mercantilism. The modern term, neo-mercantilism, refers simply to an evolving modern condition in which a national government begins to work hand in hand with its economic institutions to provide for the highest possible economic productivity. We should understand, however, that neo-mercantilism is not socialism. Indeed, it is not like any of the four industrially generated ideologies. It is a matter of an equal partnership, a settlement upon a state of cooperation between the public and private sectors rather than the dominance of one. It is public-private cooperation that plays an important role in determining how a nation's political and economic structures are combined.

GLOBAL IMPACT UPON STRUCTURE

How, then, does the new worldwide economic consideration of investment capital interact with the question of political structure, particularly with respect to public and private institutions? Again, you should be able to discover the answer, for what we are dealing with is the ability of public political institutions and economic institutions to be positioned so that economic productivity can be maximized in keeping with the other requirements of a national political society.

Is there an optimal relationship between the public, political structure and the economic structure? Drawing from terms that we already know of, there may be two answers to this question: there may be an optimal relationship when only the internal equilibrium of the political system is taken into account (cohesion,

myth, culture, etc.), and there may be a somewhat different relationship when the external equilibriums are also taken into account (see Figure 9–2). Let's say that again. When we consider only
the internal equilibrium, only the questions of social cohesion and
political culture are important in the matter of cooperation from
public and economic institutions. However, when the external
equilibrium comes into play, then the level of performance of public and economic institutions in coordinating their work becomes
at least partly a question of the requirements of the global or external equilibrium. The public-to-private structure equilibrium, in
other words, works much like the traditional post-Industrial Revolution equilibrium did on the ideologies of pure capitalism and
communism.

As we blend the comparison of elitist systems to the question
of neo-mercantilism, we should do so within a framework of the
new global economic competition. With this framework of thought,
and with the understanding that external economic equilibriums
will have some effect upon political structure, we should be able

FIGURE 9–2.
Traditional and modern influences on national political structures.

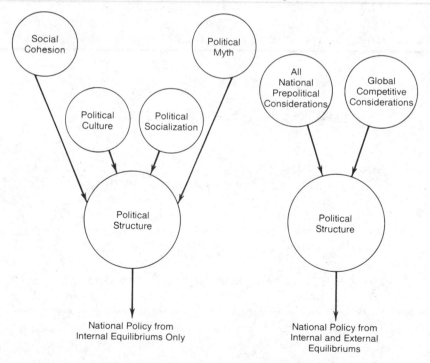

to examine the roles of internal and external equilibriums simultaneously and evaluate different political structures on the continuum of economic performance.

NEO-MERCANTILISM: PLURALISM VERSUS ELITISM

To complete our analysis of neo-mercantilism and the productivity question that now reflects the emerging world economic system, let us compare the abilities of pluralism and elitism to deal with the new national productivity challenge. We know that the fragmented structure of pluralism has traditionally dealt with economic productivity in a more nearly capitalist manner. Stated another way, the ideological commitment to capitalism, and the low social cohesion that logically accompanies a pluralist structure has accompanied modern liberal capitalism rather than some ideology that is closer to socialism. The best example of that marriage of structural pluralism and economic liberal capitalism, of course, is the United States.

From the other side of the continuum, the ideological commitment to greater state or government involvement within the economic sphere clearly dovetails better with elitist forms of government. Here, the obvious examples are the Western European nations and, perhaps, even the Japanese.

But now we have come to neo-mercantilism within a new form of international economic competition. We are talking about the ability of national public and economic systems, if and when they combine, to combine in such a way that the nation will survive global economic competition. There is no clear sense of which structure will do better in this competition, but elitists will argue that their improved integrated structures and history of public involvement with economic issues will serve them far better.

Pluralists, of course, respond to this elitist argument by saying that the less well-integrated nature of the pluralist governments and the looser linkage between public and economic institutions provide greater flexibility for the economic decision making of private economic institutions. The pluralists contend that the ability of individual companies to seize opportunities for new products and new markets without governmental approval or guidance makes the pluralist structure more competitive in the age of neo-mercantilism.

With regard to labor, the advocates of the elitist structure say that the linkage between economic management and the government includes the worker, and that workers cooperate better with productivity goals when labor is in a partnership with management and the government. European elitists cite the use of devices like *productivity bargaining*, where increases of wages are tied to labor acceptance of more productive work methods, as a beneficial example of labor-management-government cooperation. Elitists also cite income policies, where wages, and promises on costs of products to workers are linked in order to prevent national inflation, as examples of helpful neo-mercantilist cooperation.

Pluralists, on the other hand, feel that linkages among labor, management, and government should be approached more cautiously. They feel that the free market will encourage the improvement of productivity and that the market will also keep incomes within internationally competitive bounds. They are prepared to let the investment of capital flow according to less comprehensive policy, just as they are prepared to let the pyramid of national and international distribution move to whatever height that it naturally finds under the new world economic order.

Finally, with the issue of *labor retraining*, elitists believe that the political system has an obligation to ensure the updating of workers' skills. The government in elitist systems works with management and labor to make sure that technological innovations do not cost workers their jobs without training them for new employment. In fact, the Japanese government, which is a kind of hybrid elitist system based upon an exceptionally close relationship among management, labor, and government, has gone one step farther in the area of worker retraining. It ensures that workers who remove themselves from a job because they discover how their work can be done more effectively will be rewarded for their innovative ideas and retrained for another task at a higher level of responsibility and salary.

As a general statement, it is fair to say that the pluralist or liberal capitalist system has accepted economically integrative and cooperative ideas more slowly under the pressure of global economic integration. Its advocates feel that the free market of labor will encourage workers to train themselves and move on their own to where work may be more profitable for them. Although the United States supports a more substantial college and university system than does any other country, cooperation among government, industry, and labor on the updating of industrial skills and the training of young workers is generally considered to be the responsibility of individual corporations and the workers themselves.

CONCLUSION ━━━━━━━━━━━━━━━

With this chapter, we have expanded upon our comparison of the pluralist and elitist structures of government with the notion of external equilibriums within a changing and increasingly inter-dependent world. We have begun to discuss how the issue of political structure has emerged from an historical notion of either internal concensus or internal conflict and how it now faces challenges of a very different nature. No national political structure today is free of the pressure of the external economic equilibrium. What all political structures must do, more than ever before, is continue to provide for the continuing allegiance and identification of its own citizens while adopting to an increasingly singular world standard for governmental and economic performance.

Glossary

TERMS

consensus

separation of powers

interdependent world society

investment capital

multinational corporation (MNC)

global economy

distribution

productivity

neo-mercantilism

productivity bargaining

incomes policy

labor retraining

CHAPTER 10
THE GRAND EQUILIBRIUM

Although these examples of the economic challenges to pluralism and elitism are not exhaustive, they should give you a notion of how the pluralist-elitist contrast currently manifests itself within a changing world. You should also have a sense of the ways in which the two structural alternatives deal with modern problems that are fundamentally different from the internal problems that these systems have traditionally faced. We have moved, therefore, from descriptions of prepolitical conditions such as social cohesion, national culture, and national myths into a description of governmental institutions. We have also examined the internal patterns of interaction, and the interaction between governmental institutions and economic institutions.

Our evaluation of pluralism and elitism began with our discussion of the assumptions of cohesion and the adaptability of these governmental structures to the challenges of the modern world. We should now be prepared to analyze which structure is better able to do certain necessary tasks more fairly and more efficiently. These two broad categories of evaluation—fairness and efficiency—encompass the idea of economic performance, but they also include a full range of considerations concerning the desirability or undesirability of pluralism and elitism.

What exactly do we mean by fairness? We mean that the essential policy outcomes of a political system are perceived and adjudged to be just and equitable by at least a healthy majority of the population. No system, of course, will ever satisfy all citizens. But a system that is free from the wrenching tension that occurs when significant segments of its population are chronically disaffected can generally be called a fair system.

And what about efficiency? The question of efficiency is a somewhat more subtle matter. If we assume that government has little or no role in the managing of public affairs, then the efficiency question is not important. If, however, we acknowledge that modern government is concerned with a problem such as global economic competition, then the ability of a government to function efficiently becomes important. Economic productivity is not necessarily the core of public efficiency; rather, the ability of a nation to maintain its global competitiveness is so often at the core of national well-being that it will serve well as an example of efficiency.

FAIRNESS—THE PROMISE

Let us divide the analysis of both fairness and efficiency into separate categories. Let us look at what the promise of fairness is and then at the reality of fairness within pluralism, elitism, and totalitarian systems. It will be important to remember that each of these systems is falling under the influence of emerging external or world equilibriums at the same time that each remains under the influence of its own internal equilibrium. Understanding the potential strains that these influences may cause, let us turn first to the promise of pluralism.

Pluralism

The traditional view of the pluralist system describes a highly fragmented form of government. The pluralist model, remember, is the result of a feeling that government has comparatively little to do with a nation's well-being. In a country like the United States, there has always been a broad consensus over this notion, at least until the Great Depression of the 1930s. A limited government is still favored by most Americans today. The consensus on a limited governmental role and a procedural form of democracy has always promised a certain degree of political fairness. Elections have been open to all citizens. The franchise, that is, the right to vote, has been extended throughout the Republic, and other procedural guarantees have also promised democratic fairness.

As for representation within the government after the election has been held, there has always been an understanding within the American polity that various interests should have free, unlimited access to their government. The promise of such an idea was that if every interest were able to petition the government and interact with it, then the government would be fair to all. Using the original notion of voluntary associations, it would be clear in a pluralist nation like the United States that all groups could organize themselves and impress their views upon the government.

Yet many traditional writers, including David Truman and even Robert Dahl in his early writings, went farther in their praise of pluralism. They suggested that open access for all groups would assure that each would receive proper attention in the policy judgments of government. These writers argued that the distributional pyramid of pluralism would always tend to be fair. They argued, although Dahl changed his view in later works, that the representation of one's interest before a governmental access point that should exist for everyone's group, along with the openness of the electoral system, would almost guarantee fair value distribution. The history of the United States, with individuals being free to prosper economically and governmental leaders often emerging from humble backgrounds, seemed to confirm that promise within pluralism. Individuals could improve their condition, and insofar as the government played any role in that improvement, the door of a very open government seemed to be a sure guarantee of public fairness. Whether open access really resulted in fairness is something we will examine shortly, but, first, let us examine the concept of fairness within the promises of elitism and totalitarianism.

Elitism

Elitism, as we know, grows from a very different base of social cohesion and political culture than does pluralism. Elitism was founded upon a Platonic notion that a more or less naturally stable social order exists and that some people play more important public roles within that order than do others. In Europe, the social order was clearly more fixed and more involved in the awarding of individual opportunity than it was in America. Although that European order did not always bring forth its most meritorious citizens for its leaders, the idea of leadership itself was deeply a part of the European experience.

The promise of elitism today is still structurally akin to that traditional European notion of leadership. What has changed in the elitist promise is that modern political institutions, such as political parties, legislatures, the executive, and the bureaucracy, now generate leadership that, at least according to the promise, is free of class and family privileges. There is an acceptance of strong public institutions in Europe, and a promise that those who seek government office will take clear, result-oriented positions.

Hence, the promise of fairness within elitism today is the promise of a secure public order. A sense of stability exists, together with a less individualistic and less competitive set of social and economic values. Further, the promise of elitism holds that a nation will be administered within a more cohesive policy framework and that, therefore, it can face its problems in a more organized and comprehensive fashion. The elitist promise also stresses that the entire society is the concern of the government. It permits weaker groups to join more readily with other groups and political parties that affect public policy. The elitist system, therefore, encourages a reasonably high degree of political process, and it is far more procedurally open than is a totalitarian system.

Totalitarianism

It would be difficult to prove that any culture is cohesive enough and has such a level of universality or salience within its citizens' values that no democratic process at all would be necessary. Some observers argue that there are "national cultures" that are more likely to have a totalitarian government than are other cultures. Yet it is probably more accurate to say that most totalitarian governments have imposed themselves upon their citizenry.

What is the promise of totalitarianism? Although the stories of imprisonment without trial, deportation, torture, and execution are horrifying realities, they are the *results* of totalitarianism, *not its essence*. The essence of totalitarianism involves government centrality and singularity, a feeling that the oneness in the purpose and structure of the institutions of a totalitarian state, gives the citizenry the public policies it requires. The promise of totalitarianism holds that the government already knows what the appropriate policies are for that system and how these policies should be implemented. To be sure, there is always some pulling and hauling within any political system. Even within the Soviet Union, which is still a relatively totalitarian state, a certain degree of public policy competition exists among the military, the bureaucracy, the intelligentsia, the technocratic elite, and even different elements within the Communist party. The differences among these groups, however, is severely minimized because the overwhelming influence over governmental orthodoxy that stems from one political party and one clear strain of political ideology does not permit vastly differing views.

The promise of totalitarianism is usually very clear within each system. The promise of communism is that industrial and other wage distributions will be appropriately addressed from a Marxist perspective. The totalitarianism of the German fascist state under Adolf Hitler held that the national destiny of a supposedly mistreated Germany was to be fulfilled. In all totalitarian systems, some dominating theme prescribes what will be the unity of public policy.

In most instances, the promise of totalitarian politics includes an economic promise. Usually the promise says that the pyramid of distribution with which we began our model will achieve a particular height and remain constant. Even German fascism assured the continuation of capitalism, guaranteeing a continuation of private wealth and, in effect, a high pyramid of distribution. The cost to democratic process, again, is certainly high within a totalitarian system, but the promise of totalitarianism is that a singular mode of doing things permits virtually every effort to be put into the fulfillment of the totalitarian result. Little effort is spent in discussion over the method used to achieve that result, and little is done to determine whether that result reflects the desires of the citizenry.

Although our examination of the promises of pluralism, elitism, and totalitarianism has been brief, the fundamental linkages among prepolitical considerations, political structures, and the promise of each political mode should now be clear to you. With the development of our earlier discussion of the valuational or pyramid height question, we should now concentrate on the outcome of each political system. We know that these outcomes are what a political citizenry argue over through the institutions of its political structure.

FAIRNESS—THE ACTUALITY

Pluralism

You should now be able to see the patterns of policy preferences of a people as they impact upon the governmental structure (see Figure 10-1). All governments, although by a variety of different means, create public policy and present it to a people who both

FIGURE 10-1.
Contemporary equilibrium of political cohesion and structure.

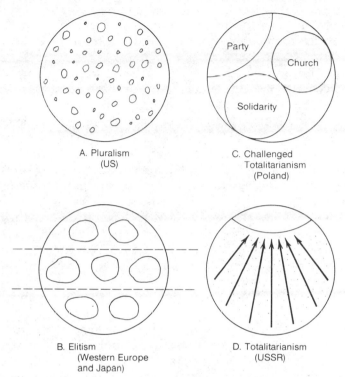

A. Pluralism
(US)

C. Challenged
Totalitarianism
(Poland)

B. Elitism
(Western Europe
and Japan)

D. Totalitarianism
(USSR)

live with and react to that policy. The degree to which a citizenry may participate in the creation of policy and respond to it can vary a great deal. Even in a totalitarian system, leadership cannot completely ignore a citizenry that is discontented over a long period of time. No government can ignore a citizenry that is not eating well or is suffering declining standards in housing, job opportunities, and the like.

As we turn from an examination of promise to actuality, let us first consider a somewhat secondary but nonetheless important point. The positions of individual nation-states along the spectrum of pluralism, elitism, and totalitarianism are not permanent. Consider, for example, the extent of the unrest in Poland in recent years. Why has the performance and structure of the Polish government been brought into question?

The answer is complex but, at a structural level, Poland is clearly a more pluralistic nation than what its totalitarian government may wish it to be. The Catholic Church has always possessed a separate identity within Poland, not at all a part of Communist party singularity. More recently, the church has been joined by *Solidarity*, an independent labor union, that, currently, has been driven underground and is still under attack from the Polish government.

The prepolitical considerations of such a nation as Poland, which has incidentally known democratic process in its past, also accounts for the difficulty of maintaining the totalitarian state. The outcome of the Polish confrontation between its workers and government may not occur for some time. It is clear, however, that throughout Eastern Europe, and even within the Soviet Union, strong internal, if not also external, equilibrium pressures are straining to pull these nations' governments from totalitarianism. The internal pressures of a pluralistic culture, and the external pressures of serious economic difficulties have affected all the Eastern European states. The increasing pressure of both equilibriums is the principal reason that the position of nation-states or the pluralist-elitist-totalitarian continuum is not permanent.

The promise of pluralism, we remember, has always included procedural openness, representative balance, and ultimately, the continuation of ethnic, regional, and religious pluralism as a condition of a free society. The method of pluralism's attempt to fulfill its promise was based upon a wide separation of institutions and a dispersion of the powers of government. The pluralist government was designed to have many access points, and to promise all citizens the right to be heard by government. In the United States, particularly, the plan fit the design of its Founding Fathers, but it also fit the design of the nation's basic social cohesion and political culture. We can now ask how well that promise has been fulfilled.

Without question, the record of the American pluralist system, at least until the years before the crest of the Vietnam war period, was an enviable one. The American economy, at the close of World War II, made up fully one half of the gross domestic product of the entire world. Its technological lead in virtually every scientific field went unchallenged, while individual Americans prospered as no people in the world ever had before. American productivity provided for an enormous variety of "creature comforts," such as the automobile, television, reliable telephone service, and other "luxuries" that only a few years earlier were not available to large segments of the population. Further, the eradication of many childhood diseases was attributed to the extraordinary efforts of medical research. Illiteracy was almost completely overcome, and nearly one of every two postsecondary students entered at least some form of higher education.

What political and economic jurisdictions were responsible this level of success? The economic argument that "200 million decision makers" could make the best economic judgments supported the idea of a highly restrained governmental role in business and industry that the American citizenry typically held. Perhaps also important to many was the "breadth" of America's economic success that permitted many American citizens to be concerned with the more associative or bonding values within society. The arts flourished as people had leisure time to enjoy them, and citizens of all backgrounds engaged in such political activities as the civil rights movement and the war on poverty of the 1960s to redress what they considered to be the remaining injustices of the American pluralist system.

The Radical Critique

Inevitably, however, there were criticisms of the American pluralist system that went beyond the specifics of particular injustices. The most fundamental criticisms of the American pluralist system fell into two categories, one stemming from a reformist point of view and the other from a more radical point of view. The radical critique, voiced by such writers as the late C. Wright Mills, stated that the procedural openness of the United States government was fundamentally a false openness.[1] This view charged that the U.S. government was in fact dominated by a small, but extremely powerful and closely knit group of individuals. In The Power Elite, Mills argued that this ruling clique overwhelmingly attended the prestigious "prep" schools and colleges for their education and then elevated themselves, through a closed network of family connections, into the upper reaches of American society. The key to Mills's notion is that the linkages within the American corporate world continue within each generation and that a military-industrial complex, made up of the chief executives of American corporations and the nation's top military leaders, has kept the country in a state of perceived insecurity over America's military safety. They have done this, Mills charged, to maintain high profits for the armaments industry, and also to keep a tight reign on what is argued to be a "threatened" country.

This view, which essentially argues that corporate and military dominance in the political system makes government institutions relatively unimportant, is, again, a radical one. Mills did not claim that there was one grand conspiracy that made his criticisms valid, yet, in fact, there is more conspiracy within his perspective than he wanted to admit. In any event, only a few observers of the American governmental system accept Mills's view at face value.

The Moderate Critique

There is another and much less radical and conspiratorial view of American pluralism that is still somewhat critical of the overall fairness of the political system. This perspective is taken by such writers as Grant McConnell,[2] Theodore Lowi,[3] as well as others. They argue that although conspiracy or a closed, political network of individuals do not consciously dominate the American political system, the everyday impact of certain powerful interest groups upon pluralist access points is far greater than the impact of less powerful groups. Remember our discussion of the ongoing movement of policy from one result orientation to another in the "democracy as process" model? We concluded that the principal elements of political power were money and numbers of people, with one balancing the other in the argument over the height of the pyramid of distribution. Both McConnell and Lowi concede that in the general arguments over distribution that may occur, numbers tend to balance power and to keep the pyramid at a moderate height. But these authors also point out that the very nature of a fragmented pluralist political structure is that the general questions concerning the pyramid's height are only seldom asked. To repeat, although the height of the pyramid of distribution is supposedly subject to a good deal of direct influence, critics argue that much of what happens in government is transacted at those singular, minute access points where only a few groups have power. As a result, pluralism never addresses the pyramid by itself as a central political question.

These advocates argue that by having no general policy as such, the height of the pyramid is higher than it normally would be because the *individual* efforts of wealthy and more powerful groups are stronger than the efforts of weaker groups. The tax loophole, the favorable inclusion in a trade protection bill, or the favorable specific ruling from an agency like the Interstate Commerce Commission are the real decisions of government. These decisions, according to McConnell, Lowi, and others, are made in a piecemeal fashion in favor of the more powerful interests. Thus, although it is accomplished little by little, these critics argue that decisions are continuously being made that, in sum, make the pyramid stand taller than it would if the entire populace addressed the question of the pyramid's height as a general issue.

Remember again that we are dealing with a government that is highly fragmented and open to day-to-day decisions and rulings. The height of the pyramid is an aggregate, that is, something made up of a collection of small pieces. We should recall here what it was that John Locke feared as he looked at the emerging democratic legislature, and what James Madison feared in his *Federalist #10*: that allowing the citizenry to aggregate into large groupings would lead to very different policies then when the citizens and the governmental structure were broken up into small pieces. As Mc-Connell and Lowi would argue, the very "breaking up" that Madison advocated has been very helpful to those who want a tall pyramid. These groups are able to gain access to the government for their individual interests. In short, the promise of open procedure under pluralism and the actuality of a pluralist government that is influenced in different ways by different interests may vary considerably. Based within both its culture and its history upon the idea of a substantial procedural openness, pluralism may in fact be a facilitator of the highly staggered or 10-to-1 valuational pattern of economic reward as opposed to the 2-to-1 pattern.

From a Pyramid to a Diamond

In closing this review of the actuality of pluralism, let us consider a circumstance that reflects very clearly upon where pluralism rests today. In our discussion of valuation, we have used the pyramid to illustrate the distribution of rewards in political societies. Certainly, we were justified in using that model historically because, throughout history, the less wealthy citizens have outnumbered the wealthy and a pyramid was an appropriate symbolic representation of society's distribution. In recent years, however, something has begun to happen to that pyramid, and it is something that, at least from the perspective of many, alters the very shape of the pyramid for the first time in history. What we suggest is that in America, although perhaps also in a smaller way in Western Europe and Japan, the shape of the pyramid is changing to something that is more similiar to a diamond (see Figure 10–2).

This diamond configuration signifies that there is a group of Americans who, for reasons that are still debated, seem to be locked

FIGURE 10–2.
Modern income distribution: From pyramid to diamond.

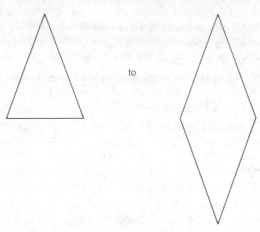

quite firmly at or near the bottom of the economic distribution. Some of these citizens are aged or infirm, and some are untrained for the kind of work that a modern, increasingly technological, economy requires. Others, however, are simply members of the working class who are having economic difficulties. What is unusual, by historical standards, is that this bottom group now clearly makes up a *minority* of the population. The middle class outnumbers the lower class for the first time in history.

Of course, when considering political power and pluralist access, the working class has always lacked money and political organization. Now, however, it also lacks the substantial numbers that it once possessed. As a result, the citizens at the lower level have far less influence upon the political system than when the distributional pyramid was shaped more like a pyramid. Hence, the economic result of the changing shape of the distributional pyramid is that the upper echelons of income are again increasing their share of the common wealth. Further, a large and powerful middle class is now withdrawing its support from a number of liberal capitalism's compromises that had typically been the core of liberal capitalism within our ideological equilibrium. Indeed, the middle class seems to be withdrawing its support from such issues as industrial and trade labor unions, governmentally encouraged safety and health regulations, and even the Keynesian countercyclical government investment programs that had typified liberal capitalism's separation from pure capitalism. The arrangement of numbers, money, and organization—the three principal elements of

FIGURE 10–3.
Ideological flow of policy with diamond distribution.

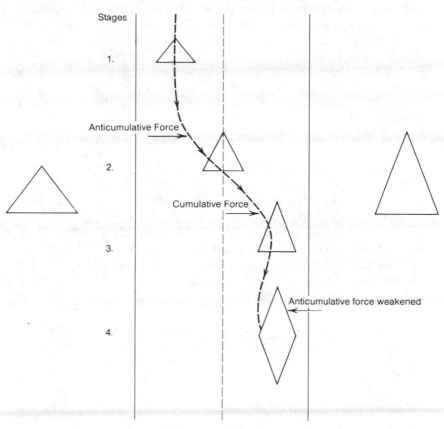

political power—exist within the pluralist diamond today in a way that might return public policy to a more conservative, and perhaps more purely capitalistic, political ideology (see Figure 10–3).

FAIRNESS—THE ACTUALITY ━━━━━━

Elitism

Whether the actuality of pluralism has lived up to its promise is something that is left for you to decide. We need now to look to the actuality of elitism, for it too may have developed into something very different from what it promised some time ago. Whether that promise has been realized or not is, again, something which you should decide. Yet, clearly, the actuality of elitism, particularly as it is represented in the traditional West European governments, is far different from what it was in the immediate aftermath of industrialization.

The sometimes painful birth of democratic political institutions on the European continent has altered European elitism considerably. We use the term "painful birth" because the continental Europeans, in contrast to the English, were slower to introduce the democratic processes that we spoke of earlier in the model. As we know, the notions of land and aristocracy, although holdovers from an ancient feudal order, maintained a level of political power for some time. Voting, political parties, regular elections, and the like only sporadically entered upon the European political stage after the period of industrialization, and even then, the principal families of Europe still largely dominated the far more class-oriented politics of these nations. It was not until the growth of both the middle-class "liberal" parties and the socialist-dominated labor parties (later in the century) that the old order was effectively challenged. Even today, the idea of social class means far more in Europe than it does in the United States.

While many reformist or Socialist movements, like Bernard Shaw's Fabians, had been the creation of people of distinction in the nineteenth century, today's political leadership within Europe's left-of-center parties is more in the hands of politicians of common origin. Important social mobility tenets such as entrance into higher education, or the "third level," are now almost universally open to all capable citizens. Jim Callaghan, the most recent English Labor prime minister, and French prime minister François Mitterand, are from other than prominent families. And even recent U.S. presidents such as Lyndon Johnson, Jimmy Carter, and Ronald Reagan are from still more humble origins. School systems throughout Europe have largely dispensed with what the English called the "11+" exam that coldly decided the academic fate of Europe's youngsters and *tracked* them into either precollege or a technical educational path.

Let us also consider the distribution of wealth within the various European systems. Although the history of European elitism would suggest that the European pyramid of distribution should be quite tall, the actuality of European distributions has in fact changed substantially. Why has an "elitist" system moderated its distributional pyramid so greatly? Or why has a system that we still call elitist dealt so extensively with industrial retraining, preventive health, adult education, and other advanced kinds of policies? The reason is quite clear, for if there was a "class" system within Europe that afforded privilege to those of family name and stature, so too there was an increasingly conscious class within Europe that chafed at its position at the lower rungs of the ladder.

The politics of class, which of course contrasted sharply to America's traditionally individualistic and interest group politics, may have often created nonconsensual politics. Such a form of politics often created conflict between citizens at opposite points on the pyramid. Also, intense result-oriented political pressure pitted industrial labor and some portions of the middle class against those who rested on their aristocratic privileges as well as against the new industrial entrepreneurs. These struggles were sometimes bloody, the years 1830, 1848, and 1871 marking significant confrontations of European class against class. Yet, when the calmer moments after the European struggles came, it was clear that two changes had occurred. First, the position of the lower, working classes and their allies had developed a true social "solidarity," and this evolving solidarity was increasingly organized politically. Second, the question of valuation and distribution itself became very much a part of the general, nonfragmented dialogue of the elitist governments in contrast to the specifically interest-oriented politics of the United States. Although different countries within Europe have very different distributions, some steeper than the United States and some less steep, there is no question that the European governments were forced to greatly modify distributions throughout the nineteenth century. During the same period, private economic activity accounted for fewer distributional arrangements.

Otto von Bismarck, for example, the late-nineteenth-century chancellor of Germany, was without question an autocratic and a ruthless leader, but he found it necessary to respond to pressure from an active German labor movement. He did so by establishing an extensive system of aid for the unemployed, the elderly, and the handicapped that in many ways foretold modern welfare programs. Certainly, the traditional political culture of the Germans, with its long history of charitable societies that had in turn been established as auxiliaries of the workers' guilds, served as helpful underpinnings for these generous policies.

As elections were slowly accepted in Europe, they almost immediately incorporated distribution-oriented issues. This, again, differed from the individualistic candidacies and the weak party

TABLE 10-1.
Distribution of Household Income, by Percentile Groups of Households.

	Year	Lowest 20%	Second Quintile	Third Quintile	Fourth Quintile	Highest 20%	Highest 10%
UNITED STATES	1972	4.5%	10.7%	17.3%	24.7%	42.8%	26.6%
FEDERAL REPUBLIC OF GERMANY	1973	6.5	10.3	15.0	22.0	46.2	30.3
THE NETHERLANDS	1975	8.5	13.6	17.8	23.0	37.1	22.5
FRANCE	1970	4.3	9.8	16.3	22.7	46.9	30.4
UNITED KINGDOM	1977–78	7.4	11.7	17.0	24.7	39.5	23.3

SOURCE: *World Development Report*, The World Bank, New York, August 1981, p. 183.

orientations of American elections. Although the legitimacy and the authority of many governments (Napoleon III in France and the Hapsburgs in Austria-Hungary, for example) were suspect for their heavy result orientation toward the privileged, these governments eventually began to deal with the issue of the distributional pyramid in a more modern sense. They learned to address the distributional issue in ways that permitted virtually all political groupings to have electoral and representational input in government policy.

Again, it is clear that the European pyramids of distribution are not nearly as "elitist" or as tall as they once were (see Table 10–1). It should be clear that the structure of a coordinated and integrated government, together with the existence of mildly ideological political parties, legislatures, and executives, have turned a structural elitism into a set of public policies that, in many instances, produces a more moderate pyramid than once was thought possible. Clearly, the strong internal social cohesion of European elitism has played a role in the forming of more cohesive structures of government. Further, internal cohesion has served as an effective countercumulative force in the evolution of public policy within elitist systems.

PLURALIST EFFICIENCY: PROMISE AND ACTUALITY

Now let us proceed to the question of efficiency, one that is very different from the question of fairness. Most citizens want government to be both fair and efficient. Although the question of fairness varies among nations, it has constantly evolved to a point at which certain procedural and result-oriented protections are increasingly recognized as fundamental to human freedom and human rights. Many nation-states still violate these rights, but international awareness of such violations and the public condemnation of such outrages as torture, imprisonment and exile are growing. The standard of having at least some degree of democratic process within all governments is increasingly gaining recognition if not full acceptance.

The question of efficiency, however, is a very different matter because there is little agreement over the question of what should constitute the business of government. Without question, the citizens of all nations have a right to have their public monies, almost invariably raised through taxes, spent wisely. The issue remains, however, regarding how these monies are to be spent. The positions of pluralist and elitist nations on this and other issues differ dramatically. Reaching back into their political histories and cultures, different nations have different views of what legitimately exists within the public sphere of consideration as opposed to what exists within the private sphere. As we have said, America's history and political culture did not permit the government to grow into a major force until the reaction to the Great Depression of the 1930s. The huge American frontier, with its abundant land, the benefits of extraordinary material resources, and the impetus of new and eager immigrants who wished to fulfill their dreams, made private initiative appear sufficient for anything the nation wished to do. In times of war, of course, the government often was allowed to serve as an organizer of public concerns. It was permitted to impress young men into the military and to create industrial productivity. Following times of conflict, however, the American culture dictated the return of the governments to its original, limited boundaries.

What, then, was the promise of efficiency based upon within the American pluralist system? What was it that held together a fragmented federal government with limited powers that would work best for the American people? The answer, again, lies deep within the American political culture, for the efficiency of the American system was always believed to be locked within the doctrine of private initiative working through enterprising economic institutions. The role of the government was restricted in its relationships to those institutions, but as the modern age turned a wiry, small-town America into a brawny, industrial nation, it may have become more difficult for the ethic and the institutions that it fostered to remain the same. The rules of the private system of productivity had said that corporations were to remain competitive. They were to maintain low prices and constantly search for new and effective production techniques while keeping the ranks of their own organizations lean and vibrant. These rules were upheld by the American internal equilibrium of private economic activity and, in later years, the external equilibrium would insist that productivity remain high for *foreign competition* as well.

Within this more competitive economic world, and under the influence of the external equilibrium of foreign structural organization and economic competition, what has been the actuality of the American pluralist promise? There is no question that through World War II and even through the 1950s and early 1960s, the worldwide economic dominance of the United States seemed to speak for American political efficiency. Since then, however, there has been a dramatic slippage in the American world economic position. By 1982, the 50 percent of the global domestic product that the United States claimed after the war had slipped to only 25 percent. American productivity increases that had averaged 3 percent per year between 1946 and 1968 fell to 2 percent between 1968 and 1973, 1 percent between 1973 and 1978, and then to zero from 1978 to 1983. Also, European Economic Community's (EEC) production, which had been only one fourth that of the United States in the six-member Community of 1958, equaled the American output when the EEC had grown to ten members in 1981.[4] Finally, these events occurrred when U.S. dependence on the world economy was growing and U.S. foreign trade was expanding from 10 percent of total GNP in 1970 to 20 percent in 1980.

Although the causes of these circumstances are still subject to debate, there is no question but that the lag in American productivity, the oftentimes higher rates of inflation, and the high unemployment of recent years has caused concern over the American economic future. Certainly, the excessive military burden that the United States carries for the Western world has had a part in the American decline. The fact that the United States spends approximately 5.1 percent of its gross domestic product on military expenses while Japan, now a major economic competitor, only spends .9 percent, clearly has an effect on American economic competitiveness.

Aside from such variables, however, there are many who now claim that the very structure of the American government must share the blame for the recent decline. What is the argument of those who relate America's recent economic difficulties to its political structure? Those who make this "structural" argument claim

two points, one pertaining to economics and the other to the relationship of economics to the political system. The first, the economic point, notes that throughout the history of American
enterprise there has been a tendency toward what Adam Smith
warned about so vigorously in his *Wealth of Nations*. The corporate
tendency to combine and merge with competitors rather than to
compete as vigorously as free enterprise would dictate has, for
better or worse, existed within American industry for some time.
In the United States, the Sherman Antitrust Act was passed in
1890, and the Clayton Act and Federal Trade Commission Act were
passed in 1914. These and other legislative efforts attempted to
prevent or slow down the tendency of large corporations to in some
way come to understandings with competitors about markets and
therefore not compete as vigorously as they should. What has caused
this lack of incentive to compete? Much of the problem lies in the
need for some degree of security or permanence in employment.
Perhaps there are a few of us who wish to be competitive all the
time. Perhaps only a few would risk the poker game where you
might lose all you have saved with one deal of the cards. The
internal equilibrium, even of an individualistic America, seems to
have never permitted absolutely free enterprise to ensure pure competition (see Figure 10–4).

But what else could cause a pluralistic America's economic slowdown? Why has the American dominance of the global economy
eroded so significantly in the last years? Some would refer to a
cause that goes beyond the lack of economic competition. Some
would suggest that we need to examine the relationship of the
public sector or the government as a whole to the economic sector.
They argue that if world economic competition is more demanding
than it once was, and if the competitive positions of national econ-

FIGURE 10–4.
The world economy

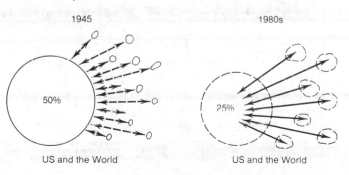

US and the World   US and the World

omies are now more vulnerable to other national economies and to the investment decisions of the multinational corporations, the attractiveness of investment of any national economic system will be determined by the production arrangements of that system. Production arrangements will be important in determining how modern and efficient a nation's economic plant will be. Ultimately, they will determine how well a nation is competing in the world market for the sale of goods and services by indicating such standards as the *balance of payments* between the purchases and sales among nations.

What can a national pluralistic government like that of the United States do about the current challenge to its competitive position? There are many responses, of course, but some citizens, including prominent economists, have begun to argue in the same vein as *The Report on Manufactures*, which Alexander Hamilton wrote for President Washington. They advocate what is called an "industrial policy,"[5] that is, an acceptance of the idea of neo-mercantilism and an acceptance of the higher degree of structural cohesion that neo-mercantilism requires.

To be sure, industrial policy is an idea that Americans may take some time becoming accustomed to. It may also take time for the American political structure to adopt, for industrial policy is a full-blown economic policy, a broad design that makes a number of difficult decisions concerning economic investment and productivity. An industrial policy, for example, decides what industries are capable of long-term competition in world markets and it also decides which industries, because they are not competitive, should be abandoned. An industrial policy might also decide where monies are to be spent for research and the development of new products, and it may even decide where an outright subsidy for sectors of the economy that are in trouble should go.

Has America ever done anything like this? Except for the very early years of the Republic and during periods of wartime, it has not. More important, perhaps, we should ask whether America has the kind of political institutions that would be able to plan and carry through a policy of this kind. For those who believe that the continuation of exclusively private planning, along with the structual denial of majoritarian, comprehensive governmental guidance is still of benefit to the country, the traditional model of governmental pluralism is still preferred. Yet, for those who believe that the internal equilibriums of America were never quite as competitive and economically oriented as some traditionally argued, as well as for those who believe that external, global equilibriums now require greater cooperation among management, labor, and government, the actuality of the American economic performance over the last years has been a sign of the need for change. Such advocates now argue that the institutional separations of power under the American political structure, along with the lack of allegiance to party or institutional leadership on the part of office-holders, prevents necessary public attention to the question of economic productivity. We know that America, and to a great extent the entire pluralist model, has traditionally held that it is better to have difficult problems solved piecemeal than it is to risk comprehensive decisions that may, if decided wrongly, harm the entire nation. But those who are displeased with the recent performance of the American pluralist system would tend to agree with the noted political scientist and biographer James MacGregor Burns that the greatest threat to nonmajoritarian, pluralist democracy is not the making of a mistake, but the institutionally encouraged deadlock over comprehensive public policy.[6]

HEGEL VERSUS LOCKE

Before we look briefly to the promise and actuality of elitism, pause for a moment and reflect upon one theoretical consideration that may shed additional light on the contrast between elitism and pluralism. We have discussed the contrast between the thinking of Plato and Aristotle who had very different visions of the natural political order nearly 2,500 years ago. Plato, as we said, held society to be deeply interrelated, with a natural leadership directing the society from the position of a "philosopher king." Aristotle, on the other hand, saw the natural fabric of society as being somewhat looser, with people having a more distant natural relationship to each other and political leadership thus being selected more openly and competitively.

With the complexity of modern society, differences in the theoretical vision of the human polity have changed substantially, although linkages to the thoughts of Plato and Aristotle still exist. We discussed the work of Hegel earlier when we introduced the dialect of thesis, antithesis, and synthesis. We discussed the work of John Locke as well when we spoke of the concept of property as it emerged as part of the modern age. Hegel and Locke were responsible for important considerations other than the dialectic and property. One consideration to review now is the difference between what is called the *utilitarian* view of society and the view of society that stresses the importance of what Hegel called *consciousness*.

Utilitarianism versus Consciousness

What is the utilitarian view of society? It is a philosophy that covers many matters, but as a method of understanding, it is a perspective that urges each element of the society to seek its own good because the sum of all individual "goods" will reflect the general good.

Of course, utilitarianism, like so many other philosophies, is either bad or good, depending upon how different viewers perceive it. However, utilitarianism contrasts very sharply to the thinking of Hegel. What you should know about the Hegelian dialectic of thesis, antithesis, and synthesis is that each of the new stages of history, that is, each of the new syntheses of the old and new way of looking at things, is supposed to bring a new level of consciousness or awareness of what the world is all about. In a somewhat simplistic but accurate fashion, Hegel suggested that humankind became smarter about itself and the surrounding world at the same time that it improved its real world condition.

Now, can you identify the key difference between the philosophies of Locke and Hegel? Locke and utilitarianism argue that if all the pieces of a whole do what is right, the whole or the entirety of those pieces will fall together in a natural way, and without much thought about the whole. Hegel, on the other hand, argues that within any situation, if the entirety of anything is to be right, the whole must be thought of consciously, and directly as a whole.

Once again, you must decide which of these philosophies appeals to you more. Is it necessary for you to think of the whole to achieve a sense of order, or do you think about each part? You are not alone in your consideration of this issue. Many have pondered the issue and argued vigorously over it. You should, however, focus on the differences between the Lockean and the Hegelian view as being a reflection of how people think about a wide range of important public concerns.

In the valuational question, for example, supporters of the market method of valuation argue that if markets are kept free and prices are allowed to rise and fall as supplies and demands of products fluctuate, then the fairness of those prices should not be questioned. The rationalistic view, as we know, believes that it is necessary to look at the skill, risk, and training that goes into a product or a service and think consciously about what constitutes a fair price or wage.

Clearly the Lockean method of thinking, that is, the utilitarian view, would argue that if all interest groups are free to influence and if each part of the government serves its interest well, then the whole of governmental policy must be for the best. You should recognize, of course, that this utilitarian way of thinking about things corresponds very closely to the political justification for pluralism.

What, then, of the other side? You should also understand that the Hegelian method of thinking, that is, the view of consciousness, is generally the method of elitism. It argues that the conscious formation of comprehensive and deliberate policy is the best way to deal with public matters. In short, the contrast in the justifications and specifications of pluralism and elitism is very much a part of how we actually think about the problem. In the sense of preferences of thinking styles themselves, how do we like to consider the problems of government? In the final chapter, we will add this consideration to our discussion of how we think about politics. However, let us first complete our review of pluralism and elitism.

ELITIST EFFICIENCY—PROMISE AND ACTUALITY

With this review of the promise and actuality of the efficiency of pluralism, we can turn to the promise and actuality of efficiency within elitism. When George Washington warned his countrymen to beware of foreign entanglements, it was a statement that reflected a view of Europe that many Americans still hold today. The European continent has seen the intrigues of shifting national alliances and the inevitable stumbling into war that often accompanied national competition. The geographical proximity of the nations themselves contributed to these tensions, of course. More important, the promise of leadership that elitism made has often meant a willingness on the part of aristocratic government to use its "lesser" citizens as pawns in selfish wars. In recent years, however, the nations of Europe have lived very differently, the European Economic Community's political emergence from the Common Market virtually assuring the end of national wars within the Western European region. The possibility of Germany going to war with

France, for example, as it did three times within 70 years (1870, 1914, 1939) is now very remote.

The economic promises of the European political culture kept Europe from a full acceptance of highly individualistic and capitalistic notions of wealth creation. Europeans, perhaps sooner than Americans, recognized that individuals and economic units like giant corporations were not fully competitive nor did corporate managers wish them to be fully competitive. The Europeans long ago embraced the idea of the *cartel*, a collection of producers that wished to share markets and technology, and generally, cooperate more than compete. The Europeans have traditionally embraced these cartels with governmental assistance as well as with governmental protection from harsh internal and foreign competition.

The typical European business was in great part an instrument of national policy, and the relative European absence of vast resources, unlimited land, as well as the luxury of secure borders further encouraged each European political system to involve itself in the promotion of economic productivity. In areas such as energy, transportation, and communication, these policies led to moderate socialism with government ownership, or at least to government involvement, ensuring the operation of important businesses in ways that were consistent with public policy. We use the phrase "moderate socialism" because the governmental role within Europe that responded to the demands of newly politicized workers was never a full socialistic role. Governmental involvement, aside from the protections of workers, was in great part a response to the intensity of international economic competition. It was, in a sense, a continuation of preindustrial mercantile policies as they existed throughout the industrial period. Although it would be a slight exaggeration to say that European nations were dealing with international equilibriums of competition and structure from an early time, these countries did deal with a very competitive international environment, which, in turn, fostered a more cooperative set of internal governmental and economic policies. To put it another way, while the pluralistic Americans were able to (1) develop their vast land and resources, (2) rely very little on foreign trade, and (3) have little fear of foreign economic or military intrusion, the Europeans, from an early time, needed to (1) coordinate public policy with far less bountiful land and resources, (2) engage in vigorous and favorable foreign trade, and (3) be wary of the potential military danger from close neighbors.

Politically, the level of coordination that the European nations required naturally dovetailed with the European style of government. Parliamentary governments are geared to handle major comprehensive decisions, and they believe in acting in anticipation of problems, rather than reacting to problems once they have occurred. The European elitist governments embrace modern problems in as comprehensive a way as possible, as does the other principal parliamentary, elitist government in Japan.

The Japanese government also organizes its institutions in a far more cooperative manner, and indeed, some observers argue that Japan, or *Japan Incorporated* as it is sometimes called, engages in a cooperative political-economic enterprise that is more vigorous in research, product development, and trade policy than any other industrial country.

As we close our discussion of the actuality of elitist efficiency, what can we conclude about the elitist model's ability to guide its government and citizenry through the difficult problems of adapting to an emerging economic globalism? Although there is some variance among the different European nations, the overall record for the Europeans since World War II has been quite good. Although the original successes, as some have suggested, may well have been aided by both American postwar generosity and the ability to begin again with the most modern of industrial machinery after the war, there is more to the success than these factors can account for. Most of the European states, as well as the Japanese, have had greater increases in productivity, smaller levels of inflation, and lower unemployment levels during the post–World War II years than has the pluralist United States. Again, whether the effectiveness of the European and Japanese systems can be ascribed to a closer "fit" of internal and external equilibriums with their structure of government is something that reasonable people can debate. What does seem clear is that two regions on the globe that are largely deficient of a basic resource such as oil and have had a history of fierce mercantile and even military competition, have now settled into a pattern of considerable prosperity and more secure internal peace. Ironically, the only military conflict that now threatens the formerly warring nations of Europe comes from the larger conflict that simmers between a totalitarian nation, the Soviet Union, and a pluralist nation, the United States. The economic efforts of the Soviet Union and the United States have been less successful in recent years than those of the Europeans and Japanese.

We do not suggest that the elitist model has clearly or suddenly risen above other models in its ability to deal with modern problems. We do suggest, however, that the kind of analysis that embraces the study of the structure of public institutions, along with the level of cooperation between public and private economic co-operation, is the analysis that will answer the difficult questions surrounding how best to arrange national economic productivity. Modern times have brought changes to citizens' expectations about their government just as they have brought changes to citizens' expectations about medical care, communications, and the comforts of everyday life. The structures of yesterday are rarely sufficient for the challenges of tomorrow.

THE TOTALITARIAN CASE

Before we leave the questions of fairness and efficiency, we need to examine briefly the promises and the "long-term" actualities of totalitarian systems. We use the phrase "long term" because several totalitarian systems have brought their political doctrines to their nations with such intensity that war with that country's neighbors was almost inevitable within a short time after that government came into power. The experience of Hitler in Germany and Mussolini in Italy are examples of how the dictatorial compression of governmental structure into a singular design and purpose can lead to the war that many foresaw as inevitable by 1939. Whether you believe that the Soviet Union has been restrained from war since 1945 because of the overwhelming Western strength that it has faced, or because the Soviet Union has genuinely sought peace, the U.S.S.R. is nevertheless a totalitarian state that has existed long enough to permit a close look at her governing patterns. Yet the record of the Soviet Union is not a happy one. It is clear that within the Soviet Union, as well as within the Eastern European bloc of Soviet influence, a "new class" of government bureaucrats has begun to push the pyramid of distribution far above what Karl Marx envisioned for a communist state.[7] Also, the economic performance, that is, the productivity of the Soviet Union has never fulfilled its promise. Each year in the Soviet Union, agricultural quotas are unfulfilled as large communal farms fail to bring to the market all of what is harvested in the fields. Finally, the availability of consumer products continues to lag behind consumer demands, although the record in this area has improved slightly in recent years.

It is clear that if one were to examine internal equilibriums, the largely individualistic Soviets, or at least the European Russians who live west of the Urals and north of the Caucusus, have never responded well to the largely collectivist institutions and incentives that dominate Soviet productivity. The Stakhanovite ideal that we spoke of earlier is not something to which all Soviets respond. Most prefer a bountiful economic reward for the economic productivity that they contribute. Externally, the Soviet Union is finding that the absence of a healthy interaction among government institutions, as well as between governmental and economic sectors, leaves the Soviet economy well out of serious global economic competition. With the exception of one simple, well-made farm tractor that sells rather well in world markets, the Soviet Union competes in almost no significant world product areas. Indeed, to satisfy even its minimal production goals the Societ Union has had to turn to the West where either purchases on the open market or the benefits of a fair amount of industrial spying bring them needed technology.

Concerning pluralism, we questioned whether the institutions of economic productivity and the realities of public policy were too fragmented to create comprehensive economic policy. Innovation has suffered throughout the Soviet Union as a result of the dominating influences of the Communist party upon governmental bureaucracies, the educational system, the scientific community, and the bureaucratized military. The most common reaction to the word "totalitarian" conjures images of prison, torture, exile, and the like, and certain totalitarian systems, such as those within Latin America, still often fulfill that vision. Although the Soviet Union has improved the treatment of its own citizens since the days of Joseph Stalin, the cost of a singular orthodoxy in both ideology and political structure still hangs over this totalitarian system. Despite a few genuine efforts at opening the channels of discussion, and despite the somewhat more imaginative leadership of recent prime ministers such as Krushchev and Andropov, the Soviet government still finds itself debating only the more narrow issues of policy implementation and short-run production difficulties. Totalitarianism, apart from the often accompanying brutality and sometimes hidden privileges of a few leaders, is still plagued by deep inefficiencies that public exhortation cannot seem to correct.

CONCLUSION

The standards of fairness and efficiency are illusive and subtle. Nonetheless, it is possible to test the promises of modern pluralist, elistist, and even totalitarian systems by such standards. We are able to evaluate the actuality of pluralist fairness against its promise and find that in an originally egalitarian social climate, structural separations encourage a high degree of personal competition and a resultant high pyramid of distribution. The efficiency of a pluralist system has been a topic of much discussion, and most agree that the strict preservation of high levels of private initiative certainly worked well for the pluralist system in the past. Global competition, however, may require a higher degree of cooperation among America's public and private sectors, as well as among its governmental institutions.

Elitism has also had to make some compromises with its past. The traditional high pyramids of distribution have faced moderation in the last century as class-based worker's parties have challenged traditional European perogatives for the well-born, and the efficiency of European industry seems to have, in part, benefitted from coordinated governmental policies.

In one sense, however, the questions of institutional cohesion, fairness, and efficiency may not be complete without the introduction of a new and increasingly understood technique for the analysis of politics. The importance of the relationship of human psychology to politics, and to the fundamental questions of political structure and political value is now clear. In our final chapter, we will introduce this new variable into our own political model.

Reference Notes

1. C. Wright Mills, *The Power Elite* (New York: Oxford University Press, 1956).
2. Grant McConnell, *Private Power and American Democracy* (New York: Alfred A. Knopf, 1966).
3. Theodore J. Lowi, *The End of Liberalism* (New York: W.W. Norton, 1969).
4. Geoffrey S. Carroll, "Multinational Reshuffle," *Europe*, No. 231 (May–June 1982), p. 12.
5. Lester Thurow, *The Zero-Sum Society* (New York: Basic Books, 1980).
6. James MacGregor Burns, *The Deadlock of Democracy* (Englewood Cliffs, N.J.: Prentice-Hall, 1963).
7. Milovan Djilas, *The New Class: An Analysis of the Communist System* (New York: Praeger, 1957).

Glossary

TERMS

Poland

Solidarity

civil rights movement

war on poverty

The Power Elite

military-industrial complex

11 + exam

tracked

foreign competition

inflation

growth rate

unemployment

antitrust

industrial policy

balance of payments

Report on Manufactures

utilitarianism

consciousness

cartel

Japan Incorporated

new class

NAMES

David Truman

Robert Dahl

Adolf Hitler

C. Wright Mills

Grant McConnell

Theodore Lowi

Jim Callaghan

Francis Mitterand

Otto van Bismarck

Napoleon III

The Hapsburgs

Lester Thurow

Alexander Hamilton

James MacGregor Burns

Joseph Stalin

CHAPTER 11
POLITICAL PSYCHOLOGY:
THE NEW PERSPECTIVE

In this short final chapter, let us think of something that should be worthwhile for your understanding of the element of political change. Change is an important element in all of modern life. As we move into the future, we tend to think of such clichés as "times are changing" or "this is the modern age." We often, however, do not make an essential distinction about the two things that we often mean. As "times change," two very distinct things happen. You may recognize each of them because the two together, return to an old argument.

Do you remember the theoretical discussion concerning (1) whether history moved according to what actually happened in the world, or (2) whether it moved as people thought about the world in a different way and then spread that vision into reality? As you recall, Hegel took the view that the human mind was where history's evolution began. Marx argued that the material world was the originator and that human analysis followed.

Within the real world, it is clear that history is moving quickly. We have been to the moon, and our breakthroughs in telecommunications, medicine, and the breaking of the DNA and RNA genetic codes are truly extraordinary achievements. But what of the other half of the debate? What has happened to the way that humankind thinks of things? Is it at least keeping pace or, from the perspective of Hegel, is it staying ahead of what is happening in the real world?

These questions are difficult to answer, but even within the single discipline of political science, there has been a major and significant change in the way we look at fundamental political questions. Over the last few years, a subdiscipline within political science called "political psychology" has emerged and has begun to present a new perspective upon how we look at something as fundamental as the valuation or distributional question.

THE EMERGENCE OF POLITICAL PSYCHOLOGY

Where did the great breakthrough of the psychological perspective begin? You know, of course, of Sigmund Freud and probably of that other great pioneering psychologist, Karl Jung. In a sense, the beginning of the discussion of psychological issues, starting at the close of the nineteenth century and reaching full flower in this century, mirrored the discussion of the economic distribution questions of 100 years earlier. As Ricardo and Malthus argued over "labor embodied" and "labor commanded," Freud and Jung argued over whether (1) understanding neurosis caused repression of subconscious drives, or (2) understanding the range of human personalities was the key to understanding human psychology. Freud, of course, was the first to consider these factors, and his studies of various neuroses were the key to a good deal of early work in political psychology. Harold Lasswell, in *Power and Personality*[1] and *Psychopathology and Politics*,[2] borrowed Freudian forms of analysis. He also considered power to be the essential element of politics.

Initially, Jung's work seemed less well adapted to politics, but in recent years his perspectives on what he called *introversion* and *extroversion* have become very relevant for political psychology.[3] How does Jung's work relate to the model we have built? Our model, and in fact virtually all traditional models of politics, seem at their root to be economic. They deal in some manner with valuation and with the "vertical" question of the height of a distributional pyramid. Jung may have anticipated that politics was more than a power-oriented, vertical, and ultimately economic matter. He realized that people's attitudes often depend upon views of human nature, that is, upon the competitive versus cooperative continuum with which we began our model.

Objectively, how you feel about the distributional pyramid may have something to do with whether you or your family are currently near the top or the bottom of the pyramid. But how you feel about the pyramid is also influenced by the subjectivity of your own nature or by what your own nature tells you about the values that you place upon your employment and those of fellow citizens. In other words, your ratio of the difference in valuation between the physician and the street sweeper may have more to do with your psychology than it does with any view of economics you may have. In reading about Jung's psychological types, as you may someday, you should have no difficulty seeing that Jung's extroverts are basically competitive people and that his introverts are basically co-operative people. We now have evidence of how this differentiation works within politics in a way that goes well beyond Jung.

The recent material on human psychology has also led to explorations into human physiology. Recent findings tend to confirm Jung's insights concerning the introvertive to extrovertive range of personalities: one dramatic area of research, for example, has already led us to an understanding of the two different halves of the human brain. Although there is a complex series of reciprocal and substitute functions on each side of the human brain, a general pattern has emerged that assigns particular functions to either the left or the right half of the brain. As a rule, the left half of the brain tends to be *analytic*; that is, it prefers to deal with problems that are of a mathematical or logical type. What do we mean by "mathematical" or "logical"? Think of how two simple numbers, say 5 and 7, interact with one another. They can be added, subtracted, multiplied, and so forth on up through difficult functions of the calculus. However, the numbers are common in that they are both of the same quality, and they interact with each other *because* they are of the same quality—they are both numbers.

The right half of the brain does not perform the analytic function as well because its primary role is to engage in what is called the *synthetic* function, that is, putting things that may not be of same quality, together. If I were to ask you to add 5 and 7, you would have no difficulty finding the answer of 12. But what if I were to ask you for the total of 5 and the color blue? That's a different question, is it not? You understand the number 5, and you also understand the color blue, but why can't you add the two of them? The 5 plus blue question is what has often been called the "apples and oranges" question, the comparison of things that at least initially seem to be noncomparable.

If we understand the left-brain, right-brain distinction and the difference between the analytic and the synthetic functions of the mind, we need only add the simple notion that there are different kinds of minds, and consequently, different preferences for different kinds of thinking.

THE IMPACT UPON POLITICS ━━━━━━

Now, understanding that these differences in mental sets are on a continuum and are not simply categorized, we should be able to look at the impact of these newly discovered psychological and physiological realities on politics. I have already suggested that the preferences for high and low pyramids, based upon what we called human nature, may have a good deal to do with psychology. With ideology, even the economically-based notions of distribution possessed a real psychological element, although Ricardo, Smith, and the others never thought in psychological terms during their period of history.

Within political structures, however, the element of psychology is even more apparent. In our discussion of the internal equilibrium of prepolitical considerations and structure, we emphasized political culture, myth, symbols, and socialization. But in recent years, it has become clear that terms like David Singer's *psychoculture* give a more comprehensive description of what is going on.[4] The DeGré model of social cohesion held that cohesion levels came from the history or the social patterns of a society. A more encompassing view today would recognize that different psychological orientations prefer the different levels of social closeness or cohesion that DeGré discussed.

Can you guess which of the psychological types would prefer which level of social cohesiveness? Can you also guess which type would prefer which political-economic ideology and which height of the pyramid? The answers should not be difficult to find. The analytic mind likes separate parts, it prefers the pieces of the puzzle rather than the whole. Also, the analytic mind tends to see people as individuals, not as part of a larger social whole, and therefore it has a more competitive view of humankind. The synthetic mind, on the other hand, sees the whole more readily than the parts, and it also, therefore, tends to view humankind as being more integrated. The pyramid is shorter in the synthetic mind, and work tends to be performed more cooperatively and with more intrinsic than extrinsic motivations.

But what of political structure? The analytic type tends to prefer an existence in which people are farther apart, sometimes called the contractural configuration of existence. The synthetic personality, however, prefers a more interpersonal relationship, or a level of social cohesion that is more dense and involved. How does this link to pluralism and elitism? It should be obvious that the pluralist model is more psychologically akin to the analytic mind. It is psychologically more conservative. The synthetic mind, however, tends to prefer the more cohesive structures of the elitist model. It is psychologically more liberal.

With this final chapter, we are developing our understanding about such things as psychology and physiology, and these new understandings are throwing a new light on some very old problems. Does this new light mean that all we have learned is now out of date? Not at all. Although the psychological variable may to a certain degree alter our thinking, in most instances it merely adds a new richness to what we already knew. What remains from our old economically based model? Virtually everything remains, for the human nature and ideological distinctions are embellished and the structural notions are deepened with an understanding of the psychology that underlies the different arguments.

Also, there is one additional point that you should keep in mind. The knowledge of psychology, human physiology, and the resultant understanding of the analytic and synthetic range may help in the understanding of traditional and more current arguments over a number of political matters. How do we want to value contribution? Do we prefer the market or the rationalistic valuation? The arguments go on, and fortunately, the pressure of the equilibrium has brought the arguments nearer the center of the equilibrium in democratic nations. Does psychology have something to do with how people argue over this matter? It certainly does, and as a final exercise, I am going to ask you to think about the market method of valuation versus the rationalistic method of valuation in terms of psychological preferences.

In market valuation, with what kinds of variables do you deal? You deal with supply and demand, but what are the qualities of those variables? Both supply and demand, we believe, are easily quantifiable, or because they are numbers they are easily dealt with in a mathematical or logical way. Using our example, they are 5 plus 7 kinds of questions.

What then of the rationalistic method of valuation? From a psychological perspective, how do you evaluate risk, skill training, and scarcity? The answer is not always obvious, for something like scarcity may be a fairly mathematical calculation. Yet how do we evaluate risk? Or how do we evaluate skill? These two variables are relatively nonmathematical, and something like training, again, may be mathematical, although we may also have to consider the quality of the training in addition to some measure of the time involved. The rationalistic method of valuation, in short, often necessitates a 5 plus blue kind of thinking, something that should

FIGURE 11–1.
A model of politics from human nature to human physiology.

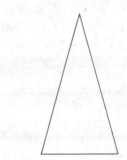

- 2:1 Distributional Ratio
- Cooperative Human Nature View
- Rationalistic Natural Law View
- Rationalistic Political Result
- Synthetic Structural Perception
- Right-Mode Cognitive Map

- 10:1 Distributional Ratio
- Competitive Human Nature View
- Market Natural Law View
- Market Political Result
- Analytic Structural Perception
- Left-Mode Cognitive Map

now be added to your understanding of the model. (See Figure 11-1).

The remaining segment of our model should easily fall into place, for you can see that the rationalistic valuation has not only a preindustrial historical lineage and a reinforcement from left-of-center political economic ideologies, but it also has a psychological propensity toward the left half of the political spectrum. The market method of valuation, coming historically from the rising middle class and from conservative ideologies, finds that it is also supported by the analytic perspective of the psychologically right-of-center view. Yet, beyond rationalism and market evaluation, two additional examples of how analytic minds work should solidify your understanding of the analytic-synthetic distinction.

TWO ANALYTIC-SYNTHETIC CONSIDERATIONS

Within the short period of history since World War II, a number of terribly important difficulties have begun to spill across the boundaries of nation-states. The issues surrounding nuclear armaments, hunger among many people of the world, and the protection of air, water, forests, and arable land have increasingly concerned citizens world wide. In the recent past, more citizens have attempted to address these problems without regard to national borders. They have, in short, begun to develop a kind of transnational politics beyond that of the European Economic Community.

Perhaps the best and most recent example of transnational political activity is the antinuclear movement, wherein citizens from all the nations of the world have attempted to persuade their own national governments to work toward the control and elimination of nuclear weapons. The issue of nuclear weapons is a controversial one, with many citizens feeling strongly about their respective positions. What is clear, however, is that some kinds of minds are more prepared than are others to look beyond national boundaries and participate within a truly global political movement.

Can you tell which kind of mind, the synthetic or the analytic, will more naturally look beyond boundaries? The answer is clearly the synthetic mind because it more naturally perceives the world as a whole. The synthetic mind is better prepared to consider humankind as one being rather than as a loose collection of people that live in competing nation-states. The analytic mind, in contrast, is more concerned with the well-being of a single nation-state and its people. It is more prepared to look at a question like world hunger as being a single nation's problem.

A second consideration that the new psychological variable may help us understand concerns the existence of a new ideological equilibrium. You will recall that we discussed what happened to the pyramid when the middle class grew larger in developed countries and the working class became the minority. We noted that the shift in population caused the equilibrium between the ideologies to swing toward the conservative side. In other words, as fewer people were prepared to argue for a flatter pyramid the flatter pyramid view was increasingly defeated.

Yet again, new issues are intruding on the political stage, and they increasingly concern psychological issues. They often ask how individual work should be structured and how leisure time should be spent, as well as how cohesive or how fragmented governmental institutions should be. Even insofar as the pyramid of distribution is still debated, much of the argument stems from different psychological perspectives. You have probably realized that the psychological disposition concerning a competitive or cooperative attitude toward your fellow citizens is not related to your position on the economic distribution pyramid. Often, citizens at the top of the pyramid who are psychologically inclined to a more cooperative view of humankind are the same citizens who lead the political debate for a flatter pyramid.

Remember that what we are looking for, again, is a new equilibrium, one that can reflect the impact of the new issues of the modern age and the psychological balance between the synthetic and analytic minds of the society. The point that you should remember about the psychological equilibrium is that whether the pyramid is flat or tall, a balance or a kind of equilibrium will exist among people of different kinds of minds. Don't forget that psychological identifications have little to do with whether the individual is near the top or the bottom of the economic pyramid. Thus, a psychological equilibrium can be maintained within societies that recognize the existence of two different views on political questions and a need to permit citizens to express those views.

There is one simple notion that may assist you in remembering the psychological variable and how synthetic and analytic minds

FIGURE 11–2.
Ideological flow of policy on psychological issues.

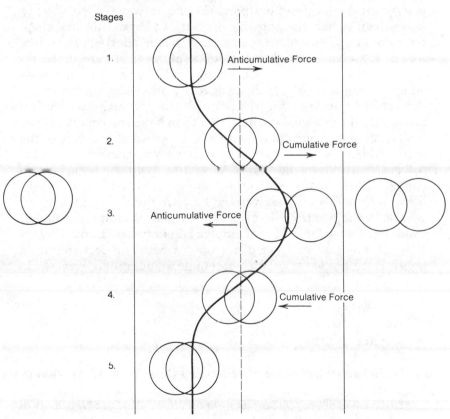

think about political ideology. It is that all of us have at least some capacity for both synthetic and analytic thinking. None of us, in other words, is entirely synthetic or analytic, or entirely liberal or conservative. Therefore, if the policies of a nation move too far to either the analytic or the synthetic side on a whole range of psychological issues, countercumulative forces not affected by the pyramid of distribution will help return public policy to a more moderate position. The idea of an equilibrium, or the balancing of cumulative and anticumulative forces, in other words, will work as well or better for the new kinds of issues as it did for the more traditional economic issues (see Figure 11–2).

CONCLUSION

Thus the model grows and accommodates change. It adds new layers that do not upset our previous understandings but serve to make them richer and more meaningful. We began this final chapter with a hope of understanding how change affects modern life. Again, the changes within the fields of medical care, telecommunications, outer space exploration, and a variety of other areas are important and often fascinating real-world events. However, as the ancient Greek Protagorus pointed out, the real study of humankind is humankind itself. Rather than have you conclude your understanding of our model with a sense of what is a part of the real world, it is probably better to have you see how our very *perceptions* of humankind and, of course, politics are subject to change. More important than a fleeting day or time are how we learn to think about ourselves and how we think about where we will be in the future. Indeed, it may be that our improved understanding of ourselves as very complex and imperfect human beings is what will lead us toward not only a better understanding of political science but toward a better understanding of the real world of politics as well.

Reference Notes

1. Harold Lasswell, *Power and Personality* (New York: W. W. Norton, 1948).
2. Harold Lasswell, *Psychopathology and Politics* (Chicago: University of Chicago Press, 1930).

3. Karl G. Jung, *Psychological Types* (New York: Pantheon Books, 1923).
4. David J. Singer, "Man and World Politics: The Psycho-Cultural Interface," *Journal of Social Issues*, Vol. 24 (1968), pp. 127–156.

Glossary

TERMS	NAMES
Power and Personality	Sigmund Freud
Psychopathology and Politics	Karl Jung
introversion	David Singer
extraversion	
analytic	
synthetic	

EPILOGUE

In this description of a model of politics, you have been asked to think your way through a series of model-building steps. First, you were asked to think of the distributional question; then, you were asked what the structure of a government would be that would best provide for the people of a nation. Our discussions have led to important structural steps, building federalism, separation of powers, and the principal institutions of government into the model. But they have done so, it is hoped, within the context of a number of standards for the democratic climate of a nation, and both the degrees of respect for its institutions and the methods it uses to resolve political controversy. No one portion of this model should have been terribly difficult for you, and you should have been able to learn each component of the model as a part of a growing understanding of the workings of politics.

To remember something, it is necessary to see it as being part of something else, and to remember it well, it is better to have used it, at least in your mind, as it impressed itself upon your consciousness. You should recall what we have spoken of here for a long time, but even more important, you should remember it as a whole and at least reasonably well remember where all the pieces fit within that whole.

If you can do that, then you will not only retain what you have learned, but you will also be in a better position to learn a good deal more about politics as time goes on. As you come upon new events and new understandings of your own perceptions; you should be able to place your knowledge of them next to what you already understand and in that way, the model will continue to grow for you as long as you continue to learn new things about politics.

INDEX

access points, 137–141, *138, 139*
adjudication, 160, 162–164
Africa, 129–130
aggregated interests, 147
Altgeld, John Peter, 44
American Bill of Rights, 77
American Cancer Society, 138, 139
American Indians, 95
American Revolution, 77
American Tobacco Institute, 138, 139–140
analytic mind, 210–216
anticapitalism, 77–78
anticumulative forces, 87–88, *88*
Anti-injunction Act, 45
antinuclear movement, 214
antithesis, 61
Aristotle, 4–5, 23, 72, 92, 93, 95, 106–108, 110, 128, 170, 199
art of the possible, 161
Articles of Confederation, 164
association, values of, 13, *14*
assumption of risk, 40
atomistic cohesion, *93, 94, 97, 98*
authority
  delegation of, 160
  power and, 118–120, *119*

balance of payments, 198
Bill of Rights
  American, 77
  English, 77
Bismarck, Otto von, 193
bourgeoisie, 63
brain, studies of halves of, 210–212
bureaucracy, 159–162
  adjudicatory function of, 162
  American, 141
  "new class" of, in Eastern Europe, 204
Burke, Edmund, 153, 154
Burns, James MacGregor, 199

cabinet governments, 164
Callaghan, Jim, 192

Canada, 96, 131, 156, 159
candidates, 148–150, *149*, 157
capitalism, 32–49
  beyond Industrial Revolution, 32–34
  democracy as process and, 77–78
  democracy as result and, 78–79
  distribution in liberal and pure, 45, *45*, 55, *55*
  human nature and, 36–37
  liberal or state, 32, 37–49
    cycles affecting, 46–49
    industrial safety under, 39–41
    industrial unions in, 41–45
    modern changes in, 190
  pure, 32–33, 35, 36
    criticism of, 37–39
captive agency, 139–141, *139*
cartel, 202
Carter, Jimmy, 166, 192
centrifugal forces, 127–129, *128*
centripetal forces, 127–129, *128*
church, as socializing institution, 126
civil law, 163
civil rights movement, 187
class system, 52, 53, 56
  elitism and, 96
  in Europe, 108, 111, 112, 192–193
  in Latin America, 100
  Marx on, 63, 64
  middle class in, 190
  working class in, 190
Clayton Act, 197
coalition governments, 148
coalitions, in pluralist society, 99–100
cohesion, social and political, 92–98
  atomistic, *93, 94, 97, 98*
  DeGré's classification of, 93–94, *93*
  elitist, *93*, 96–97, *97*
  multipartite, *93*, 94–95, *97*
  pluralistic, *93*, 95–96, *97*, 99
  totalitarian, *93*, 97–98, *97*
Coke, Edward, 77
collective bargaining, 43
collective representation, 153–154

colonialism, 129–130
common law, 73
Common Market. *See* European Economic Community
communism, 57–64
  as dialectical materialism, 59–64
  differentiated from socialism, 56
  distribution for pure capitalism and, 57, *58*
community, 3–4
competition
  conflict and salience and, 113–118, *114, 115*
  in Europe, 202
  foreign, and American pluralist efficiency, 196, 197–198
  human nature and, 11–12, *11*
  international economic, 177–178
  in political ideology, 12–13
  public policy and, 110–118
conflict, competition, and salience, 113–118, *114, 115*
Congress. *See* United States Congress
consciousness versus utilitarianism, 200–201
consensus, 168–169
conservative(s)
  definition of, 83–84
  in ideological struggle, 85–89
contract, movement from status to, 25
contribution
  different kinds of, 12–13, *14*
  distribution and, 4–5
  evaluation of, for different occupations, *9, 10, 14*
  human nature and, 11–12, *11*
  qualitative variable in evaluation of, 20–22, *21*
contributory negligence, 40
cooperative relationships, 3
  human nature and, 11–12, *11*
  value of, 12–13
Copernicus, 69
court system, 162–164
cross-pressures, pluralistic, 100–103, *102*
culture, political, 92, 124–126
cumulative forces, 87, *88*
cycles, boom-bust, 46–49, *47*

Dahl, Robert, 182
Darwin, Charles, 52
Debs, Eugene V., 43–44, 57
DeGré, Gerard, 93–99, 105, 106, 110, 111, 124, 132, 134, 155, 156, 211
DeGré's classification of cohesion, 93–94, *93*
delegate, representative as, 154

delegation of authority, 160
demand, supply and, for labor, 34–35
democracy
  elitism and pluralism in, 108–118
  Glorious Revolution effect on, 70
  in ideological struggle, 85–89
  Locke and, 70–71
  as process, 76–77, 77, 80
  public policy in, 80
  as result, 77–79, 77
  socialism within, 56
  valuations in, 67–69, *68*
Democracy in America, 99. *See also* Tocqueville
Department of Agriculture, 138, 139
Depression, Great, 45, 46, 195
dialectic, 60, 61
dialectical materialism, 59–64
differentiation among contributions, in valuation, 8–9, 11–12
distribution, 1–2
  democratic institutions impact on, 71, *71*
  early industrial, 35, *35*
  in European countries, 192–194, 194t.
  in liberal and pure capitalism, 45, *45*, 55, *55*
  modern income, changing, 189–191, *190*
  productivity and, 174–175
  public policy impact on, 80–84, *83*
  realities of, 4–6
  in socialism, 55, *55*
division of labor, 28–29
dyadic representation, 153–154

economy, world, 170–177
  Europe in, 203
  Soviet Union in, 205
  U.S. slippage in, 196–197, *197*
education. *See also* schools
  tracking in European, 192
efficiency, 149, 157–158
  elitist, 201–204
  in grand equilibrium, 180–181
    pluralist: promise and actuality, 194–199
  standard of, 142–143
egalitarian, 82
Eisenhower, Dwight D., 165
11 + exam, 192
elitism
  access points in, 137, *138*
  cohesion in, 93, 96–97, *97*
  efficiency of, 201–204
  equilibrium in, 158–159
  evaluation of, 168–178

neo-mercantilism and, 177–178
world economy influence on, 169–177
executive system in, 165, 166
fairness of, 182–183, 191–194, 194t.
legislatures in, 152, 154, 156–157, 161–162
pluralism contrasted with, 105–112
policy process in, 136 136, 137
political parties in, 147
candidates and, 149–150, 149
Enclosures, the, 35
England
capitalism in 32–35
law in, 70–73
Locke's contribution to, 70–72
mercantilism in, 70
rights in, 77
socialism in, 51–53
English Bill of Rights, 77
equilibrium, 66–75
external, 159
global economy and national, 173
government role in, 66–69
grand, 180–206, 185
elitist efficiency in, 201–204
fairness in, 181–194
Hegel versus Locke in, 199–201
pluralist efficiency in, 194–199
totalitarianism in, 204–205
internal, 158–159
public policy and, 109,110, 113
world economic influences on, 175–177
Europe, Eastern
equilibrium pressures in, 186
productivity in, 204
Europe, Western. See also England;
France; Germany
capitalism in, 53
culture of, 126
democracy and individual rights in, 76–77
economic cooperation in, 201–203
elitism in, 106, 158–159
efficiency in, 201–204
fairness in, 192–194, 194t.
executive systems in, 164–165, 166
fairness in, 182–183, 192–194, 194t.
interest groups in, 135–137
judicial systems of, 163
labor in, 178
Left and Right in, 83
mercantilism in, 24–25
political parties in, 145–146, 149, 158
prenationalism in, 130, 131
production in, 196

social classes in, 108, 111, 112
socialism in, 56
supranationalism in, 133, 170
European Economic Community (Common Market), 133, 196, 201
evolution, theory of, 56
executive branch of government, 164–166
extrinsic value 12, 13
extroversion, 209, 210

Fabian Society, 52, 53, 192
factories, 28–29, 34–35
modern, 41
safety in, 39–41
fairness, 149–150, 157
actuality of, 184–194
under elitism, 191–194, 194t.
under pluralism, 184–191
promise of, 180–184
under elitism, 182–183
under pluralism, 181–182
under totalitarianism, 183–184
standard of, 142–143
family, 92, 95, 126
Federal Trade Commission Act, 197
federalism, 127–131, 158–159
Federalist #10, 72, 189
Federalist Papers, The, 145
fellow servant doctrine, 40
feudalism, 16–17, 62
valuation in, 22–23
fiscal policies, 48–49
France
capitalism in, 33
in social cohesion, 93
unitary government of, 132
French Revolution, 77
Freud, Sigmund, 209
"fruits of their labor," 23, 27, 72

Galileo, 69
Germany
elitism in, 159
fascism in, 184
federalism in, 131
guilds in, 42–43
labor movement in, 193
totalitarianism in, 184
Glorious Revolution, 70
government. See also U.S. Congress; U.S. government
in capitalism, 33, 34, 53
in economy, 46 49, 47
equilibrium maintained by, 67–69
under capitalism, 33, 34, 53
under socialism, 53–54

government *(cont.)*
    executive branch of modern, evolution of, 164–165
    interest groups versus society related to, 145–146
    in market valuation, 79, 109–112
    public policy created by, 80–84
    in rationalistic valuation, 79, 109–112
Great Depression, 45, 46, 195
Greece, 1, 93, 107, 128. *See also polis*
Greeley, Horace, 58
guilds, 42

Hamilton, Alexander, 146, 198
Haymarket Affair, 43
hearing, in bureaucracy, 160
Hegel, G. W. F., 60–61
    versus Locke, 199–201
Hitler, Adolf, 184, 204
Hobbes, Thomas, 94
Hooker, Thomas, 70, 77
human nature
    contribution and reward ratios affected by assumptions about, 10–12, *11*, 13
    Industrial Revolution related to, 36–37
    model of politics from, to human psychology, 213, *213*
    view of, as influence on public institutions, 145–146

idealist, definition of, 60
ideological struggle
    elements of, 84–86
    structure of, 86–88, *88*
ideology(ies). *See also* capitalism; communism; socialism
    agreement and disagreement in, 19
    competition and cooperation in, 13
    continuum of, 66–67
    core of, 8–10
    democracy as process and result and, 77
    history of, 22
    modern, 32
    natural and positive law and, 74, *75*
    productivity and, 174–175
    psychological issues and, *215*, 216
incentives. *See* work, motivation for
individualism
    American
        culture supporting, 125
        economic cycles and, 47
        interest groups and, 135–137
        labor and, 42
    in atomic cohesion, 94
    communism on, 57–58

Locke on, 70–72
    valuation of, 13, *14*
industrial policy, U.S., 198
Industrial Revolution, 26–28, 34
    capitalism due to, 32–34
    distribution during, 35, *35*, 36
    value of work after, 59
    wages following, 37–38
industrial complex, military-, 187
industrial safety, 39–41
industrial unions, 41–45
industrial wages, 34–36
injunction, 44, 45
institutions, 145–166
    national, 134–142
    public versus private, in pluralism and elitism, 173–176
interdependent world society, 170
interest groups, 134–137, *136*
    access points and captive agencies for, 137–141, *138*, *139*
    criticism of, 188–189
    political institutions and, 147
interests
    aggregated, 147
    local versus national, 155
intrinsic values, 12, 13, 55
introversion, 209, 210
investment, in economic cycles, 47, 48
investment capital, 171–172
iron triangle, 141–142

Japan
    distribution in, 189
    elitism in, *185*, 203
    labor in, 178
    productivity in, 203
    unitary government of, 132
Japan Incorporated, 203
Joan of Arc, 126
Johnson, Lyndon, 192
judicial system, 162–164
Jung, Karl, 209, 210
Justinian, 5, 23, 72

Kennedy, Edward, 166
Keynes, John Maynard, 47
Keynesian economics, 47, *47*, 48, 190

labor. *See also* unions; working class
    division of, 28–29
    in Germany, 193
    under liberal capitalism, 37–38
    market combined with, 29–30
    Marx on value of, 58–59
    in neo-mercantilism, 178
    supply and demand of, 34–35
labor commanded, 38

labor embodied, 38, 58
labor retraining, 178
labor theory of value, 59
laissez-faire, 33
lander, 159
Lasswell, Harold, 2, 209
Latin America
  classes in, 100
  political conflict in, 117
law
  common, 39–40, 41, 73
  democracy as process and, 76–77, 77
  democracy as result and, 77–79
  natural, 69, 70
    on property, 72
    valuation and, 74–75, 75, 77
  positive, 73–74
    in public policy quest, 80, 82
    valuation and, 74–75, 75
  workmen's compensation, 41
Left, 83–84. *See also* liberal
legislation, loose, 160–161
legislative veto, 161
legislatures, 151–158
  representation within, 153–155
    collective and dyadic, 153–154
    as trustee or delegate, 154
  selection of, 151–153
  structure, staff, and leadership loyalty of, 155–158
legitimacy, authority and power, in political systems, 118–120, *119*
Leviathan, 94
liberal(s). *See also* capitalism, liberal
  definition of, 83–84
  in ideological struggle, 85–89
liberté, egalité, fraternité, 126
Lincoln, Abraham, 125
Lipset, Seymour Martin, 100, 104, 105
lobbies, 135
Locke, John, 5, 23, 26, 33–34, 59, 70–72, *71*, 76, 77, 79, 189
  versus Hegel, 199–201
Lowi, Theodore, 188, 189
Luther, Martin, 17, 25, 26

McConnell, Grant, 188, 189
Madison, James, 72, 76, 146, 189
Maine, Henry, 25
Malthus, Thomas, 38
market valuation, 24
  democracy as result of, 78, 79
  emergence of, 25–26
  government role in, 109–112
  labor combined with, 29–30
  in pluralist structure, 111
Marx, Karl, 46, 57–64, 74, 75, 204
Marxism, 58, 63–64, 68, 184

materialism, 60
  dialectical, 59–64
mercantilism, 24–25, 26, 70, 175
mèson, in politics, 66
middle class, American, 190
military-industrial complex, 187
Mills, C. Wright, 187–188
Mitterand, François, 192
monetary policies, 48–49
motivation for work
  under communism, 58, 59
  under socialism, 54–57, *55*
  in Soviet system, 63
multinational corporation (MNC), 172
multipartite cohesion, *93*, 94–95, 97
multiparty systems, 148
My Fair Lady, 51, 53
myth, political, 124–126

Namibia, 129
nation-states, 128–131. *See also* unitary state
  global economy and, 173–175
National Institutes of Health, 138, 139
national institutions, 134–142
national interests, versus local interests, 155
nationalism, 138
natural law. *See* law, natural
negligence, contributory, 40
neo-mercantilism, 175, 176
  pluralism versus elitism in, 177–178
"new class" of bureaucrats, in Eastern Europe, 204
Newton, Isaac, 69
Norris-LaGuardia act, 45
notice, in bureaucracy, 100

observed truth, 69
Olney, Richard, 44
Origin of Species, The, 52
ownership. *See* private property

Paine, Tom, 77
parliamentary system, 70, 72, 73
  executive in, 164–165, 166
Parsons, Talcott, 103–105
parties, political, 145–148
party discipline, 157
party platforms, 147–149
peer group, 126
Phillips curve, 46
philosopher kings, 107, 199
platforms, party, 147–149
Plato, 106–108, 110, 125, 199
pluralism. *See also* pluralist cohesion
  access points and captive agencies in, 137–141, *138, 139*

pluralism *(cont.)*
  criticisms of, 187–189
  efficiency under, 194–199
  elitism contrasted with, 105–112
    on access points, 137, *138*
    on policy process, 136, *136*, 137
  equilibrium in, 158–159
  evaluation of, 168–178
    neo-mercantilism and, 177–178
  executive branch in, 165, 166
  fairness in
    actuality of, 184–191
    promise of, 181–182
  legislatures in, 152–157, 161–162
  political parties in, 146–147
    candidate and, 149–150, *149*
  stability of, 99
  trust as element in, 103–105
pluralistic cohesion, *93*, 95–96, *97*, 99
pluralistic cross-pressures, 100–103, *102*
Poland, pluralism in, 185–186, *185*
polis, 1, 13, 92, 95, 107, 128
political cohesion. *See* cohesion
political culture, 92, 124–126
political parties, 145–148
  responsible, 148
political psychology. *See* psychology
political science, definition of, 2
political structures, 92–93, 105–106
  conflict in, 114–118, *114*, *115*
  legitimacy, authority, and power in,
    118–120, *119*
  model of, from human nature to hu-
    man psychology, 213, *213*
  modern, 123–143
    continuum and equilibrium, 124
    federalism and unitary states,
      127–133
    myth, culture, symbol, and
      socialization, 124–126
    national institutions, 134–142
  other side of circle in, 98–105
  policy and, 108–118
  similarity of poles in, 98
  social cohesion model in, 93–98, *93*,
    97
  traditional and modern influences on,
    176, *176*
  world economy effects on, 175
politics, definition of, 2
positive law. *See* law, positive
power
  authority, legitimacy and, in political
    systems, 118–120, *119*
  concept of, 2
  in social cohesion, *93*
Power Elite, The, 187
Power and Personality, 209

prenational systems, 129
  artificial, 130
  disintegrative, 130–131
  evolutionary, 131
prepolitical conditions, 126
prepolitical considerations, 92
price(s)
  Adam Smith on, 30
  of labor, 34–35. *See also* wages
"priming the pump," 48
printing press, 69
private institutions, versus public, 173–
  176
private property
  American Constitution on, 72
  Locke on, 72
  Madison on, 72
  Marx on, 62
  natural law as protector of, 72
private schools, in example on cross-
  pressures, 102, *102*, 103
procapitalism, 78–79
productivity
  American, slippage in, 196–199
  distribution and, 174–175
  in Eastern Europe, 204
  Marxian analysis of, 61–62
  neo-mercantilism and, 177–178
  in Western Europe and Japan, 203
productivity bargaining, 178
proletariat, 63, 64
property. *See* private property
psychoculture, 211
psychology, political, 208–216
  emergence of, 209–210
  impact on politics, 211–213
  two analytic-synthetic considera-
    tions, 213–216, *215*
Psychopathology and Politics, 209
public versus private institutions, 173–
  176
public policy
  equilibrium of, 80–84
  government activity related to, 69
  ideological flow of, changing modern,
    190–191, *191*
  law and, 75
  in pluralist and elitist governments,
    108–118
  quest for, in two forms of democracy,
    79–80
Pullman strike, 43–44
Pygmalion, 51

qualitative variable, in valuation of work,
  20–22, *21*

rationalistic valuation, 23–24
  of Adam Smith, 30

democracy as result due to, 78–79
   in elitist structure, 111
   government role in, 109–112
Rayburn, Sam, 161
Reagan, Ronald, 88, 192
reason, 16–31
   in early attitudes toward value, 16–17
   in history of valuation, 22–29
   in market and labor combined, 29–30
   qualitative variable and, 20–22
   in valuation, 17–19
Report on Manufacturers, The, 198
representation, 153–155
   collective, 153–154
   dyadic, 153, 154
   level of, 155
   as trustee or delegate, 154, 155
   virtual, 153
Republic, The, 125
responsible party, 148
resources, and work, 3–6
result orientation, of democracy, 68, 68
reward
   distribution and, 4–5
   evaluations of, for different occupations, 9, 10
   human nature and, 11–12, 11
   proportionate, concept of, 7–8
Ricardo, David, 37–38, 42, 46, 58, 59
Right. See conservative
rights, individual
   American Bill of Rights on, 77
   English law on, 73, 77
   Locke on, 70–72
risk
   assumption of, 40
   in valuation of work, 18
Roosevelt, Franklin, 45, 88
rule making, in bureaucracy, 160

"safe district," in campaign, 165
safety, industrial, 39–41
salience-competition-conflict continuum, 113–118, 114, 115
scarcity, in valuation of work, 18
schools, private, in example on cross-pressures, 102, 102, 103
separation of powers, 169
Shaw, George Bernard, 51–52, 53, 192
Sherman Antitrust Act, 197
Silas Marner, 27
Singer, David, 211
skill, in valuation of work, 18
Smith, Adam, 29–30, 34–37, 57, 74, 75, 197
social cohesion. See cohesion

socialism, 51–57
   democratic versus Marxist, 51, 55–56
   distributions for, 55, 55
   emergence of, 51
   European, 192
   Marxist, 58–59
   "moderate," 202
socialization, political, 124–126
solidarity
   in Europe, 193
   in Poland, 186
Soviet Union
   federalism in, 131
   Marxism in, 63
   productivity in, 203, 204–205
   totalitarianism in, 183–184, 185
specialization, in work, 6–7
Spencer, Herbert, 52
stability, pluralist, 99
Stakhanovite medal, 63, 205
Stalin, Joseph, 205
status of work, 25
stratification, 96
structures. See political structures
supply and demand, of labor, 34–35
supranationalism, 133
surplus value, 59
survival of the fittest, 52, 53
synthesis, of Hegel, 61
symbol, political, 124–126
synthetic mind, 210–216

Taft-Hartley Act, 45
taxes
   in economic cycles, 48
   in example of public policy, 83
thesis, of Hegel, 60–61
Tocqueville, Alexis de, 99, 108, 135
totalitarian cohesion, 93, 97–98, 97
totalitarianism
   fairness under, promise of, 183–184
   political parties under, 146
   promises of, 183–184, 204–205
tracking, in European education, 192
training, in valuation of work, 18
Truman, David, 182
trust, in political system, 103–105
trustee, representative as, 154
truth, observed, 69
Tuchman, Barbara, 128

unemployment, in economic cycles, 46
unholy trio, 39–41
unions, industrial, 41–45. See also labor
unitary state, 127, 131–133
United States
   capitalism in, 33, 42–43, 47, 53
   cycles of, 46–47

United States(cont.)
  constitution of, 72, 77
  controversy in, 112–113
  cross-pressures in, 101, 102, 102
  democracy as process in, 76–77
  distribution in, 189–190, 190, 194t.
  evolutionary prenationalism in, 131
  fairness in, 181–182
  government of. See also U.S. Congress
    access points and captive agencies to, for interest groups, 137–141
    bureaucracy of, 141
    executive branch of, 164–166
  individualism in. See individualism, American
  judicial system of, 162–163
  liberals and conservatives in, 88
  myth, culture, symbol, and civilization in, 124–126
  pluralism in, 95–97, 99, 101–103, 108
    critique of, 187–189
    efficiency and economic slippage in, 195–199
    promises of, 186–187
  political parties in, 145–146
  private property in, 72
  productivity in, 177, 178, 196–199
  socialism in, 56–57
  taxes in, 83
United States Congress, 141, 155–158, 161, 165
utilitarianism versus consciousness, 200–201

valuation, 1–15
  Adam Smith on, 30
  for communism, 57
  contributions and, 12–13, 13
  distribution in, 1–2
  early attitudes toward, 16–17
  extrinsic and intrinsic, 12, 13
    in socialism, 55
  history of, 22–29
  human nature and, 10–12, 11
  ideology affecting, 8–10, 10
  market. See market valuation
  modern debate on, 66–90
    democracy and law in, 76–79
    equilibrium concept in, 66–75
    ideological struggle and, 84–88
    moderate state and, 89
    public policy in, 79–84
  natural and positive law and, 74–75, 75
  political structures and, 109–112

qualitative variables in, 20–22, 21
rationalistic. See rationalistic valuation
reason in, 17–19
resources and work in, 3–6
work. See work, valuation of
work performance in, 6–8
value(s)
  of association, 13, 14
  concept of, 2
  labor theory of, 59
value theorist, definition of, 38
veto, legislative, 161
village, 92, 95
Voltaire, 77
voluntary associations, 99, 135, 136
von Pufendorf, Samuel, 70

wage(s)
  industrial, 34–36
  iron law of, 37, 42
  under pure capitalism, 37–38
  union influence on, 41–45
Wagner Act, 45
war on poverty, 187
Washington, George, 125, 164, 198, 201
Wealth of Nations, The, 29–30, 197
white-collar employment, 43
work. See also industrial entries; labor
  allocation of, 6–8
  characteristics of modern, 5–6
  communal ownership of, Marx on, 62
  motivation for
    under communism, 58, 59
    under socialism, 54–57, 55
    in Soviet system, 63
  resources and, 3–6
  reward for, 7–8
  specialization in, 6–7
  valuation of
    early attitudes toward, 16–17
    history of, 22–29
    due to Industrial Revolution, 34–36
    by kind of work, 8–10, 10, 12
    modern, 28–29
    qualitative variable in, 20–22, 21
    reason in assessing, 17–19
    resources and, 3–6
working class. See also labor
  American, 190
workmen's compensation laws, 41
world economy. See economy
world society, interdependent, 170

yellow-dog contract, 45